WITH THANKS

As always, my words are inadequate to express my gratitude, but I'll have a go:

Jonathan Frank – *muchas gracias* for going through this with a fine-tooth comb and giving me pointers that have really sharpened the final thing. I hope I can return the favour soon.

Stephen Ashcroft – our chat about this over Broadway Market's delicacies was pure gold. The safest pair of hands. Thank you.

Stephanie Vernier – thank you for taking the time, despite how crazily busy you are, to share your insights with me. They truly were valuable.

Terrell Cole – thank you for our boundless talks around topics that informed this story and kept me on the straight and narrow.

Cally Higginbottom – thank you for being an eternal sounding board and a pillar of support throughout the entirety of this process. Big love.

First published in Great Britain in 2021

Copyright © 2021 Arton James
www.artonjames.com

The moral right of Arton James to be
identified as the author of this work has been
asserted in accordance with the
Copyright, Designs and Patents Act, 1988

All rights reserved. No part of this publication
may be reproduced or transmitted in any form
or by any means, electronic or mechanical,
including photocopy, recording, or any
information storage and retrieval system,
without permission in writing from the publisher.

All characters in this publication are fictitious and
any resemblance to living persons, living or dead,
is purely coincidental. Their thoughts, words and
actions do not represent those of the author.

ISBN 979-8-48611-186-0

Cover design by Cally Higginbottom

TARGET MAN

The First Half

Arton James

CHAPTER 1

He stared down beyond his gleaming black boots to the shiny blood-red concrete beneath them. The stadium noise reverberated from the cold ground up through his metal studs into his cold, aching bones. A pair of heavy hands slapped down onto his shoulders, amplifying the vibration passing up through him. They lingered for a moment before slapping down twice. Go time.

As he emerged from the tunnel, the white glare of the floodlights assaulted his eyes, overexposing his vision momentarily. As his sight returned, a sea of red shirts confronted him from every stand. The din their wearers made was loud and shrill. The air hung heavy; almost resisting his first step out onto the turf. Even though he had not kicked a ball yet, his legs felt unusually heavy as he led the line out to the centre circle. Saturated by the vitriol from the crowd, his walk dragged on. As he reached the centre circle, the referee and his assistants stood in its middle. Clad in black, they looked through him expressionlessly. His insides fluttered as he took his place next to them and his teammates filed alongside him.

The jeers loudened; their pitch climbed. His ears grew uncomfortable. He had never known an atmosphere like this. Leaning a little forward, he peered past the officials to the opposition players. All he could see were faceless red streaks. He scrunched his eyes closed, scrubbed them with his fists, then reopened them. Still blurred. Hot blood gushed like a geyser up the artery of his neck. The shrieks grew higher still, piercing his mind.

Something was not right. He turned back to tell his teammates. They were gone. The panic spun his head back towards the officials. They were gone too. As were the reds. His gaze shot down. His feet stood astride the centre spot. His face contorted. He looked towards the dugouts. All he saw were black gutters that the crowd bled into. Screams now. Women's screams.

Brightness blinded him again, but this time the glare was not white but red. Heat stabbed his chest where the Weavers' badge sat. He looked down at his white jersey. The badge was not there. A red spot of light hovered over his heart.

His breath halted. The screech surged. *Bang.*

Dmitriy snatched for breath as his eyes snapped open and his torso jolted out from under the covers. Over the next second, the dream fell away from before his eyes and left him surrounded by darkness. A glowing aquamarine shard of light from the window helped him reorient himself. He checked down next to him. Andriy faced his way, still fast asleep. He peeled the light cover off his sweat-drenched skin and rolled out of bed as quietly and softly as he could.

The aquamarine light shone through a crack in the curtains near his side of the bed. He turned away from it and tiptoed around the bed to Andriy's bedside table. He silently slid its drawer open just enough to be able to fish his phone out of it, then crept back around the bed, picking up a bath robe from a nearby chair en route, and eased himself between the curtains and out of the sliding glass door.

The patio floor was cool from the night, refreshing to his overheated skin. He placed his phone into the pocket of the plush white robe before putting it on, tying its belt, then sitting down on a nearby lounger that faced out onto the glowing turquoise infinity pool and the beach and sea down beyond it.

He pulled the phone straight back out and immediately noticed there were no new message notifications. After unlocking the modern, minimalist handset – a special model designed to limit distraction through reduced functionality – no apps appeared on its white facade; just a contact list with six names. Andriy. Cas. Kazimir. Emily. Mama. Papa.

He clicked Emily's name, opening her message feed, and gazed at the spot underneath a column of messages from him. His finger hovered over the message creation button. The waves lapped onto the white sand below. He looked out to the horizon. The dawn light was nowhere to be seen yet. He attended back to the phone, exiting Emily's feed and entering Papa's. It contained no messages, just records of outward call attempts. He locked the phone, set it down on the patio floor, and folded his arms to stop his warmth from escaping so quickly. He turned his attention back to the horizon ahead and the swishing tide.

The cry of a gull pierced his sleep. He peeled his eyes open to the cloudless blue sky. The golden sun warmed his face and neck, below which a blanket covered him.

'Good morning, Mr Star Gazer.'

Dmitriy turned his head to find Andriy walking out onto the patio carrying an espresso cup and a glass of pomegranate juice, which he placed on the floor by Dmitriy's lounger before kissing him.

'Thanks,' Dmitriy said as he picked up the juice. 'And for this,' he said, pulling the blanket off himself. 'Did you just put this over me now?'

'No. I came out hours ago. You looked so peaceful under all those stars, in front of the sea. Thought it was best to leave you to it.'

Dmitriy smiled gratefully and looked out across the crystal-clear water ahead. The only manmade thing in sight was a small fishing boat. 'There he is,' said Dmitriy in a childlike tone, pointing out to it.

'I leave you in peace, yet you insist on tormenting me with this game,' replied Andriy with a sardonic smile.

'You started "Where's Oleg?",' said Dmitriy.

'That I might have, but you're not even playing properly,' said Andriy playfully. 'He's not coming in something so quaint. There'd be a speedboat with a few heavies and then a yacht off in the distance.

You think he'd let a Saudi princess get a better snatch-and-grab than me?'

Dmitriy shrugged. 'Maybe that fisherman will offer to take us out to see some dolphins and there'll be a submarine waiting for us.' He laughed and picked up his juice.

'Hold it right there,' said Andriy.

Dmitriy stopped short of taking a sip.

Andriy raised his cup. 'Seriously, cheers to a delightful final day in paradise.'

Dmitriy kept his glass near his mouth. 'If I don't cheers you, that means it can't be our final day, right?'

Andriy tilted his head in consideration. In the blink of an eye, a jovial grin spread across his face as he abruptly clinked his cup against his partner's glass, spilling some juice onto his robe. 'Cheers.'

They laughed as Dmitriy tried to wipe the juice off himself, making the stain worse.

'It'll wash out,' assured Andriy.

Dmitriy nodded, took a sip, and placed his glass on the floor. His hand automatically searched for his phone.

'It's back where it belongs for now,' said Andriy. 'Like the bloody Pink Panther, you must have been. Save your tippytoeing for chasing silverware this season.' He paused. 'For now, let's enjoy the quiet while we can. I can't see much of it ahead of us this season.'

Dmitriy pulled his robe belt tight, dropped his head back against the lounger, and let out a guttural sigh. 'Me fucking neither.'

Cas surveyed the rack for the right bottle. There it was – the Bodegas Hermanos. He swept it out and flipped it like a flaring bartender before skipping over to the elegant glasses ready on the counter, each large enough to contain a full bottle's worth. He gathered them by their stems, spun on his heels, and looked out of the window to eye Amber sat at the garden dining table, where she basked in the summer sunshine whilst admiring the mosaicked playhouse. He savoured the whole scene. A cosy warmth rose inside him. As he closed his eyes and took a deep breath in, the copper of her hair remained with him. *Ring ring.*

He controlled his exhale and slowly opened his eyes, giving himself a moment before a measured march over to his phone. He flipped it over to see the caller ID and immediately answered it. '*Hola,* Ali. For what do I owe the pleasure this day?'

'It's not much of a pleasure, I'm afraid.'

'What is it? They not make the announcement until tomorrow, yes?'

'Officially that's right, but I have word from a reputable source that we've lost the appeal. The result of the game and the league stand, but he still has his stadium ban.'

'*Maltadita prohibición del estadio. No hay justicia ¡Me cago en tu puta madre!*' hissed Cas in rapid fire. 'Are you sure?'

'My source is solid. I wouldn't have brought this to you if it wasn't.' Silence hung on the line. 'I'm sorry. We did everything we could.'

Cas raked his teeth over his bottom lip. 'I know . . . I know. Thanks for all of your work.'

'It's no problem. Speak soon.'

'Yes.' As Cas took the phone away from his ear, he heard his name again and re-raised it.

'You still there?' asked Ali.

'Yes.'

'Take those fuckers apart this season.'

Cas nodded. 'We will. *Adiós.*'

'I thought you'd gotten lost in there,' said Amber with a chortle as he came out, her eyes still closed, enjoying bathing in the summer rays. 'What were you doing?'

He clinked the glasses against the bottle. 'Finding the perfect one for the celebrating.'

She immediately opened her eyes; a smile spread ear to ear instantly. He placed her gigantic glass on the table and began pouring with the bottle rested across his forearm, sommelier-style. A large glass would have been a third full. He kept pouring.

She smirked his way. 'I don't think the boss of this establishment would approve of you serving such loosey goosey measures. You'll pour this place bust like that.'

He tilted back the bottle just enough to stop its flow. *'Bombón* . . . I am the boss.' He resumed his pour. 'And I would make everything bankrupt . . .' He stopped the pour again and slid the glass closer to her.

Her cheeks flushed as her gaze locked onto his as he sat down. He poured himself a glass and lifted it.

'To the real boss. Head physio, *men's* first team. *Salud.*'

'*Salud.*'

They clinked glasses, their eyes not veering a degree off each others' as they each took a sip. Cas settled back into his seat, widening his visual field to take in the greens of the garden, the blue of the sky, and the golden light framing Amber. A satisfied grin emerged on his face.

She raised her glass again. 'And good luck with the verdict tomorrow.'

He determinedly kept his facial expression exactly as it was as he gratefully nodded.

'Fingers crossed you and the guys get what you deserve and that prick finally gets put in his place. Champagne tomorrow!'

He strained inside to keep his tone cheerful as he re-raised his glass. 'Champagne.' He took a swig. 'So, they only ask you today about the promotion?'

'Yep. Completely out of the blue. I hadn't been sounded out about it, hadn't expressed an interest in it, nothing. Rob's gone all of a sudden and they've come to me before advertising it. I'm probably a bloody diversity hire.'

'Don't say that. Are you sure you want it?'

'I mean, it's a massive opportunity. Big pay bump. Profile. I'd be crazy not to have taken it.'

Cas eyed her. 'Big opportunity. But I feel some hesitation . . .'

Amber swirled the red around her glass. 'It'll just be bizarre sat on the bench opposite you twice a season.'

'Ha. I guess it will. But where you sit a few hours in the season is not the most important. Where you sit all the rest of the time, that's the main thing. Sitting across from me here, now, is not bizarre. Is *correcto. Destinado. Infinitamente,*' he said, holding his wedding ring.

She smiled cautiously.

'Come home. Please,' he said, putting his hand on the table, asking for hers.

She glanced away, towards the playhouse, then back at him and his outstretched hand. Her eyes flitted down as she deliberated. Then it came – she placed his hand on his.

'I want to . . .' Her eyes welled up. '. . . but you hurt me so bad.'

Cas dipped his head. 'I know . . . I know.' His words barely made it out.

'What you thought about me.' Her lip trembled.

'I know, *mi amor*. But trust in me, if you can, when I say to you . . . it was not about you. I always feel like . . .' he contemplated his words and gulped, '. . . I am not a real man—'

'What are you talking about?' Amber protested. 'Of course you're a real m—'

He squeezed her hand as tears rolled down his face. 'Look at me. At these hands . . . they can't protect you. I can't even protect myself.'

'Look at where we live.' She waved her hand towards the house. 'This is because of what *you're* capable of. We don't live in a slum. It's not dog eat dog here. What could you possibly have to protect me or protect yourself from?'

He remained silent.

'I don't need a barbarian. I don't want one. I love *you*. I married *you*. Being big and strong means nothing. The sort of strength that *you* have is what I want. You're a good man. That is strength. You're a loving man. That is strength. You're a smart, creative man. That is strength. You love me – I know you do – and despite how deeply you hurt me, I love you too. Our love is real strength.'

His free hand clasped their hands together as tears streamed down both their faces. *'Te quiero.'*

'I love you too. *Infinitamente,*' she said, lining her ring up beside his. The two leaned in towards each other and softly kissed – the salty tears running between their lips – before hugging each other with all their might.

He planted a few kisses on her cheek. 'I missed you so much. You don't know how much. This is no home without you.'

She ran a hand through the back of his hair and cupped his face with her hands, brimming with affection. 'I missed you too,' she said, her tears still streaming as she met his lips with a full-lipped, luscious kiss. 'I just need to know one thing,' she said as she took her face back and wiped some of her tears away. 'You won't keep any more from me.'

He wiped his face somewhat dry, then looked at her. 'Of course, *mi amor*. No more.'

'Complete transparency.'

'Totalmente.'

'There's nothing else big you haven't told me? Nothing else that could come between us?'

His mind hurtled back to the tightening chokehold, his abject terror, and finding his trousers and underwear around his ankles, hurting down below. 'No,' he replied, his solitary word squeaking out of him as he tried to maintain eye contact.

Her hold of him went limp. 'What is it?'

'What is what?'

'What is it you're not telling me?'

'Nothing, *mi amor.*'

'Don't *mi amor* me. Tell me,' she said.

'I don't know what you mean.'

'Cas. Don't pretend you don't know what I mean.'

'I don't,' he insisted desperately.

She relinquished her hold, screeched her chair back, and rocketed to her feet. 'You lied to me for years. I see you now. There's something else. Just tell me, for God's sake.'

'Is nothing, *mi amor.*'

'It's bloody well something. I don't even care what it is. Just tell me!'

'Amber . . . is nothing.'

She stepped around her chair, pushed it back in, and took a deep breath. 'I love you, Cas,' she stated, her tone low. 'But if you're going to wedge a lie between us, I can't do this.'

'I'm not—' Her look stopped him dead in his tracks.

'Goodbye, Cas.' Deflated, she turned away and took off.

'Amber,' he called.

She carried on without response.

'Amber,' he said, louder this time.

She stopped and looked back at him.

He stood up and pushed his chair in. 'Don't go. You stay here now, in your home . . . until I make you believe me.'

'You're not going to make me believe a lie.'

'You stay until we fix this. It's my turn for the hotel now. I just get a bag and I go. This is your home too.' He lowered his gaze and headed past her for the house. As she watched his every step, he never looked back her way.

CHAPTER 2

The tiny fingers randomly wiggled like alien tentacles as they tried to latch onto his finger, which was so huge that it would make a handful. Gunnar leaned away, taking his finger out of range of the jet-black-haired baby gawping up at him from the mat. His own expression was not dissimilar as he studied every little incoherent movement. In the background, he heard the intercom from the front gate buzz.

'I'll get it,' shouted Penelope, Gunnar's wife, from a far-off room. 'You keep him entertained.'

Gunnar put his head in his hands with a sigh and sanded his hands up and down his face. As he removed them, the baby laughed. Gunnar looked on blankly. Suddenly, the baby's lip began quivering.

'Don't,' pleaded Gunnar.

The baby sobbed, then howled, screwing its eyes shut.

Gunnar closed his too as the squawky tone went through him. After a moment, he reached down and scooped up his tiny son, holding him away like a feral animal that may bite if too close. Arrhythmically, he began rocking the baby back and forth. The screams escalated. 'Why?'

A bassy, Icelandic voice came from the doorway. 'You've got to hold him like you mean it, my boy.'

Gunnar's breathing seized for a moment as he instinctively brought his son tighter against him. He turned as his son's crying raged on. Towering over Penelope, who stood six foot one barefoot herself, was a broad-shouldered, rangy man in his sixties with circular, black-rimmed glasses and a head thick with unruly white hair that looked styled by a touch with a Van de Graaf generator.

'What are you doing here?' asked Gunnar, a deep scowl on his face.

'Gunnar!' said Penelope.

'It's OK, darling,' the man reassured her. 'There was never much room made for pleasantries in our house. I hope yours is different in that regard.'

'What are you doing here?' repeated Gunnar over his still-crying son, more insistent for an answer this time.

'My boy. I know you don't care much for me, but I'm hoping you can find the grace to let an old man hold his first grandson. May I?' he asked, stepping closer.

Gunnar dead-eyed his father for a long moment. 'We're going out in a minute, so now isn't a good time,' he replied, adjusting his son against him as he continued to wail.

'Gunnar, Magnus has come straight from the airport,' said Penelope.

'So? Nobody asked him to come here.'

She shook her head at her husband's bluntness. 'So let him have a hold before we make tracks.' She turned to their guest. 'I really am sorry. We'll have to do this properly another day.'

'It's my fault for showing up unannounced. I'm lucky you're even in. Gunnar, may I?' He stepped closer and put his hands out hopefully.

'I don't think he's in the mood,' said Gunnar as the baby bawled away.

'That's true, but he certainly can't get any worse,' replied Magnus.

Devoid of any further easy excuses and with Penelope urging him on with her eyes, Gunnar stepped towards his father. Magnus came the rest of the way and put out his gigantic hands. He stood a couple of inches taller than his son, even. The two exchanged the baby with the care of a robber swapping a fake for a Fabergé on a pressure sensor. Within seconds of the baby being in Magnus's arms, he ceased crying and laid peacefully, transfixed by the reflection from his grandfather's glasses. Having softened during the cushioned passing of the baby, Gunnar's demeanour resolidified.

'Look at that,' said Penelope as she slipped her lithe, defined arm into her jacket. 'Love at first sight.'

'It's in our blood. It couldn't have been any other way, could it, little one?' Magnus offered one of his digits to his grandson's lively hands. The baby eagerly gripped it. 'What have you called him?' The question was aimed at Gunnar, but only a glare came back his way.

'Our little man is called Jokull Magnusson,' said Penelope, pronouncing the J as a Y.

'Jokull Magnusson?' asked Magnus, mildly surprised.

'Yes. We call him Joki. I can't say I was a fan when I initially heard it, but Gunnar said it's your word for joyful?'

'That it is,' replied Magnus.

'What's more important than being joyful; happy?' she said.

'What indeed?' Magnus grinned. 'And you went with Magnusson?'

Gunnar stood by, stony faced.

'Yes. I know it's your tradition, but going with Gunnarson in this country was just going to get all kinds of confusing,' said Penelope.

Magnus contemplated her point for a moment, looked over to his scowling son, then back to his grandson. 'Little Joki Magnusson,' he said softly with a warm, prideful smile.

'Is he squelching there, Granddad?' asked Penelope, already making her way over to him.

'Granddad is *Afi* in our language,' he said in baby talk, his eyes never leaving little Joki. 'Yes, maybe.' He tenderly handed Joki over to his mother.

'Let's get you changed, Joki,' said Penelope as she knelt down, put her son on the mat and pulled his little trousers down. 'It's lovely to finally met you,' she said, aiming her words back at Magnus as she peeled open one side of Joki's nappy. 'We'll have to do this properly in the next few days. Are you staying close by?'

'Yes, practically down the road.' He turned to grin at Gunnar, whose eyes barely blinked.

'Do you have any time tomorrow evening?' asked Penelope.

'I came for my family so all I have is time for you but if tomorrow is at all inconvenient, we needn't do it so quickly.'

'How long are you in town for?'

'Quite a while, it turns out,' replied Magnus. 'I signed a three-year deal, so I'd hope at least that long.'

'What did you say?' blurted out Gunnar.

'I've taken the manager's job with the Surgeons. Somebody's got to keep you on your toes, my boy.'

Gunnar's nostrils flared as the veins in his neck and forehead visibly throbbed to his skin's surface.

'But seriously, it was an unmissable opportunity. What was I to do? I get to be close to my grandson, to manage in this league, maybe even to make things better between us. You wouldn't begrudge your old man that, would you?'

Gunnar glared through his father.

'Dear.' Penelope pulled the wet nappy out from under Joki and turned to her silent husband. 'That sounds nice. We only get one family. Plus, he looks like he has the magic touch of a babysitter.'

Magnus smiled. 'Naturally.' He pulled a scrap of paper from his inner jacket pocket and set it on the floor by Penelope. 'That's my cell number. Message me so we can organise something soon.'

'Of course. I'd get up to give you a hug, but I think you don't need my wee covered hands around you.' She pulled a fresh nappy out from under the edge of the mat as Joki wriggled tirelessly.

'It's no problem. Thank you for welcoming me into your home. It's a pleasure to finally meet you. I'll be seeing you soon.'

'Say goodbye to *Afi*, Joki.' She took Joki's wrist between her thumb and middle finger and gently made him wave.

Magnus seized his chest, heartbroken by the cuteness of it, then walked over to Gunnar. 'It's good to see you, son.' He held his hand out for a shake.

Gunnar eyed him, not moving a muscle.

'Too formal.' Magnus stepped forward and wrapped his arms around his inanimate son before lowering his voice and flipping into Icelandic. 'That little man is the greatest thing you have ever done and will ever do. You should be proud, my boy.' He patted Gunnar's granite-hard back and stepped back to look him in the face. 'But *that name*?' He grinned sourly and shook his head before turning away. Flipping back to English, he aimed a 'farewell' back towards Penelope and Joki, then left.

Gunnar's eyes followed him until he disappeared from sight, then flicked back towards those still in the room. They fell upon the used nappy – still open next to the mat – and its straw-yellow stain.

*

With a jiggle and a few splashes into the dirty honey coloured liquid, he was done. He tucked himself away, flicked the seat down, and darted out, leaving the wooden frame to rattle off the toilet bowl. As he careered down the stairs, he heard a car pull into the drive. Reaching the hallway, his friend – a short, baby-faced teen with shoulder-length fair hair – was zipping up his tracksuit top.

'That your mum?' asked the animated fifteen-year-old Gunnar in his native tongue. He stood almost his full adult height but was gangly; yet to fill out.

His friend nodded, resigned to leaving as he flung his holdall over his shoulder.

'Alright. See you tomorrow, Jóno,' said Gunnar. The two bro-shook – clasping hands, bumping shoulders, and finishing with a custom elbow bump – before Jónsson turned and headed out of the door, giving a thumbs up over his shoulder as Gunnar closed up behind him. Instead of stepping away from the door, Gunnar stepped to the right just so that his right eye aligned with a gap where the edge of the lace curtain did not cover the side window. Out of it, he watched his friend climb into his car.

'Gunnar!' came the booming shout from upstairs, startling him. 'Up here, now.'

Faster than before, Gunnar took off on the return journey, blazing along the hall and pounding up the stairs. He dashed to his parents' bedroom at the end of the landing. It was empty. The door to an adjoining room, usually locked, was open a crack. Gunnar crept in towards it.

'Where the hell do you think you're going?' boomed the marching Magnus – his unruly hair as black as coal – from behind him as he entered, causing his son to spin round.

'I just thought you might be in—'

'A million times I've told you. Will you not learn?' As he reached Gunnar, he grabbed his collar but instead of a straight yank, he pushed the collar away then circled it around Gunnar's neck, like a matador *pase*-ing his cape, unbalancing his son before dragging him round and back out of the bedroom door. Gunnar did not resist, just making sure that his stumbling feet kept up with his body. Magnus let go of him as they entered the bathroom. He pointed into the toilet. 'What's this?'

Gunnar peered in to see the dark urine. 'I'm sorry, Dad.'

'Boy. Do you know how far we are past sorry? This is not difficult stuff. The information is right up here in front of your fucking eyes multiple times per day.' He pointed to a laminated graphic on the wall depicting different shades of urine, ranging from almost colourless with a large green tick next to it, right the way through to an orangey-brown colour with a large red cross by it. 'There's a one litre bottle of carbohydrate replacement drink in the car every day. There are the electrolyte solutions pre-made in the fridge all the time and all the water in the world. And still, day after day you squander your chances. When will you get it through your thick skull that if you have any chance to make it, you *must* do it all? You can't play like some of those boys. You can't run like them. You need every percentage point you can scrape out of the depths of yourself and *this* is such low-hanging fruit. I'm giving you everything you need to make up ground on them and what do you do? You piss your chances away.'

Gunnar stood utterly downcast. 'I just forget sometimes, Dad. I really am sorry. I'm fucking stupid.'

Magnus examined his face and stepped in close to him. Gunnar's entire body braced. Magnus slowly lifted his palms, showing them empty, and then wrapped his arms around his son. 'My boy. No son of mine is stupid,' he said in a soothing tone. 'Acuity is in your blood. You're just easily distracted and don't understand the damage you can do to your future by taking your eye off the ball.' He laid his head on Gunnar's shoulder and took a deep breath. Gunnar eventually put his arms around his father.

'You know I only ultimately want the best for you, don't you?' asked Magnus. Gunnar rested his head against his father's shoulder and nodded before Magnus tenderly lifted it off and placed his forehead against his son's, resting a palm on his nape. 'Good.' Magnus slid his arm around his son's neck and suddenly heaved him down into a headlock.

'What're you doing, Dad?!' gasped Gunnar, trying to rag his way out of the hold.

'Teaching you the only way you seem to learn, my boy,' said Magnus, sounding regretful as he removed a large empty plastic plunger syringe from his back pocket. Using his foot, he pushed the back of his son's knee down, buckling it to the floor, and then knelt himself, bringing Gunnar's head near the toilet. Gunnar flurried punches against his father's back with his closest hand, trying to get free. 'Stop fighting me, boy. This is for *you*.' He lowered the syringe into the toilet bowl and drew up a plunger of the dark urine. 'Smell that.' He held it close to Gunnar's face. His mouth was locked shut as he still flapped around, trying to squirm free. 'And that's diluted by the toilet water. Your piss should be so clear you could quite happily drink it. But it isn't, so now you have to find out the difference for yourself.'

Gunnar scrambled around, trying to lever his way out of his father's hold in any and every way he could. Magnus tightened his grip. 'Beating me here is just beating yourself, boy. I can't allow it. Let's just get this over with. It's just medicine.' Magnus leaned against his son, pinning his side against the floor, then partially removed the headlock to clamp Gunnar's nostrils closed.

Gunnar kicked and jostled, desperately trying to get free but within a few seconds, his air ran out. When he gasped, the syringe was ready waiting.

*

'Gunnar,' said Penelope.
His gaze broke away from the nappy towards her and the baby.
'Get your jacket on. Can't miss our first night out.'

Dmitriy tugged both sides of his seatbelt. The buckle held rock solid. He gulped as he pushed himself back into the plush seat. Across the table from him, Andriy watched on as the airport became visible out of the window. He reached a hand across to comfort Dmitriy, whose hand leapt off the seat's armrest like a viper, grabbing and not letting go as he closed his eyes and lowered his head.

The plane levelled out. The few seconds before contact felt like an eternity to Dmitriy. *Thud.* The plane bounced and clattered, rattling his organs uncomfortably inside him. It felt like it would never stop for all of two seconds, then the plane resumed smooth forward motion. He opened his eyes.

'You're lucky I get plenty of calcium,' said Andriy, jokingly shaking his hand off as he took it back. 'You seemed OK on the flight out?'

'That was to paradise. Now we come back to hell.'

Dmitriy went to the next available passport control booth just ahead of Andriy. As the midfielder arrived and handed his document over, the guard – a middle-aged man with a crew cut – looked at it, then at him, then cast a glance sideways to Andriy at the next booth before thrusting the passport back towards him and nodding him through.

As they met after their checks, Dmitriy spoke quickly in Russian. 'The fucking look he just gave us, that arsehole at passport control.'

Andriy let the comment go.

Dmitriy continued. 'The media is going to be like a pack of ravenous vultures here. You saw how they were at Emily's.'

'You're a good penalty taker, yes?' asked Andriy.

Dmitriy frowned. 'What're you on about?'

'Well?' Andriy waited for an answer.

'Umm, yeh. Well, I would be if Victor ever let me near one.'

'What do you do if the goalkeeper does a merry dance, jumps up and down flapping his arms around and shouts at you as you're placing the ball and running up?'

'Ignore him.'

'Exactly. That's all the press are doing. It's their job to get a reaction; to make you miss. You win by giving them nothing; not a flinch. They'll be doing this all season, as will many others. If you want to be the best now, dealing with this is part and parcel.' They came up to the doors that led to the arrivals lounge. 'Ready?'

Dmitriy nodded determinedly.

Andriy stepped in front and took the doors first. During the moment between them opening and closing, Dmitriy saw the sea of photographers, camerapeople, and reporters waiting; so many that the airport had stationed extra security by the doors and put up a retractable belt barrier. There was no turning back. When the door re-opened for him, he carried on through into the frenzy of flashes, clicks, and shouts. But the tone of the calls for his attention was different to what he experienced during the final night of last season outside Emily's. They were less interrogatory and more respectful; even complementary. His ear picked a shout out that asked, 'How does it feel to be a hero to millions all over the world?' Passing this gaggle, vast as it was, was a breeze. He just fixed his eyes on Andriy's feet in front and kept moving.

'Gordost' nashey natsii!' The friendly shout instinctively turned Dmitriy's and Andriy's heads. A man with sharp Slavic features and a black bomber jacket over a red Russian national team jersey was at the front of the crowd near them, holding his hand over the barrier for a shake. As Dmitriy move towards him, his face soured. *'Ty merzost'!'* As quickly as his tone turned vicious, he launched something at Dmitriy, who reflexively tried to dodge it, snatching his hand back and turning his back to protect himself. He was hit. Andriy darted over to cover him as the press and security guards grabbed the offender and wrestled him to the ground.

'Are you OK?' Andriy asked as he desperately scanned the back of his jacket with his eyes and hand. Dmitriy frenziedly tried to look at and feel around his own back. Their hands came to a slimy wet patch.

Dmitriy checked his fingers, breathing easier as he saw the substance was not red but clear. 'What the fuck is this?' he asked as he sniffed it.

Andriy scanned the floor as he rubbed his fingers together, trying to get a sense of what was on them. 'There,' he said, pointing to something a few yards away on the floor, as two security guards approached them. Dmitriy looked. A trail of the clear substance led to a burst condom. Andriy sighed and shook his head, 'It's K-Y.'

CHAPTER 3

Half of the dressing room were gathered around the open cardboard box, sniggering like schoolboys. Finney hushed them, fearing they may be heard over the music playing from the speaker in the centre of the room.

'You got it ready?' Finney whispered to Charlie.

Charlie scrolled through the playlist on his phone and nodded. Some of the others close by were spluttering; one crying tears of laughter. Even those not immediately involved, just getting dressed or undressed, were watching on, mischievous grins plastered across their faces. Charlie clicked a new track and turned it up. 'Faith' by George Michael flooded the airwaves right through to the shower area.

'Rasclaart! Someone turn that whack shit off, I beg you!' shouted Victor from his shower stall. He moved the crucifix on his gold chain over his shoulder and grabbed the shampoo. As he applied some, the track abruptly ended, giving way to the unmistakable spewing base sound, gasps, and melody of Genuwine's 'Pony'. 'YES!' shouted Victor. 'Real old school vibes, bredrin. Ain't Chaz's pasty white ass choosing this shit, was it?' As he two-stepped away in his stall, lathering to the beat, a bunch of the players tiptoed into the shower area.

'Man's got bars for you, fellas,' shouted Victor at the top of his voice just before the lyrics of the song kicked in. 'I'm a don baller, I'm looking for punani, Dem gyal who'll take the Easy D, No cryin' learnin' how to walk again.' Something slid into the shower and hit his foot. He ceased singing, washed the suds out of his face, and took a look. Laid against his foot was a soap dildo, balls and all. 'What the—' Then they slid in from all directions. His feet were bombarded by soapy phalluses as his ears were bombarded by the cackles of his teammates outside the stall. 'You're sick, you dickheads,' he said as he kicked some away, only to be squirted from all angles of the top of his stall and deafened by squeaks. He looked up to see the streams washing him coming out of rubber penises being squeezed by their balls, squeaking like rubber ducks. He raised his hands in futility, trying to cover himself. The howls from the adjacent stalls and the dressing room boomed all around.

As he nudged the phallic soaps out from under the stall, his delirious teammates left the shower area, many struggling to stand upright as they heaved laughter out. The ruckus continued alongside the music, escalating as Victor, wrapped in his towel, stormed into the dressing room.

'What in the fuck is wrong with you, detty bludcaarts?!'

'What happened to "Thou shalt not swear", God squad?' taunted Charlie.

'Fuck you, Chaz,' snapped Victor.

Finney wiped the tears from his face and caught his breath. 'Stop being such a ratty ringpiece, Vic. This is exactly why we're trying to lube you up before Dimmy's return.'

Victor sucked his teeth and shook his head.

'Catch.' Nixon's voice came from behind Victor, whose eyes flickered towards him and the object whizzing his way. He snatched it out of the air. It was one of the squirty toy penises. The laughter ramped up again, some of his teammates falling about on their benches. His face scrunched up as he examined it. 'Which one of you Whammers bought this shit?'

With all the noise, nobody had noticed the sound of the door. From around the corner emerged Dmitriy. A wave of silence fell as everybody noticed him. Victor turned to see what everybody was looking at and froze, rubber cock in hand. For a few seconds they stood silently in a strange stand-off.

'What you look at me for?' asked Dmitriy. 'It not mine. Too small for me . . . like Victor's.'

The dressing room buckled with laughter, Finney slapping his hand against the bench as tears erupted from his eyes. Dmitriy scanned around his teammates before he chuckled with relief. The only stony face was Victor's. He tossed the toy over his shoulder towards the showers and walked over to his dressing area.

After Dmitriy had done the rounds greeting teammates, some of whom checked he was OK after his incident at the airport, he wandered over to his dressing area. Victor stood beside him, back turned, dabbing his legs dry through his wrapped towel.

'How was your summer, Easy?' asked Dmitriy as he sat down and opened his bag.

Victor glanced over his shoulder, said 'A'ight, man. A'ight,' and resumed drying, back still turned.

Dmitriy waited a few moments. The reciprocal question never came. He lowered his eyes, sat still for a moment, then began removing his shoes.

Victor looked at his clothes, deliberating over something. Eventually, he picked up his gold and black Versace boxers, held his towel wrap with one hand, and started to awkwardly try putting his boxers on with the other. Dmitriy could not help but notice. When Victor finally got his boxers secure, he lifted his towel to his chest, moved the gold crucifix from over his shoulder to its regular position, and began drying his front.

As Dmitriy undressed, Cas, Steve, and some of the other coaching staff entered and began mingling. On the first day back doing individual fitness testing, players were coming and going at different times and the staff had not seen everybody yet.

Steve made his way over and heartily shook Dmitriy's hand. 'You alright, kiddo?'

Dmitriy nodded his head.

Steve could see he did not want to talk about the airport incident. 'How was your summer?'

'Very good, thank you. How about yours?'

'Not too shabby, thanks. Think the missus is glad to have me back out from under her feet. How's Andriy?'

Victor half-turned his head for a moment as he dressed himself.

'He misses the beach already,' replied Dmitriy.

'Tell him if he wants a real beach to get himself along to Blackpool.'

'Black-pool. I not hear of it. I will tell him.'

Steve grinned to himself. 'You fully recovered from that bump you had?'

Dmitriy patted his ribs. 'Not perfect, but good enough.'

'Good,' said Steve, patting his shoulder before moving on.

A few moments later, as Dmitriy was down to his boxers, Cas arrived. *'Hola.'*

'*Privyet,* boss.'

'You alright?' Cas asked, nodding towards Dmitriy's ribs.

'I'm OK, thanks.'

Cas's tone sobered. 'And after yesterday? You ready?'

Dmitriy knew he did not just mean for the fitness testing or even the football that season. 'I hope so.'

Cas nodded earnestly. 'We talk properly over the next few days.' As he shook Dmitriy's hand, McGlynn entered the dressing room followed by a cameraman and a sound man. Everybody ground to a halt, some raised towels, and the music shut off.

'Welcome back, guys!' said McGlynn. 'As you were. Pretend they aren't here.'

'Fucking wish *you* weren't here,' muttered Charlie, drawing the snickers of some nearby teammates.

McGlynn and his crew made their way towards Cas and Dmitriy, who both eyed them suspiciously. McGlynn had an enormous smile smattered across his face.

'Yo, Andy.' Victor, half dressed, stepped out ahead of Dmitriy and Cas and shook McGlynn's hand, paying more attention to the camera. 'Dis shit is sick. You makin' one of those behind-the-scenes documentaries 'bout us?' He nodded to the cameraman and bounced his pecs. 'Fo' de gyal dem. One hundred percent from the spot and on your spot, ya get me?' he purred down the lens, finishing by suggestively licking his lips.

'Maybe, Victor. Maybe,' replied McGlynn, having not really heard the aside.

'Shouldn't there be more of dem?' asked Victor.

'Fly on the wall, Victor. Minimally invasive,' said the owner, tapping his finger to his temple as he repositioned himself to encourage Victor to turn and include Cas and Dmitriy in the group. 'Cas'. He gave a quick customary nod and eagerly thrust a hand towards Dmitriy. 'Dmitriy! How was your break?'

'Very good thank you, Mr McGlynn.'

'Andy, Dmitriy. Please,' he said, nearly shaking Dmitriy's hand off its wrist.

'I saw what happened at the airport yesterday. Reprehensible stuff. I just want you to know that I'm here to do everything I can to support you,' said McGlynn. 'I'm so grateful you felt comfortable enough to be yourself here. It's unbelievably brave.'

Dmitriy gave a polite, awkward smile, conscious of the camera.

McGlynn positioned himself between Dmitriy and Victor and put a hand on each of their shoulders. 'I want to show the world that we lead the game both on the pitch and off. I want every fan of every inclination, colour, and creed to know that if they want to feel truly included in this beautiful game we call football, they have a home right here with us.' He turned to the group, missing Victor's side-eye. 'Gentlemen. This is a huge season we have ahead of us. We're standing for more than just *our* football now. We stand for football itself.' He paused, waiting for a round of applause that never came. He turned back to Dmitriy and Victor. 'The profound transcends applause sometimes. Takes a while to sink in.' The duo did not know what to say.

'Is there something we can do for you, Mr McGlynn?' asked Cas.

'Andy, please, Cas,' McGlynn replied with a tiny edge. 'Firstly, I just wanted to introduce the crew to everybody.' He turned back out to the dressing room and raised his voice. 'Everyone, this is Adam and Michael. You're going to see them around a fair bit this season in some capacity.' The crew waved around, getting waves and nods back from all the players as McGlynn turned back to Cas and the duo. 'We can chat about the filming in a minute. Mostly, I was coming to give Dimmy some moral support and to let him know how much he's valued here.' He switched his attention to Dmitriy. 'If you ever need to speak, you drop me a call anytime, day or night.'

Victor exchanged a wry smile with Charlie, who rolled his eyes.

'I know talk can be cheap, but you'll see over the coming days that this club is ready to support you through our actions.'

'Thank you, Andy,' said Dmitriy. As he shook hands with McGlynn, the club's owner opened his body out so give a clear line of sight to the camera.

'Big season, fellas,' said McGlynn, projecting to the room. 'Do the shirt proud.' He beckoned Cas to step outside with him. As they headed for the exit, a voice called after them.

'Andy,' said Adam the sound man, almost apologetically. 'Your mic.'

McGlynn gave a thumbs up and flipped a switch on the transmitter pack attached to the back of his trousers.

Finney used the moment to head him off. 'Andy. How's it going?' he said with his most charming smile.

'Great thanks, Ian. Can't stop now.' He patted Finney's arm. 'Catch you soon.'

'Shall we book a meeting in?' he called after McGlynn.

'Yeh. Get your agent to ring my office,' he said as he carried on out without so much as a glance back.

'How was your summer, Cas?' asked McGlynn, sweet as saccharine, as they reached the corridor.

'I don't want the cameras,' said Cas. 'We are a sports team. Not the Kardashians.'

'Cas, my friend, you've got me all wrong. Can't you see we can be more than just a football team now?'

'We are a football team. We entertain the fans on the pitch.'

'I know that. Football always has to be central to what we're doing here, but we can be more too. We can take this club to a whole other level.'

Cas folded his arms.

'Look,' levelled McGlynn, 'I know that maybe there was a touch of . . . there was a bit of a breakdown of communication between us at the end of last season, but we're all still here, aren't we? We're all friends.'

'I don't want them, Andy. The dressing room, the dynamic, is very important. I don't want the outside interests to interrupt that. There will be too much extra attention, anyway.'

McGlynn smiled to himself and shook his head. 'I can see where you're coming from, Cas, I really can, but you can't see the bigger picture yet.'

'Tell me,' said Cas. 'What bigger picture do I not see?'

'All in good time, my friend. Tell you what. Out of respect for your position here, I won't have the crew in the dressing room until I reveal my master plan. They'll just be around like a few extra members of our club media team. Deal?'

Cas thought on it for a few moments. 'And you won't be angry if I still say no after?'

'Angry? Not at this club, Cas. We're about more than that now.'

He surveyed McGlynn's face. He still did not trust him. 'OK. No dressing room. They can be around outside.'

'Excellent. Next time you'll see them in there is at the big reveal. This is going to be an incredible season, Cas.' He offered his hand.

Cas shook it, although unable to fully shake off his own reluctance.

Through the parade of bodies kitted out in black and gold, their eyes met. Each player shook Gunnar's hand, exchanged some smiley small talk, took a GPS tracking vest from him, and headed across to a long line of cones to stand side by side. From the back of the queue as it reduced and snaked, Lawler kept catching eyes with his manager until eventually they met at the front.

Gunnar fiddled with the vest in his hand for a moment before looking at Lawler, his face devoid of the smile that had greeted all his other players. 'Polly like her medal?'

'Yeh,' he replied meekly. 'Kept robbing it from me cabinet to show her mates.'

Gunnar nodded, half a grin appearing and vanishing just as quickly before his expression hardened. 'Now show me you're one of us.'

Lawler maintained eye contact with him, eventually nodded, took the vest, then headed over to the line.

Gunnar marched over and addressed the players. 'We can't let victory defeat us. A Warrior always has to keep his blade sharp. You saw how fine the margin was last season. I don't want it that close again. And we don't just have them to worry about now. Mark my words, the Surgeons are coming for us too. For those of you who think I'm a cunt, all I can say is that you haven't met my father yet. He is *ruthless*. He will examine every detail he can gather about us, he'll try to dissect every weakness we have, and his team will run us into the ground if we don't start sweating blood today and sweat a river more of it every day that passes.' He signalled one of his coaches to turn the pitch-side PA system on. 'Sweat those black shirts red, men.'

The audio track blared out, announcing the beginning of the Yo-Yo intermittent recovery test level two. If level one was like the bleep test on steroids, level two was like the souped-up level one on speed. As with the bleep test, pre-recorded bleeps marked the time when participants must reach a point twenty metres away and return to the start. Every minute, the test track announced the start of a new level within which the duration between these bleeps became shorter, meaning the runner must up their pace to keep up with them. One of the major differences from the bleep test that counterintuitively made the Yo-Yo test tougher was the ten-second rest period between each there-and-back run. This recovery time – which made the test more specific to stop-start sport like football – spent in a five-metre *recovery zone*, allowed the running to occur at a faster pace throughout than the bleep test, meaning it attacked the body's energy systems more sharply. The test subjects run for as long as they could keep pace with the bleeps, again and again, literally *ad nauseam*.

The first beep sounded. Lawler and the pack set off. Thoroughbreds, they breezed through the first few minutes of the test, which would see most mere mortals off. As the going started to get tough, the first players to bow out of the test were, unsurprisingly, the goalkeepers. Nobody wanted to be the first outfielder to drop out but eventually the pace broke Denton, a second-string centre back in his twilight years. Pouring with sweat, the troop kept rushing back and forth, tearing up the turf. This was a battle of the will as much as it was the lungs and the legs, and nobody wanted to be the next to break. Gunnar would look on them differently than the old steed; they would be less for putting out to pasture and more for the glue factory.

A few more lengths in and Ayissi failed to stop at the line, walking out of the test. The newish big money striker had only been around seven months or so; he would be OK. Right as the bleep went to signal the next ten second rest, Hardison spewed all over. When the next beep went, he ran again. They galloped now.

Lawler knew that as a midfielder, he had to finish in the top three or four for his effort to be respectable. Doubled over, sucking in the air during the next rest, he saw the pack starting to thin. His legs and lungs felt as if they had been dipped in acid. Again he went, meeting the beep and making it back. A few more bit the dust.

A few minutes later, only three weary runners remained: Lawler, Botterill, and Hardison. Fatigue saturated their sloppy movements yet somehow, they were almost sprinting, cheered on by their retired teammates, who had regained some of their breath. On the next run out, Botterill missed the beep by a hair's breadth.

'Second warning, Botsy!' yelled the fitness coach over the PA system. A third warning would mean he was out. Botterill made it back to the rest zone just in time. Lawler forced himself to stay upright, linked his fingers behind his neck, opened his elbows as wide as he could, and snorted in some precious oxygen through his burning nostrils.

'You're fucking done,' growled Hardison at Lawler, barely getting his words out before having to suck in some more air. 'Give it up.'

Lawler dropped his hands and stepped to the line. *Bleep.* They went again. As the squad urged them on to beat the next bleep, Gunnar watched on, arms crossed. He had not uttered a word of encouragement so far. As the trio ran back to the recovery zone, Botterill lagged behind. Leaning like a sprinter for a photo finish, he met the bleep at the line but toppled forward to the turf. His race was run.

Hardison vomited again then spat the afters Lawler's way as he squared up to the line. Half aware, dazed by pain, Lawler lolled forward to go again. *Bleep.* They ran out, almost shoulder to shoulder. At the turn, Hardison veered across, bumping into Lawler. In a sort of agony-induced fugue state, Lawler didn't notice. All that existed to him was the bleep, the line, and Gunnar's unwavering gaze. His legs readjusted under him, keeping him going.

The bump had slowed Hardison down. He was half a yard behind Lawler and not catching up. The entire squad and coaching staff, barring Gunnar, rallied them on. Hardison veered towards Lawler again, trying to shoulder barge him and make it look accidental, but missed. Knowing he was done, he tumbled to the ground, tangling legs with Lawler on his way.

Lawler lost his balance, clawed at the ground, and somehow managed to correct back into his stride, just missing the beep, which was almost drowned out by the cheers of his teammates.

'Warning one, Bry, but you can leave it there,' called the fitness coach as he reached down to turn the track off.

'No!' shouted Gunnar. 'He's still in.' He looked over to Lawler. 'Aren't you?'

Hands on his knees, struggling for air, he squinted over. Gunnar looked like a photographic negative in front of a black sky to him. He shoved himself upright but before he could step to the line, the bleep went. Heaving, he launched into this sprint. His arms furiously pumped as he propelled himself forward through what felt like treacle. He met the beep at the line and mustered the sharpest turn he could. An involuntary groan escaped him.

'Show me, Bry!' yelled Gunnar. Lawler reached the line just short of the bleep.

'Second warning,' announced the fitness coach. 'You still going?'

Delirious, Lawler nodded. He closed his eyes to stop their rolling around dizzying and tilted his face to the sky, hoping that his wandering feet found the line for him. He faced forward. The test announced its highest level yet. *Bleep*. The squad willed him on as he fell forward into a raggedy sprint.

'Show me!' repeated Gunnar, louder still.

Lawler's legs churned away. The groans came with every breath now. He planted his foot on the line just about with the beep and flailed back towards the recovery zone. Snot streamed out of his nose.

'SHOW ME, BRY!'

His eyes wobbled around in his skull, unable to focus on the recovery zone entrance, which he could barely see now the whole image was washed out to him. His muscles seared as they kept the momentum of his legs going just long enough for him to crash land over what he hoped was the line on the bleep.

The players went berserk and ran over. A couple rolled him onto his back, lifted his legs and shook them, helping the blood back to his barely conscious brain.

When Lawler eventually got up and regained his senses, a few of his teammates accompanied him on a stroll to help get freshly oxygenated blood back to his shrieking muscles. Gunnar was gone.

A while later, as the group stretched off, the fitness coach came over and tapped Lawler on his shoulder. 'Unbelievable effort that, Bry,' he said as he crouched next to him.

Shattered, all Lawler could muster was a grateful nod.

'Obviously got your level recorded, which is great, off the charts . . .' He sheepishly covered his mouth for a moment. '. . . but I think there was something wrong with your vest. We didn't get any of your heart rate and force data and the boss wants it all; you heard him before, they're going to scrutinise every detail, so we have to as well. Sorry but we're gonna need to re-test you next week or the week after.'

'You got my score though!' exhaustedly snapped Lawler.

'I know, Bry. I know. I'm just the messenger.'

Lawler clenched his jaw, took a deep breath, and nodded.

'I am sorry. Here – while I'm here, pass me your vest.'

Lawler peeled the sweaty, skin-tight tracking vest off over his head and passed it to him.

The fitness coach checked the small processing unit zipped into it and shook his head, bemused. 'I sorted all these myself. Dunno what's gone on here.'

Lawler's jaw muscles bulged as he began to grind his teeth.

CHAPTER 4

Charlie spluttered out the takeout coffee he was sipping and nudged Finney to get his attention as the black Ford Focus rolled into the carpark. They led a bunch of teammates to the car as it parked up. Out climbed Victor.

'Fuuuuucking hell! Where's the Golden Gyal gone?' teased Finney, referring to Victor's gold-wrapped Lamborghini.

'Big man. I am blessed. What am I needin' such garish trinkets for?'

'Gotta give it to Chuks,' said Finney. 'This is the best ventriloquism act I've ever seen. Operating you from miles away and I can't see the hand up your arse or anything.'

Everybody laughed except Victor, who stood tall, his nose raised to them. 'This ain't Chuks, fam. This is humility. One of the ten commandments. Educate yourself.'

Charlie piped up. 'Vic – I went to a Catholic school. Humility isn't a commandment.'

'Chaz, don't embarrass yourself. Catholic Bible ain't the real Bible.'

'Neither's your bloody LADbible.' The gang chuckled. 'Go on then. Tell us a Commandment.'

'Oh, you want me to lay that shit out for you?'

'Yeh.'

'For all you pagans?'

'Yeh.'

Victor checked his watch – an all-gold Rolex. 'We runnin' late, fam. Ain't got no time for your games.' He turned and made for the facility entrance.

'Oy!' Charlie shouted after him, signalling his mates to up their pace. 'Mr Humility's wearing a fake Rolly!'

Victor broke into a sprint as they chased him, cackling.

The indoor pitch was a makeshift studio, with lighting rigs, background drapes, reflectors, and various cameras and video cameras scattered around.

McGlynn, accompanied by his own film crew, beckoned the squad over. 'Over here, gents. Come on over.'

The players sauntered over. Scattered around behind McGlynn was a collection of arched podiums of different sizes. Each had a different odd number of spots for people to stand on, but unlike regular medal podiums, these were symmetrical around their highest spots – one metre high at most. The structures were also gently curved depth-ways, with the highest spot set back relative to the outermost spots. This multidimensional curve played an optical illusion to make the arches look taller than they were.

Directly behind McGlynn, on the seven-spot podium stood seven mannequins draped in black sheets. He dramatically pointed over to somebody across the studio. The main lights cut, spotlights illuminated the covered mannequins, and an instrumental version of Seven Nation Army pumped out of some nearby speakers.

The players looked around at each other, mystified.

Finney nudged Dmitriy. 'Bit grand for showing us the bloody third kit, isn't it?' he whispered.

Dmitriy shrugged and whispered back, 'Too grand for *him*?'

After letting the music build for a few seconds, McGlynn pulled a microphone from his back pocket. 'Weavers, I welcome you. Last season, we made club history with our highest finish ever. On the final day of the season, our place in football history was unjustly taken from us. We played with our hearts on our sleeves against the ultimate regressive football and won, only for the footballing structures to fail us. For a moment, I'm sure we all lost hope in this beautiful game of ours.' He pressed his microphone over his heart and closed his eyes. The players exchanged minute eye rolls and mocking grins.

'But on that very same day,' said McGlynn as he opened his eyes, 'something awoke the hope in my heart. Love. And bravery.'

Dmitriy shrivelled in anticipation.

'Dmitriy,' said McGlynn, 'you and Andriy, your love, your bravery; it has changed football forever.'

Dmitriy glared at the floor, praying for it to swallow him.

'You've given us more than a league title. To trust us to shepherd you through this historical turning point is an unbelievable honour. You have made this club, whose very foundations are built on the motto "From The Same Cloth", a beacon for hope, a symbol of progressiveness, a gamechanger for diversity and inclusion. We will proudly play our hearts out to show all those who never thought this game was for them that we welcome them too; that this is their footballing home. And our hearts won't just be on our sleeves.' The big chorus guitars kicked in and the black covers swept off the mannequins.

Dmitriy's insides sank as he gawked, straining to smile, at the row of headless models donning striking rainbow-coloured shirts. The podium even lined them up in the subtle arc of a rainbow. Rainbow-coloured stripes in restrained tones, pink having replaced violet, ran diagonally across the torsos of the shirts. The background pattern of these stripes mimicked a woven fabric – a common design feature of Weavers' kits down the years. The multi-coloured body sections contrasted elegantly against off-black sleeves and V-necks that connected via wide strips of the same colour along the top of the shoulders. The shorts and socks were the same colour as the sleeves and were accented with rainbow-coloured woven-style stripes.

Nobody could deny the tasteful nature of the new third kit apart from one key feature.

Across the chest from the badge, there was no kit manufacturer's logo. This was instead much larger, in the stylish off-black, where the shirt sponsor would normally be. The manufacturer and sponsor were one and the same: MCG. Andy McGlynn's sports retail and manufacturing empire – where he had made his first fortune before diversifying his entrepreneurial interests into the service and technology sectors – had made the club's kits since his takeover a decade ago. This was the first time they had sponsored a shirt too.

The players applauded the rousing speech and reveal, Dmitriy's clap only coming a fraction late.

'To Dmitriy and everybody who wants to be themselves in this beautiful game of ours . . .' The big screen behind McGlynn sprang to life with a burst of colour, displaying the same words that simultaneously left his mouth. 'Weave got you.' He waved the players over to admire their new third kits.

Dmitriy was practically swept aside by his teammates as they patted his back and offered supportive words on their way past. Uneasy, he arrived at the beaming McGlynn, who unfolded a shirt bearing 'Lebedev 10' on the back. 'We're with you, Dimmy.'

Dmitriy grinned and took the shirt, having never felt so alone in a crowd.

'EasyMoney; over here,' called McGlynn.

As most of his teammates were inspecting the kits, Victor was detached from the pack, scrolling on his phone. He traipsed to McGlynn and Dmitriy.

'Let my crew get a snap of us together; my top scorer and assist master. One second.' McGlynn stepped away to rummage through a box behind the arched podium and came back with Victor's printed shirt. 'Shirts on, gents.'

Both players hesitated.

'C'mon. No need to be shy. We're all friends here.'

Both peeled their tops off and slipped into their new shirts as McGlynn's cameraman swapped to his stills camera. McGlynn beckoned them over to stand one either side of him, where he wrapped around an arm around each of them. 'Ready?'

The photographer nodded.

'Right, gents,' said McGlynn, puffing out his chest. 'With pride.'

'That's a very generous offer indeed,' said Andriy into his phone, eyebrows raised, as he closed the front door behind him. 'Yes . . . yes, I'm sure you can appreciate we have a lot on the table. We'll be having conversations over the coming days about best fits and so forth,' he said as he followed the thumping noise deeper into the house 'Yes, you have my word . . . As soon as I can . . . OK . . . enjoy the rest of your day.' As he hung up, he reached the source of the noise in the gym. Dmitriy was whacking boxing mitts held by a hulking man, whose quick hands were occasionally trying to hook Dmitriy's head off his shoulders. Nimble on his feet, Dmitriy danced around, punching and slipping shots before stopping.

'Like a young Drago!' said Andriy.

Dmitriy smiled and came over, putting his gloved fists out. Andriy grinned and banged his fists down against them, Dmitriy determinedly keeping them in place as best he could before playfully Andriy wrestled them down and kissed his cheek.

'Hello, I'm Andriy,' he said, offering his attention and a hand towards the gigantic mitt-wearing guest.

'Alright, buddy. I'm Otis,' said the bruiser as he removed his mitt, wiped his hand on his T-shirt, and shook hands. 'Pardon the clam. It's hotter work than I was expecting for session one.' He turned to Dmitriy. 'They didn't fuck about in Mother Russia, did they?'

'Not so much,' said Dmitriy, bittersweetly. 'Just over the border too. The training seemed very proper.'

'It shows,' said Otis. 'Good luck to any more dickheads trying to get cheap shots. You want a few minutes before we get onto the bag?' he asked, nodding over to the brand-new freestanding punch bag.

'That'd be great thanks, Otis,' said Andriy.

As the trainer made himself scarce, Dmitry took his gloves off.

'Enjoying blowing off the cobwebs there?' asked Andriy.

'After today, definitely.'

'Go on,' urged Andriy.

'The third shirt – they make it rainbow colour.'

'Oh,' said Andriy, pausing a while. 'Well, at least their hearts are in the right place.'

'McGlynn?'

'Ha. You make a compelling point.'

'Doesn't matter anyway why he do. It still makes even bigger target on me. A nice bright one.' Dmitriy shook his head to himself and took a deep breath. 'How was your day?'

'Hectic. You, Mr Lebedev, are in demand. Major demand.'

'With the strangers, at least.'

Andriy smiled sadly at him.

'Did you hear back from *Khrabryy*?' asked Dmitriy.

Andriy shook his head.

Dmitriy blew out a disappointed sigh then perked himself up. 'So, in demand? Are there any good offers for me to take?'

'Honestly, there are some *extremely* lucrative deals on the table. Just with the money comes more visibility.'

Dmitriy mulled it over for a few moments.

Otis walked back in. 'Ready?'

Dmitriy nodded and started to glove up. 'We wait. See a little bit how things go. Focus on the preseason. Get ready.'

'I think it's a wise stance.'

Dmitriy banged his gloves together, raring to go, as he paced towards the punch bag.

'Just take it easy,' said Andriy. 'Save plenty for the pitch.'

Dmitriy tippy-tapped the bag with a few jabs, grinning over at Andriy. 'Easy enough, boss?'

Andriy shook his head and smiled as he left, only to hear the blows louden.

The haze of weed smoke hung heavy, swirling in front of the only light in the room, which came from the TV. The rattle of machine gun fire blasted from the TV and simultaneous vibrations came from the gaming chair he sat in. The gamer's slightly crooked eyes fixed on the game action through his thick glasses as he clutched his controller by his chest. The screen showed the first-person perspective of his in-game character lining up a sniper shot down a scope across a seemingly derelict courtyard. His thumbs moved the tiny joy sticks delicately until only his hand in front of the badge on his football shirt made the final adjustments. The crosshairs hovered over the quarter-exposed head of a character hiding behind a crate down below in the distance.

'You're mine,' he whispered to himself as his target moved a few more centimetres into view. He lifted his trigger finger.

BANG BANG BANG.

He flinched at the loud knocks on the door, accidentally firing and missing.

'Washing?' shouted a woman outside.

'Just give me a few minutes,' he whined back in teenage fashion, although he was in his mid-twenties.

'You said that three hours ago, Winnie,' she replied.

'Stop calling me that, Mum. I'm a grown man. Gimme ten minutes?' he asked, glancing towards the door.

Footsteps walked away from the door. 'Ten.'

His attention returned to the screen only to see blood oozing down it. Dead. He smashed his controller to the floor and tore his headset off, steam almost hissing from his ears and nose. After burying his head in his hands and eventually calming his breathing, he grabbed his phone from beside him and checked his messages. He clicked a video link in one and cast it to the TV. The selfie video featured a bearded man in his late thirties wearing a camouflage jacket and a black cap bearing the Weavers' badge. He stood in front of the corner of a billboard.

'My name's Rory Johnson. I was 'oping this day would never come but the way the world's been going, I suspected for a while it would. I might cause bother for myself 'ere, but someone 'as to say something.

I'm a sports fan through and through. I spent my youth kicking about with my mates on the street, against any wall we could find. I've travelled the world watching the national team in qualifiers and tournaments. I was there on that night in Berlin. I saw that ninety-third minute winner in Belgrade. I've watched our best boxers smash it out in Vegas. I work in sport, coaching kids in various sports on the estate I've lived on all my life.

I've seen our culture crumble over the last ten or twenty years. What sort of society do we live in now where we can't let our kids kick a ball about in the street? Why is everyone so precious? Is it their cars, the noise, the fear of a broken window every now and then? Are people really that scared of the safety of their kids in the safest society we've ever known? Is it cos the elites 'ave decided that our games aren't ours anymore? That with their gentrification, they've managed to bamboozle us into thinking we need more than jumpers for goalposts and that everything 'as to be organised and monitored? Maybe.

But I'll tell you what the biggest factor is. The society doesn't want boys being boys anymore. Boys being boys makes men being men and in this day in age, manhood is the most toxic of things. Manhood, which at least 'alf-built the world as we know it, is being castrated. And when's the best time to take someone's balls? When they're young.

Don't let the poorest ones play cos they're probably a bit feral. If they can maybe afford it, make them jump through 'oops for it. Loads of 'oops. Make sure they're compliant. When they do play, give 'em all medals, even the shit ones. But don't let 'em touch each other. Make it no-contact. No shoulder-to-shoulders. Despite almost every fucking animal in existence needing rough and tumble during childhood, our kids can't 'ave it. It'll make 'em too *aggressive*.

They're wrapping the kids in cotton wool. They're creating generations of weak, low-testosterone men from the bottom up.

At least from the top, the pro game's been a beacon for boys. They've rounded the edges off it a bit but there's still blood and thunder. There 'as to be because ultimately there are still winners and losers. No fucking participation trophies at the top. Until now.'

He tilted his camera up and edged out of frame to show the full billboard behind him. 'Look at the fucking state of this. From the club I've followed all my life.' The poster showed Dmitriy in its centre, with Victor and Finney just behind him in a shallow V formation, all wearing the rainbow third shirt. The poster's headline read "Leading The Way".

'*Leading*. He's not even playing bloody preseason. 'Urt his shoulder, they say. Probably rubbing one out onto this shirt.

This is the beginning of the end. What you see 'ere is the celebration of what those who pull the strings want; a nail in the coffin of traditional masculinity's last bastion – professional sport. Till now, we've celebrated winning in this game, plain and simple. Now, drop by drop, they'll use their bright colours to paint over the dark truth – that they want our game away from us.

This is the ultimate participation trophy, dedicating A SHIRT to somebody based on something that 'as sweet F.A. to do with winning. Tell me any player in this club's 'istory who's 'ad a shirt dedicated to them *even for* winning.

Look . . . look down 'ere.' He moved the camera to show a rainbow-coloured heart in the bottom corner of the poster. The slogan next to it read "Weave Got You." 'They've set up a charity to encourage *participation* in sport for all sexual orientations. Tell me where there's been a rule banning gays in sport in this country since it was legalised fifty-odd years ago. There are already gays in sport. Navratilova was out about thirty years ago.

They've castrated us from the grassroots. Now they'll use their idol and their propaganda to do it from the top down, mark my words.'

The gamer watched on, mouth agape.

'The elite – the fucking *bourgeoisie* – already crush the working man – the man's man – but it's not enough for 'em. They want us even weaker, so we'll work even closer to the bone for them and be too feeble to fight back and take our part of the spoils.

Not only are they taking one of our only pleasures away by making football more and more expensive and less accessible, but they're using *our* game as a trojan horse that'll weaken us as they do it.'

'I'm not 'aving it. This is *our* game! We deserve *our* place in this world we 'elped build with our blood and sweat. This is *our* sanctuary where we can shout and talk shit and drink and 'ave a bit of a tear-up if we want. Nobody's taking that from us or our sons after us.'

The gamer leaned forward in his seat, his body vibrating with excitement.

'Stand with me against this shirt. Dads, granddads, uncles, brothers. Let us be men so that our boys can be boys.'

CHAPTER 5

Amber slowly raked her oiled elbow along the hamstring of the player lying face down on the physio table, applying deeper pressure on the knots as she went. A knock came on the open door. 'Come in,' she called.

In walked Magnus holding a black gift box that looked to contain a bottle of some sort of alcoholic spirit. 'May I?' he asked, gesturing to an empty chair.

'Rob?' she asked the player she was treating.

'Yeh. No bother,' he replied.

'Then no bother with me neither. Do you need me for something? I'm going to be a while unless you need me urgently,' she asked, slowing in anticipation.

'No, I'm just familiarising myself with how everybody works. Don't mind me. Just a quiet observer.'

'OK. It's not the most enthralling spectator sport – you might need to crack that open for entertainment,' she said, gesturing towards the bottle. 'Take a seat.'

Magnus sat and studiously watched on.

'See you later, Magnus,' said the player as he left the treatment room.

'Indeed,' said Magnus. After the player's treatment and farewell, Magnus climbed to his feet. 'Do you have a few minutes to talk, Amber?'

'Yes. Nobody's due in for another fifteen,' she replied as she typed a sentence in to her laptop before folding it closed. 'And how can I say no when you come bearing what may be a gift?' she said, flashing a hopeful grin his way.

'Ha, indeed. Just a little welcome gift for you from my motherland.' He handed the box, bearing the name *'Brennivín'*, to her and took the seat across the desk.

'Thank you very much. I'll be sampling that shortly,' she said, setting it down. 'Not shortly like when you leave shortly. Like *tonight* shortly. Aren't I making a first impression to remember?!' She giggled awkwardly.

Magnus smiled warmly. 'I knew what you meant. And your first impression was just fine. Better than fine, actually. I have to tip my proverbial hat to you. That's the first time I think I've ever seen a physio using an electromyograph to check the results of their treatment.'

She smiled. 'Ha. Thanks. I have to tip my proverbial hat right back at you. I don't think there are too many managers who know what an EMG is. But then with that nickname, I probably shouldn't be too surprised. What was your study in?'

'I started in the hard sciences, then moved into sports science before it was really a thing, and now, many moons later, here I reside in the soft skills job of management, trying to bring that rigor with me. I cannot do it alone so thank you for bringing your rigor too.'

'Thank you for the opportunity, sir.'

'None of the "sir" please, Amber. We are a family here; there is no room for such formalities.'

Amber warmly nodded.

'The opportunity is well-deserved. I did my research before I arrived. Watching you work now, I didn't just see a rigor and keenness of attention. I saw a deep caring in what you did. The older I get, the more I appreciate the role of care, of connection, in what we do. I was not a natural. You are.'

'Thank you very much. That's very kind of you to say,' said Amber.

'It's the truth. You are essential here. I want success and generally, the best way to get there, to be maximally competitive in the league, is to have an environment that perfectly balances intra-squad competitiveness and also cohesion. We need these boys, these men, to be like family, like brothers to each other. They need a perfect dynamic tension between rivalry and chemistry with one another to make them formidable. Your role here is more than just fixing the broken. Can I count on you to help keep it all together in the first place, to keep the compassion alongside the combativeness? To balance out this family?'

Amber's wide eyes filled with pride. 'I'm honoured you see my role as larger. Of course, you can count on me.'

'Magnificent,' he said, standing to leave. 'Your children are very fortunate to have such a capable woman raising them.'

Amber flushed bright red. 'Oh no. I don't have children.'

'You don't?' asked Magnus, mortified. 'Oh my. I'm so sorry. I was told you . . . I'm misinformed. This is utterly embarrassing. Please forgive my idiocy.'

'Don't be silly. There's nothing to forgive,' she said, trying to calm him and, inside, herself.

He nodded gratefully. 'OK. I shall carry on my welcome chats, trying to keep my foot out of my mouth. Thank you for letting me view your work and for accepting a wider role in this footballing family. Together, we multiply our chances.' He stood up and headed to the door. 'Here you can say "cheers" for thank you, yes?'

'You can indeed,' she replied with a smile.

'Cheers then!' he said as he left.

Amber leaned back in her chair and sighed before pulling the gifted bottle over for closer inspection and fetching her phone from across the desk.

Finney laid on his back on the physio table; his scarred knee bent slightly in the head physio's hand. With one hand hooked behind the top of Finney's calf and his other applying pressure just above his kneecap, Neil gently pulled Finney's lower leg, as if trying to shear it off at the knee joint. 'How's that?' he asked as the shin displaced forward a couple of millimetres.

'A-O-kay,' replied Finney.

Neil pulled again to check his conclusion. 'OK. On your feet. We'll chat in my office.'

As Neil headed off to his office, Finney sat himself up. Dmitriy laid facing him on a nearby table, receiving ultrasound treatment on his shoulder.

'Don't worry, Dimmy. I'll have that heavy armband from you soon. Not all shoulders can take it,' said Finney.

'Ha, you can have it,' replied the playmaker. 'I think the bright shirt will be heavy enough for me this year.'

Finney snuffed a laugh out and nodded up to alert Dmitriy to something across the room behind him. Dmitriy peered over his shoulder to see McGlynn's film crew recording.

Finney wandered over, sat by Dmitriy, and lowered his voice. 'Listen, mate. I can barely imagine what you're going through. Just know absolutely nowt has changed for the lads. You're one of us. Andriy's one of us. We can't know exactly how it's gonna be for you once the season gets under way, but I'm assuming there's going to be some chew. Do you what you can to block it all out. None of it matters, none of it. You need anything at all, you speak to me, yeh?'

Dmitriy thankfully nodded. The two fist bumped.

'Now, I've gotta go see a man about a dog-eared knee. Wish me luck,' said Finney as he turned to head away.

'I pray for Clooney,' said Dmitriy, drawing a smile from the club captain.

Finney arrived in the office as Neil was putting up some MRI images. 'Dr Finney gives the all-clear,' he joked.

'Come here, Ian,' said Neil in a gentle yet sombre tone.

Finney walked up to the image and hovered his finger in front of it, tracing the black line from the tibia diagonally up to the back end of the femur. 'Good as new.'

'Ha. Not quite. You're right. It is intact, but it's not achieved anything like the thickness we need yet. Your knee is still quite unstable. I can't sign you off to get back into full training yet.'

'C'mon, Neil. All my life they tell me I'm *too* thick. Don't flip the script on me now.'

Neil smiled wryly.

'Neil. Mate. I've been doing the graft.'

'I know. Jason's said your numbers are superb.'

'Exactly. I've been taking so many vitamins if you pushed down on my head, I'd pop one out my arse like a PEZ dispenser. So, what've I got to do to get back on that pitch?'

'Unless you can get younger, there's nothing more you can do other than what you're doing. Healing just takes a little longer at the back end of your thirties, with growth hormone and your body's other natural elixirs on the decline.'

'I don't really have a little longer. McGlynn's been fobbing me off with extension talks. I need to get back out there. There's gotta be something I can do. Can't I just get some growth hormone signed off by the doc?'

'No. Chris won't give you that without a medical exemption for it. That's not happening without a recorded medical issue going back years.'

Finney's mind whirred. 'What about legal boosters? To up my levels through diet or some other supplement or whatever?'

Neil gurned as he mulled it over. 'Let me look into it. Until then, just keep grafting.'

'Of course.' He headed to the door and turned back. 'Will watching Benjamin Button do me any good?'

'It won't do you any harm,' said Neil.

Cas shut his laptop and picked it up off his office desk. He turned over his phone, which had been face down and turned to silent. A new text waited.

> **AMBER**
> Just tell me what it is and come home

He watched the cursor blink in the reply box, acutely aware of the ticking of the office clock, and rubbed his neck. Eventually, he sent his reply:

> I told you everything already my love.
> Please believe me x

As he left his office and headed for the auditorium, he received another text.

> **AMBER**
> Stop lying to me! I can't be with part of
> you anymore. It has to be everything.

He stopped and stared at the screen, as if unable to walk and text simultaneously. His thumbs froze above the keyboard.

'You coming?' called Steve. 'They're just starting to head in.'

Cas nodded, powered down his phone and caught up with his assistant.

A few moments later, the auditorium was full, bustling with anticipation. McGlynn's filming duo stood in the back corner. Cas tapped the lectern's microphone. Beside him was a waist-high object covered in black cloth.

'Good afternoon, everyone.'

His team echoed their greetings back at him.

'I know we've been back a few days, but I wanted to wait for the right time to do this. I hope you all have a good holiday. It was well-deserved.' He took stock for a moment.

'Deserved. This is the interesting word. You saw the result of our appeal. The association . . . they acknowledge with the long stadium ban that what he made was not a normal offence, but they still keep the result. There is nothing more we can do about this now, but I still don't accept this decision. Victor put that ball in the net . . . he would have even if the goalkeeper tries properly to stop him. We won that game zero-three. The record doesn't say the truth.

You guys . . . we, we won that league. I want you, no matter what they say, to know that you did enough to be champions. Here, I know you *are* champions.' He stepped away from the lectern to the unveil the object beside him. It was the Alpha League trophy, or at least an exact replica of it. A gasp filled the auditorium. 'You think I care what the bureaucrats say? We know the truth even if they don't have the balls to make it right.'

'Yes, boss man!' shouted Victor, instigating a round of applause and more yells.

'I want you to see this every day before we train and remember you are already champions.'

The ovation built.

'I want you to know how proud I am of what you did. How we perform at the start of the season, how even with the problems we never fall too far, and then how we play in the final game. How we play in that game, guys . . . it was incredible. That is the blueprint for this season.'

The cheering built.

'How we express ourselves; the way we let them know we are ready to fight too. You are ready to fight again, yes?'

His players agreed at the tops of their voices, some up on their feet.

'All I want from you this season is more of the same identity. We sharpen more, we toughen more. We make it so that this year we go so far away, those fuckers can cheat and it doesn't matter!'

Everyone rose to their feet, clapping and hollering.

'At the end of the season, nobody will be able to deny what we deserve and he,' Cas gestured to the replica, 'will have a brother in the stadium trophy cabinet.' He reached down grabbed the trophy by its handles. 'Better get some practise.' He lifted it overhead, pumping it up and down.

The players went wild, streaming out of their seats and down the stairs to get their hands on the silverware.

CHAPTER 6

The sound of jazz cymbals brushing away in his earphones, Andriy opened an incognito tab, went to Twitter, and searched #lebedev. He scrolled down the endless page of Tweets. The rainbow colours, be they on a photo of Dmitriy in the third shirt or in the form of heart or rainbow emojis, illuminated the feed. But every now and then, the feed darkened. 'Fuck #lebedev . He should take that shit back home, see how they greet him,' said one Tweet, finished with a skull-and-crossbones emoji. 'Are rainbow laces strong enough for someone to hang themselves with? #lebedev' said another. 'WFC got fucked like good pussy last season. This season, they'll take it right up the arse #lebedev.'

Andriy kept scrolling and skimming. Some of the abusive Tweets were in his native language. His eye stopped on his own name in an English Tweet. 'Always suspected agents shafted players. Who knew it was literal? #romanov #lebedev.' The more nasty Tweets he came across, the more he noticed another hashtag: #BWBB. He typed it into the search bar and as he was about to hit return, 'BOO!' Hands grabbed him from behind. He jumped and instinctively slammed his laptop shut as Dmitriy kissed his cheek.

'Twitter that scary?' asked Dmitriy.

'I'd like to say no,' replied Andriy.

Dmitriy pulled up a seat next to him and sat. 'Whatever you're seeing there, I'll see it in the flesh soon enough. You still think it's a good idea for me not to see what they're saying?'

'Absolutely,' said Andriy. 'There are going to be enough distractions we can't help, so it's best we limit the ones we can.'

Dmitriy took his minimalist phone out of his pocket. 'So how come I'm in the stone age but you get to look?'

'Because your job is to look after the football while mine is to look after you and for me to do that, it's useful for me to see some of the bigger picture. All you need to be seeing to be at your best is the ball, your teammates, and the opposition. None of the rest of this need enter your mind.'

'Simple as that,' said Dmitriy with a laugh.

'I know it's easier said than done, but it must be the aim.'

Dmitriy knowingly nodded. 'Can you at least put some of the guys' numbers in here for me please?' he asked, handing Andriy his phone.

'Of course.'

'I can't only have you to speak to.'

'Why not?' Andriy grinned. 'I've been told I'm exceptional company.'

'You are but I can't have any of your camp rubbing off on me,' Dmitriy joked as he tried to scarper.

'Cheeky bastard,' said Andriy as he grabbed him. 'Didn't hear you complaining the other night,' he said, letting him go.

Dmitriy laughed and walked out of the room. As he reached the foot of the stairs, Andriy shouted him. 'Dmitriy; Iryna's calling!'

He dashed back to meet Andriy to grab his phone, desperate to make it before the call rang out.

'Good luck,' said Andriy as he handed the phone over.

Dmitriy took the call and wandered away for some privacy. 'Mama.'

'My boy,' she said, her words caked in the heavy residue of longing.

'How are you?' he asked.

'I'm so sorry it's taken me this long to call.'

'It's OK, Mama.'

'Your father . . .'

Dmitriy paused too. 'I know.'

'I really am sorry. I should have called.'

'No, no. I should have told you before I spilled my guts to the world . . . I was just under so much pressure, and then in the moment . . .'

'It's OK. I can't even imagine.' She paused. 'How have you been? How's the reaction been there?'

'I don't really know yet. We went to Phuket, kept ourselves to ourselves, and didn't look at any news. Even since we've been back, I've steered clear. Andriy's kept an eye on it, but I'm just concentrating on football.'

'How have your team been?' asked Iryna.

'Sweet. Supportive, mostly. Maybe making a bit too much of it. I just want to play, you know?'

'I know, son.' She paused. 'How is Andriy?'

A surprised grin emerged on his face. 'He's good, thank you. He's good. Thank you for asking.'

'He's your partner.' She paused again. 'I want the best for him too. He always seemed very nice.'

'Thank you. He is. How are you . . . and Papa?'

'Well, I'm fine. I have no problem staying in.'

'Staying in?' he asked.

She continued as if his words had slipped by her. 'He . . . he's not dealing with things so well. You know how he is. It's driving him mad being stuck in the house so much, which is driving me mad.'

'What do you mean "stuck in the house"?'

She hesitated. 'He's had a few *issues* at work.'

'Like what?'

'Somebody vandalised the outside of the office. He got in a bit of a fight with one of his colleagues about it so he's working from home at the moment. His models have taken over the dining room.'

'Were the offices to do with me?' he asked, his voice creaking.

She took an audible breath. 'He wouldn't tell me, but I think so.'

Dmitriy sighed back. 'Tell him I'm sorry.'

'I don't know why he's so angry. If somebody would have told me to take my sewing machine and work from home back in my working days, I would have bitten their hand off. To get rid of that commute and those dead-eyed crossing guards every damned day. I'd have missed the girls, but he doesn't like half of his colleagues at the best of times.'

'Is he home now?' he asked.

'No, he's gone for a walk.'

Dmitriy checked his watch. 'At this time?'

'He's only really been going out when it's dark.'

Dmitriy covered his eyes with his free hand. 'Tell him I'm sorry, ple—'

'I've got to go,' she said, snatching at her words. 'He's back. I'll call soon, I promise. I love you.'

'I love you too. Tell him, please.' She was gone before he finished. He stared at the phone for a moment before sliding it into his pocket and heading to finding Andriy.

'How was it?' he asked.

Dmitriy burst into uncontrollable floods of tears. It was the first he had cried since the night with the weighted vest last season. Andriy rushed over and hugged him wholeheartedly.

COLIN

Welcome to the first OmniSports Friday Football Frenzy of this new season! I'm your host, Colin Samson, and I'm joined tonight by your favourite footy connoisseur, Pete Gossamere. How excited are you for the kick-off tomorrow, Pete?

PETE

I'm more wired than an electrician's house, Col!

COLIN
Wow. Where you may not have missed some of the banter, after a football-less summer, we'll bet you're still raring for the restart! Over the next hour, we're going to look at the prospects of the Alpha League's teams for the season ahead and we'll be weighing up their chances for the first round of fixtures.

But first, while there hasn't been much happening on the pitch, one soccer saga spanned our break – I'm of course talking about GunnarGate. What're your thoughts on the final verdict?

Cas watched on, his legs a blur as they kept up with the treadmill's whirring belt. The spacious grey room, situated at the top of a soaring apartment block attached to a swanky hotel named *Fuga* that overlooked the docklands, only contained the cardio machine, a massive TV, and an armchair – identical to his one at home.

PETE
I've got massive sympathy for Velasquez and the Weavers but ultimately, I think the Federation came to the correct decision. Overturning the results of a match and, in this case, an entire season would set a dangerous precedent.

COLIN
Even with such an unprecedented breach of the rules at such a pivotal moment? I mean, hasn't

> *that altered a club's place in the record books and their future?*
>
> **PETE**
> *As soon as that goalkeeper stopped due to the extra ball entering the pitch, I don't see what else could have been done. It's not as if the ref could have given a penalty for an infraction that occurred on the sideline. It's rough on the Weavers, but there are plenty applauding Magnusson. You would want a player to take a red there to stop such a pivotal goal. Why not a manager?*

Cas grabbed the remote out of the treadmill's cupholder, turned the TV off, pushed some hair back out of his eyes, and ramped up the speed.

> **COLIN**
> *Well, a manager may think twice now. Following Magnusson's trailblazing – for want of a better term – behaviour and his subsequent eight-match stadium ban, it has been announced today that any other managers who do similarly will be subject to more stringent punishments that will involve longer bans and even points deductions.*
>
> *All this brings us into this season with bad blood between these two rivals, who play each other just a few games in, but the plot thickens even further.*
>
> *Never have a father and son coexisted as managers in our league until now. The Surgeons*

have been taken over by their very own doctor, Magnus Rúnarsson, Gunnar Magnusson's old man. Known for building some of the most adaptable, tactically savvy, hard-running teams in world football, he'll be hoping to make this a three-way battle this season.

Let's take our first in-depth look at last season's controversial champions, the Warriors.

*   *

PETE
With Lawler – arguably his most important player last season – fit but having only made cameo appearances in preseason, you wonder if Gunnar is planning to shape his midfield differently this season.

Sat up in the plush super king-size bed of an unfamiliar hotel room, Lawler tapped the remote control on his lap before turning the volume down.

'Time to play here,' said a pigtailed blonde woman in her early twenties, crawling along the duvet to him wearing nothing but knee-high leather boots. She took the remote from him and threw it on the floor. 'Any position you want.'

The women either side of him – his regulars from last season – giggled, one of them running her hand along his torso as she got out from under the covers.

'Stay just like that,' he instructed the crawler, who was on all fours. He walked round to the end of the bed and pulled her back by her knees until her shins dangled off the edge of the bed. She squealed delightedly.

'Tara,' he said to the naked woman with frizzy space buns. He pointed to the spot just ahead of the crawler's hands. 'Get there.' He patted the crawler's backside. 'Give her a nice treat.' He beckoned the cherry-lipsticked bottle redhead left in the bed. 'Over here, Katrina.'

COLIN
And now onto Lawler's old team who took them right to the wire last season, the Weavers. In just their second season in the Alpha League, they lost the league on their head-to-head record only, and played some of the best football we've ever seen. With no ins or outs yet, the main question is whether they can maintain the heights they reached or whether they'll prove to be just a flash in the pan.

PETE
A lot of that will depend on their three big players. How quickly can they get the club captain Ian Finney back playing and at thirty-six, will he be the same dominant force that he was in the middle of the park?

Finney listened on as his eyes drank in the loveliness of Lulu peacefully sleeping on the lap of his recovering leg. He stroked her hair a few times then eased a hand under her head and took its weight, lifting it ever so slightly so that he could straighten his leg and bend it a few times without waking her.

As he rested her head back down, his phone pinged. He reached for it and read the new text from Nova. His brow furrowed furiously as he called her to respond. The line rang out. He tried again immediately, but this time was met by her answerphone after a single ring. He flung his phone along the sofa, bouncing it off the arm, which made it spin to the floor with a loud crack, jarring Lulu awake.

'What was that, Daddy?'

'Nothing, darling,' he cooed, trying to mask his anger. 'Nothing.'

> **PETE**
> *Can last season's Golden Boot winner Victor Ezemonye carry on his outrageous goal run?*

Victor half-listened as he opened the padlock on the built-in wardrobe and took off his backpack. The bedroom had a single bed with Pokemon covers and a poster of a younger Ian Finney on the wall amongst a host of rap video vixen posters.

'Victor. Do you want supper?' came the shout in a Nigerian accent from a woman downstairs.

'*Yes please, Mudda,*' he shouted back in a mocking thick imitation accent as he tipped the backpack's contents – wads of bundled banknotes – on top of an already waist-high stack of cash.

'The cheek of you,' she called back. 'Mark my words, you joker. You can still end up in McDonald's.'

> **PETE**
> *And after becoming the first openly gay top footballer of this generation, how will Dmitriy Lebedev fare this season? After a stellar final game of last campaign and the announcement that followed it, apart from the hateful attack he was subject to on his return from his summer getaway, we've not heard from him or seen him play. With more eyes on him than ever, will one of league's most promising creative talents be able to find more consistency this year?*

Andriy shut down the OmniSports app and removed his earphones as he arrived at the door. A resonant hum came from inside. After a faint knock, he nudged it open and crept in.

The air was thick with sandalwood incense swirling up from a pot in the middle of the floor. One side of it sat Dmitriy, legs crossed, eyes closed; the other side sat a slim South Asian man in a bright orange robe bolt-upright in the lotus position, his eyes shut. The warm sound of their collective Om-ing filled the room.

Dmitriy turned his head, opened his eyes, and made a lighthearted face that begged for rescue. Andriy did not comply, instead joining his thumbs and forefingers and inhabiting his most satirical pious posture, drawing a grin from his partner.

The meditation teacher let his Om trail off towards silence, prompting Dmitriy to re-close his eyes and Andriy to drop his mockery.

The teacher opened his eyes. 'Slowly let your Om fade into nothingness and allow your eyes to open.'

Dmitriy obliged, letting his eyes peel open and giving them a heavy look as if they had been closed for hours. The teacher raised his hands to his face in a prayer of gratitude towards Dmitriy, who politely nodded back.

'You are centred. Ready,' assured the teacher. 'All that matters is the quiet *inside*,' he said, touching his heart.

Dmitriy affably smiled. Under his breath, he muttered in Russian, 'Try keeping that with an entire stadium shouting at you.'

CHAPTER 7

Dmitriy wheeled his team travel bag to the bench, pulling up next to Charlie. Until the last few weeks, Charlie had always taken the end spot on one end of the dressing room's bench set-up with Victor always taking the one next to him. Since the day after the shower prank, Victor had taken Charlie's spot. Charlie asked at the time what Victor thought he was doing.

'Facing Jerusalem, fam.'

After a good laugh, Charlie thought no more of it but Dmitriy registered it.

As Dmitriy unzipped his bag, Finney wrapped one of his expansive hands around his upper arm where the captain's armband would go. 'Warm her up for me real good, mate. You've got this.'

Dmitriy nodded brusquely. As the absentee captain moved off, the kit man hung Dmitriy's shirt on the hanger in front of him. The playermaker's eyes drank in the colour of it before he had a chance to avert them, but he swivelled away quickly anyway, sat, and concentrated on unpacking his bag.

'Dmitriy,' said Cas from across the room, beckoning him with a tilt of the head. Dmitriy pushed himself to his feet. The pair found an empty room down the corridor.

'How do you feel?' asked Cas.

'I don't know. Lots of things.'

'Yes.' Cas looked him in the face. 'They will be loud. They will try to make you angry.'

'I know,' he said, meeting Cas's eyes with his.

'The fire they aim down at you. Don't let it burn you. Make it your fuel. Make them wish they never opened their mouths.'

Dmitriy nodded sternly before Cas brought him in for a bro-hug. 'Show them *you* define you,' Cas said into his playmaker's ear.

He breathed more heavily than usual as they stood in the tunnel, waiting for the referee to signal them out. Not only was he aware of his heart beating away in his ribcage; he could also feel the blood rushing into his heavy hands and up into his neck. Inside his head felt muddled. He struggled to keep his eyes in one place for more than a few seconds and the glare from the end of the tunnel made him squint. The noise from the crowd went through his bones like a tuning fork.

From behind, a pair of hands slapped down onto his upper back and kneaded it.

'Back in the mix, boys!' yelled Charlie.

Dmitriy clapped, bringing himself back to the moment, and looked over his shoulder to Charlie and the line behind him. 'C'mon, guys,' he bellowed.

His teammates lit up, aside from Victor, who looked down at his golden boots and made the sign of the cross.

'Let's go,' called the referee. They began the march out. The closer the tunnel's opening they got, the louder the cheering grew.

As the sunlight hit him, his vision overexposed momentarily. Walking past the crowd nearest the tunnel opening, their colours reappeared to him. He looked their way, trying to refocus. There she was. She screamed his way, pumping her hands overhead in defiance. A blink later, she was gone. It was a brunette of a similar age who barely even looked like her.

BANG. He flinched, his head instinctively snapping around. Opening day pyrotechnics. He led the line out to the centre circle, took his place by the referees, and scanned the sea of grey shirts, soaking in the din.

The match started cagily, with most of the action in the middle third of the pitch. Just after the twenty-minute mark, the Weavers got their first corner on the left, which Dmitriy trotted over to swing in. As he fetched the ball from the delve before the advertising boards, he glanced up at the obscenity-hurling home fans a few yards from him. Through the flurry of waving arms and hand gestures, his eyes were drawn to a man stood utterly still with a crooked mischievous grin on his face. The man winked, puckered his lips, and blew a kiss his way. Dmitriy turned his back, pressed the ball down into the grass of the corner segment, and swung a vicious delivery towards the back post. Cole rose well over his marker to thunder a header into the top corner. One-nil to the Weavers. Dmitriy looked over his shoulder, making sure to lock eyes with the kiss-blower. His glower lasted only a moment before joining in the celebrations.

After the goal, the Weavers dominated. Dmitriy was the main instigator, getting on the ball as often as possible, and completing more dribbles than anybody during the next twenty minutes. On forty-three minutes, after a rare push forward from the Trawlers, Xavier broke down their move just inside his defensive third and passed sideways to Dmitriy. His first touch took the ball out of his feet and took two opposition midfielders out of the game. The break was on. He charged past halfway, his head panning side to side, checking for support. He passed the ball out to the ungainly yet pacey Nixon and carried on his run. Nixon drove forward, cutting infield onto his favoured left foot before playing a no-look pass to the overlapping Charlie. The return was on for Nixon had he not got his feet tangled and fallen to the turf. Charlie carried the ball further to the byline, glanced across the box, and then cut an acute ball back to Dmitriy, who had darted back into a pocket of space just level with the penalty spot. The first-time shot was not on, as a huge centre back had spotted his move and closed the angle well, so Dmitriy took the ball out of his feet towards the byline. The touch was heavy, killing his angle for a shot. A peek across goal showed him Victor cutting across his marker, free for a tap-in if he firmly side-footed a pass immediately across the six-yard box. *Smash.*

Victor was still gesturing for the ball to be fed just in front of him when he realised the ball was in the net. Dmitriy had cracked the ball high into the near-post area, somehow squeezing it between the post, the bar, and the 'keeper's flicked-out hand. Two-nil Weavers.

The rainbow-clad Weavers nearby raced over to celebrate Dmitriy's improbable strike with him. Victor eventually joined them and as the crowd part, gave Dmitriy a limp high-five. 'I was free.'

'Oh,' said Dmitriy, blank-faced. 'I didn't see you.' He took off back to his own half.

Victor watched him go for a moment, then wiped his hands on his shorts before following.

TRAWLERS 0-3 WEAVERS
FT
(HT 0-1)

Cole (21')
Lebedev (44', 71')

As the Weavers sauntered back into the away dressing room, an OmniSports reporter called over, 'Dmitriy – awesome display. Can I grab you for the Man of the Match interview?'

With only two teammates between him and the doorway, Dmitriy kept his eyes forward, as if he had not heard the request.

'Dmitriy!' yelled the reporter.

Even the players ahead of Dmitriy stopped and looked around. He reluctantly turned.

'Please – a quick man-of-the-match interview? Just about the game, I promise.'

'Oh, you promise?' he replied with an edge. This was the reporter who interviewed him after the final game of last season when the story leaked to the wider press before he made it to Emily's house.

The reporter sheepishly clammed up.

'Mr Lebedev,' came a well-annunciated call from further down the corridor. Dmitriy and the reporter both looked to see who it was.

'Saved by the bell-end,' mumbled Charlie in his teammate's ear as he brushed past him.

The man, briskly approaching with a clipboard in one hand and a cool bag in his other, was Mr Davis, a tester from GADA – the Global Anti-Doping Association. 'Come with me, please.'

Dmitriy shrugged over to the reporter. 'Another time, I promise. Just like you.' He walked away.

Victor jumped out of the queue, arms wide, landing with a flourish. 'I'll do you an interview, big man.'

'Brilliant, Victor,' said the reporter. 'Can you just grab me a goalscorer from in there to do it with you?'

'EasyMoney is *THE* goalscorer, fam.'

The reporter sheepishly replied, 'I mean an actual scorer from today, if that's alright?'

Victor eyeballed him, then slid off into the dressing room.

'Winner winner,' said Finney as he put down the plate in front of Lulu.

'Chicken dinner,' she chirped before seeing the contents of the plate. 'I thought you said we could have some fried chicken?' she asked as she poked the spice-dusted white breast on her plate.

'This is practically the same. A little bit of mash. The corn on the cob. A bit of peppercorn gravy on the side there.'

'It's not the same. I don't have to lick my fingers after this.'

Finney laughed to himself. 'This is true.' He stroked her hair before moving round the table to his seat. 'But Daddy has to eat clean to mend up properly so you're really helping me out here, Little Princess.'

She raised an eyebrow. 'I thought captains don't make excuses, Daddy?'

He grinned. 'That's a fair point. But I think you'll find only team players get their desserts.' He raised an eyebrow back to her. 'Now eat.'

Two chicken dinners and two protein ice cream sundaes later, Finney took her ice cream dish. 'Go get your tablet. It's time to call Mummy in a few minutes.'

'But your phone's right there,' said Lulu, pointing across the table to his cracked handset.

'It's best on yours. My phone doesn't seem to connect to Mummy's properly since I dropped it. If you can get back here in two minutes,' he looked over at the clock, which showed just before seven twenty-three, 'with it, I promise your next chicken will be finger lickin'.'

She almost knocked her seat over fleeing the table.

Finney picked up his phone and checked his messages thread with Nova. Over the last two days, the plentiful string of them were all from him and went from irate to polite back to irate. The air from his nostrils blew hotter and hotter as he skimmed them.

When Lulu returned, two seconds short of the fried chicken limit, she got him to shake hands on the drumstick deal and they moved through to the living room, where he put the TV on and sat around the bend of the sofa from her, out of camera frame.

Seven thirty came and went. Seven thirty-four. Seven thirty-nine. Lulu was glued to the show.

'You try Mummy. Maybe her clocks are broken,' said Finney, muting the TV.

Lulu realised the volume was not going back on until she called so dialled the video call. Finney craned his neck round to peer at the screen as the rings continued. Eventually, the call rang out. Lulu's face sunk as she slid her tablet across the sofa.

Finney softened his clenched jaw as he looked at his daughter's sad little face. 'I'm sure she'll call tomorrow,' he said, biting his lip as he edged round to hug her. 'I know it's nearly bedtime but how about we start a film?' He unmuted the TV and hit the search button.

'A film! A film!' she squealed.

'I've got a good one for us,' he said, keying in the first few letters of the title and moving across to its full name when it appeared as an option.

'Chi . . . cken . . . Run,' she read. 'Chicken Run!'

'Well done, Little Princess,' said Finney, stroking her hair. 'That's absolutely right.'

As Dmitriy shut the front door behind him, a loud pop startled him. He shoved his phone back into his pocket as Andriy appeared down the corridor holding a bottle of champagne.

'For my man of the match!' said Andriy, who noticed Dmitriy checking out the bottle. 'Non-alcoholic, of course. You won't get to the top with the drinking habits of mere mortals.'

Dmitriy put his bag down, walked over, and wrapped a tight hug around Andriy. 'Thank you,' he said, his voice heavy with emotion.

Andriy tightened his grip. 'It didn't seem too bad from the stands. How was it down there?'

Dmitriy pried the bottle out of Andriy's hand and took a swig. 'Cheers,' he said, passing his partner a leaden look. 'Any calls?'

'Plenty. The League reached out to see if we would like any assistance with anything, which I politely declined. I think your performance today shows we can help ourselves just fine. Beyond that, request upon request for sponsorship meetings and interviews. Nothing But Pride are like a dog with a bone.'

'Who?'

'Nothing But Pride. The magazine.'

The repetition drew no recognition from Dmitriy.

'It's the number one gay magazine here,' said Andriy. 'You've never heard of it?'

Dmitriy shook his head, then tickled Andriy. 'But you seem very familiar.'

'*Otvali!*' Andriy laughed, wriggling free. 'Don't make me knock your champagne all over.'

'No adverts. No interviews. Especially with gay media. That's just going to draw attention we definitely don't want,' said Dmitriy.

'I think that's a wise strategy right now,' replied Andriy.

'Any calls from home . . . from anybody we know?' asked Dmitriy hopefully.

'Not from yours, sorry. More from mine. It'll only be his bloody secretary.'

'At least he's trying.' Dmitriy took another big swig.

'Pace yourself, lightweight,' jested Andriy. 'Dinner's just about ready.'

'Can I have ten minutes?' asked Dmitriy.

'Of course. I'll keep it warm.'

'Thank you.' He handed Andriy the bottle, kissed his cheek, and set off along the corridor.

As Andriy turned the oven down and readied plates and cutlery, the strums of funk guitar boomed through the house. The distant thuds of the heavy bag being whacked were overlaid by the Prince song 'Kiss'.

'"Come now, let us settle the matter," says the Lord . . .' The church door slammed closed, interrupting Chuka's flow. Everybody turned to see Victor entering. A shimmer of excitement passed throughout the audience. As Victor noted their attention, he removed his cap and shades, nodding apologetically to his brother behind the lectern. '"Though your sins are like scarlet, they shall be as white as snow; though they are as red as crimson, they shall be like wool." Amen.'

'Amen,' echoed the congregation, Victor joining in.

'Now let us sing in praise,' said Chuka, gesturing towards the keyboardist, which triggered everybody to stand.

At the end of the service, around a third of the congregation flocked towards Chuka. An equal proportion gathered around Victor, ravenous for Weavers' stories and gossip. After a few minutes of chatting church-business to those at the front, Chuka noticed his crowd had dwindled whereas his brother's had grown significantly. He edged over towards him, bringing his remaining cluster with him.

'And dat cloud busted aside and He shone down on me,' said Victor, his eyes wide in awe as they looked up through the ceiling. 'My name's on the scoresheet but dat was all Him, you get me?'

'Bring it in, little brother,' said Chuka, opening his arms and closing off his little brother's tale.

'Man don't know about no little,' Victor laughed, scanning the crowd for approval, drawing universal smiles. 'Younger, I'll allow, fam,' he said as he hugged his brother.

'We're all little in His Eyes,' said Chuka.

'True dat. True dat. Just so long as I ain't little in hers.' He scanned the crowd again, spotting a few laughs that stopped the moment Chuka looked their way.

Chuka heartily patted Victor's shoulder and addressed the crowd. 'Forgive my little brother, for he knows not what he does . . . yet.'

One of the congregation piped up. 'With a bit of time, Victor, you'll be shining as brightly in here as you do on the pitch. Your light will bring people from far and wide to our quaint little house of worship.' Having stopped, she realised what she had said and nodded towards Chuka. 'As will the quality of your brother's sermons, of course.'

'Bless you, Desiree. Bless you all. Thank you for bringing your full spirits to today's service. And many thanks to all of you who were able to contribute towards the fund this week,' said Chuka, gesturing towards a one-third full fund thermometer on the wall. 'We're going to make a big difference back home.'

As some of the congregation put their hands over their hearts and many nodded gratefully, Victor looked as far away from the fund thermometer as he could, mumbling *'home'* under his breath.

'I'll be seeing many of you at tomorrow's service,' said Chuka. 'Have a blessed family day everybody.'

The crowd began to disperse, many of them shaking hands, some kissing the cheeks of Chuka and Victor as they made their way out. A rotund woman in a purple dress-suit-matching-hat combo and her conservatively suited husband, both in their sixties, talked Victor's ear off before asking for a photo to show their grandchildren. After joking that he would take the photo in exchange for some help with speeding tickets owed for his old Lamborghini, The Golden Gyal – the gentleman worked for the DVLA – Victor obliged and suggested they should bring their young kin to the service.

'After we show them this, it'll be hard to keep them away, Victor,' said the woman, Esther, cupping his face and kissing both cheeks.

'Watch her, my man,' Victor said to her husband. 'I could feel she nearly went for one on the kisser there too.'

'Wouldn't be the first time,' laughed Godwin. 'The Lord be with you, boys,' he said as he turned away, receiving a slap on his arm from his wife.

Victor raised his eyebrows and grinned, turning to see if his brother had seen the interaction. The life drained out of him.

Chuka was talking to a muscular, bearded white man wearing a black western gambler hat; the same man who had held a hunting knife to Victor's belly just a few months ago. Jack, as Victor knew him. His real name, however, was Ted.

'I hope our people made you feel welcome today,' said Chuka.

Victor's breathing stalled.

'Wonderfully so. I know it might sound a bit naff, but honestly, it felt like I'd known some of you for ages. A real familial feeling to it all,' said Jack, his gaze wandering over to Victor. 'You two don't half look alike,' he said, stepping towards Victor. 'You must have got mixed up all the time growing up?'

'Yes, we did,' said Chuka as Jack looked back and forward between the brothers. 'In my less wholesome youth, I admit I passed some of my sins off as his.'

'Naugh-ty!' said Jack with a gleeful grin. 'Ah well, boys will be boys. I'm sure you've made it right with the man upstairs. Best you got it out of your system young. Don't wanna be landing your brother in grown-man bother.'

'No, sir. Those days are long gone,' said Chuka. 'We're doing God's work now.'

Victor stood deathly still.

'Dunno about that,' laughed Jack. 'As a rival fan, that is. One man's angel is another man's devil.' He paused, smiling at Victor like the Cheshire Cat. 'Anyway, we're all one team in here. Thanks for the beautiful service, Pastor.' He shook hands with Chuka.

'You're very welcome, Jack. Our door is always open to you.'

'Thank you. I travel a fair bit on business, but I'm sure you'll be seeing me again. Pleasure meeting you too, Golden Boy.' He put his hand out for Victor to shake. Not knowing how else to respond, the striker shook it.

'God bless you, boys,' said Jack before walking down the aisle and out of the door.

Chuka saw his brother's complexion and expression. 'Bro – you alright?'

'Yeh . . . yeh. Just a bit lightheaded. Gimme a minute, yeh?'

'Of course,' replied Chuka, eyeing his brother as he strode off to the toilets.

Gasping for air, Victor splashed some cold water on his face and dried his hands on his jeans before pulling out his phone. He typed a message to Jack:

> How many times I told you man? I got your money.
> Just tell me where and when

After sending it, he got an almost immediate response:

> COWBOY
> I don't want your money. I want your soul.

CHAPTER 8

Four games in, the Weavers had a perfect record alongside the Surgeons at the top. The Warriors lagged just behind, having drawn one during the first half of Gunnar's stadium ban.

It was the eve of the Warriors' visit to the Weavers. Lawler knocked on the manager's door.

'Come in,' rumbled Gunnar's voice through it.

Lawler entered the dark room. With most of the décor black and charcoal, the only hints of colour came from photo frames, pens on Gunnar's desk, and the large sword displayed on the wall behind it. Unlike a samurai sword with a colourful sleeve, this sword was heftier, and its unsheathed straight blade had a yellowy-golden tint. An intricate pattern ran from its tip almost to its base, where eight Chinese symbols were etched.

Gunnar sat marvelling at it and did not turn even as Lawler sat. 'That sword . . . the real version . . . it sat in a damp tomb for two thousand five hundred years. You know what they found when they unsheathed it?'

'No,' replied Lawler.

'It was exactly like the day they left it there. Not the tiniest speck of rust. Still sharp enough to gut a man. The sheath was almost airtight. They don't understand how they made it like that all that time ago.' He swivelled his chair towards Lawler. 'What about you, Bry? It's been a while. How sharp are you?'

'I'm ready to go, chief. I've been putting it in in training. I just need to get out there now . . . when you wanna choose me, of course.'

Gunnar's unblinking eyes studied him. 'You've been training like a beast. I'll give you that. But there's a difference between training like a beast and playing like a demon. I don't think you're up to taking souls anymore.'

Lawler eyed him, keeping his expression fixed.

'You saw what was necessary to win last season and you fucking did it, game in, game out . . . right until you didn't.'

Lawler stayed stoic. 'What you mean, chief?'

Gunnar smashed his palm down against the desk. 'Don't fucking give me that. You know exactly what I fucking mean.' He locked eyes with Lawler and leaned back. 'But you know what, I probably wouldn't admit it either.' He grinned to himself, slapped his thighs, and spun himself around in his chair. 'There's only room here for players who're willing to bleed for this shirt. Would you bleed for it, Bry?'

'You know I would. You know what I did last season.'

'Best we don't talk about last season, ey? I'm talking about now. Would . . . you . . . bleed?'

Lawler nodded.

'Go on then.'

'You mean I'm starting tomorrow?' asked Lawler.

'No. I mean go on then.' He twirled round to view the sword. 'Bleed.'

Lawler looked at the sword then back at Gunnar, confused. 'What you mean?'

Gunnar spun back round to face him. 'You said you were ready to bleed. For a man who's willing to risk loss and limb; for a man who's ready to take souls, what's a little finger prick?'

'You . . . are you asking me to cut myself?' Lawler asked, restraining his incredulity.

'You said you'd bleed,' said Gunnar. 'Prove it.'

Lawler scowled in disbelief, taking a few seconds to find his words. 'It's not normal this, Gunnar.'

'I know. This is *exceptional*. I said to you before, this life isn't for everybody. Winning is a choice and very few are willing to make it.'

Lawler got out of his chair, shaking his head. His taut muscles trembled as he deliberated walking out.

'What's it gonna be, Bry? You give blood to the medics regularly. What's a few drops here?'

'You're fucking mental,' growled Lawler, clenching his fists.

Gunnar laughed at him. 'Clench your fists all you want. It's one drop here or a few tampons full every month while you deepen your arse groove on the fucking bench.'

The skin over Lawler's knuckles drained almost bone white as he balled his fists tighter still before he snarled, let them loosen, and walked around the desk to the sword. Gunnar turned to watch as Lawler stared at the floor for a moment before raising his hand towards the sword's tip.

A feather-light touch of his index finger against it drew a long drop of crimson blood, which he thrust towards Gunnar. 'You fucking happy?'

'You should be. You're starting tomorrow,' replied Gunnar as he turned back to his desk. He pulled a tissue from a box and offered it to Lawler, who snatched it from him and pressed it to his finger as he stormed past the table. 'That energy you're feeling now, that seething fury; remember who you need to turn that against tomorrow.'

Lawler scrunched up the tissue and tossed it in the bin before slamming the office door behind him, leaving Gunnar slowly nodding in his seat.

'Go!' called Jason, watching on with Neil. Finney sprang into action, hopping back and forth over two pieces of tape on the floor, forty centimetres from each other, like his life depended on it. Hands clasped behind his back, he bounced side to side, flickering his eyes across to the digital timer.

'Over the line each time, fella,' encouraged Jason.

A grey strand of Finney's hair fell out of place and stuck on his moistening forehead as he sprung back and forth with all his might.

'Aaaaand time,' said Jason.

Finney stuck his landing on his recovering leg with a brief wobble, quickly slamming his other foot down to try to hide it as he puffed out a forceful exhale. 'Sixty-two, yeh?'

'Yep, I got sixty-two,' replied Jason.

'Fucking get in,' said Finney, pumping his fist. 'Only two short of the good leg. Back in the game.'

'Hold your horses, El Capitan. They weren't all clean. What's the foul jump count, Neil.'

'I made it seventeen,' replied Neil with a sigh.

'Seventeen is legal, Doc.'

Neil laughed. 'In this state, seventeen is jailbait, Ian.'

Finney shook his head, despite knowing he was wrong. 'Alright. Let me go again.'

'Not today, Ian. We don't run that test more than once per forty-eight-hour period. We'll go again in a few days.'

'I've been hearing "a few days" for a few weeks now. Come on, fellas. I'm right on the borderline.'

'You are,' said Neil. 'And the reason you keep hearing it is because you've been on the borderline for weeks now. Your test scores will only improve as quickly as your weakest link allows them to and your knee, internally, is still weak. Don't think I didn't see your little wobble at the end there.'

Finney looked away, knowing he had been rumbled.

'We need those ligaments thicker before we can get you back into full training.'

'So give me whatever the equivalent of bicep curls for your ACL are and let me pump iron like Arnie,' pleaded Finney.

'The exercises are dialled in,' said Neil. 'Nutrition. Treatment. It's all good. Just be patient.'

'I've been *a* patient long enough. You said I'd be healing faster if I was younger. The squad's threadbare at the moment. *Surely* there's some legal Benjamin Button shit you can give me?'

Neil shifted his jaw and exchanged looks with Jason.

'There is, isn't there?' asked Finney, stepping closer to them. 'I will pull my shorts down and bend over for you right now if you'll jab me with your sweet medicine.'

'Ha ha. This is no joke, Ian,' said Neil. 'There are some medications that boost growth hormone levels, but they're pretty heavy duty; used for Parkinson's, Alzheimer's, seizures. Not stuff to be trifled with.'

'I'm not trifling. I just need to get back out there,' said Finney, desperation creaking in his voice. 'They're legal?'

'The substances themselves are, but we'd need to make sure your growth hormone levels don't surge,' said Neil. 'If your levels were above threshold, you could get picked up by a random test and they'd assume you're taking straight HGH.'

'You could stay on top of that though, right?' asked Finney.

Neil reluctantly nodded. 'But that isn't all. I know you want your career back, but mis-prescribing medications could do some major damage to mine if anybody found out. I mean, they're kind of justifiable for a prescribing physio to dish out if I were to say they were for motor control issues, but I'm not confident that reasoning would stand up well to scrutiny.'

'Oh.' Finney hung his head for the length of a deep breath, then perked himself up. 'No bother, Neil. Cheers for looking into it, anyway. I'll just keep beavering away. Might even go'n have a pray with Vic and Chuks.' He shook the duo's hands, headed to the door, turned back, and smiled. 'You'll rue the day you turned down me getting my arse out for you.' He double patted his backside and left.

'Are you ready?' asked Steve.

'I'm ready. The boys, they trained well. Been on the good form. They know what to expect tomorrow.'

'I wasn't talking about that,' said Steve as he opened the door to *Carne*. 'I know we're ready for that. I meant are you ready for a steak so big and so tender you won't even believe it came from an earthly animal?'

Cas clapped his hands as he inhaled the aroma of chargrilled meat. 'I am READY.'

'That's the smell of grass-fed glory right there,' said Steve as they walked to the unmanned maître d' stand. 'You know they massage the cows every day with these special oils to give them unrivalled tenderness?'

Cas raised his eyebrows. 'Very nice here,' said Cas as he scanned around the restaurant, admiring the décor. 'I never really came to many steakhouses.'

'Well, this is on another level so you absolutely have to eat here. You're in for a treat, guv. Well, I guess technically I am,' said Steve. 'This'll supercharge us for battle tomorrow!'

The maître d' appeared from around the bar. 'Hello, guys. Do you have a reservation?'

'We do. It's under . . .' Steve halted, like something had derailed his train of thought. He turned to Cas, stepping across him. 'Guv – you mind if we go somewhere else?'

Cas scrunched his face up. 'Why?'

'Umm. Dunno. The smell's just knocked me sick. I can't do steak now. I need to get outside.' He barged past Cas, then grabbed his arm. 'Please. I can't be in there.'

Discombobulated, Cas followed Steve's tug and twisted back towards the maître d'. 'I'm sorry. He's not feeling well. We book for another time.'

Steve tugged his sleeve again. 'C'mon. Please.'

'It's OK, sir. I hope you're feeling better soon,' said the maître d'. As she stepped aside Steve pulled again, but something caught

Cas's eye. On a table near the far end of the bar, almost facing away, was Amber in a semi-backless top, fully made up. Opposite her sat a handsome man with cropped dark hair and slightly cauliflowered ears, wearing a dress shirt, swirling a whiskey in his hand. She raised her glass of wine and laughed as they clinked glasses, keeping their eyes fixed on each other.

'Cas. Please,' said Steve flatly, pulling him one last time out of the door. The pair walked out onto the street, with Cas almost stumbling away, his face washed out and aghast. 'I'm sorry, guv. Nobody needs to see that.'

'We're *married*,' muttered Cas.

'I know.' Steve did not know what else to say as Cas covered his eyes with his hands. Suddenly, the Spaniard's hands were down and he darted for the restaurant door. Steve lunged over and grabbed his arm. Cas tried to shake off his assistant's grip only for Steve to bearhug him.

'Don't,' said Steve, softly but firmly. 'Not like this in public. It's not good for you or the team.'

Cas stopped struggling immediately.

Steve let him go and took a deep breath. 'Let's fuel up elsewhere.'

Cas turned his gaze away from the restaurant. 'I'm not hungry.'

CHAPTER 9

Andriy rolled his tinted window back up, having chatted to the security man who granted entry into the stadium's squad car park. 'Nice to be home.'

From behind a pair of large shades, Dmitriy nodded as the song on the radio finished. 'This is Red Square Radio and the time is four o'clock,' announced the radio presenter in Russian. 'The headlines this afternoon: the President welcomes representatives from the Ukraine and Dagestan, the Education Secretary comments on last week's tragic school shooting, and in sport, Volkov announces his squad for the first World Cup qualifiers.'

Dmitriy pulled his phone out. No new notifications. He navigated his way to his inbox. Nothing.

'Calm down. Let's not jump to conclusions,' said Andriy. 'Let's listen.' He parked up as the Russian news show continued, Dmitriy fidgeting more as it went on. The football section came and went with no mention of Dmitriy, just a few new call-ups.

'Please check it,' said Dmitriy.

Andriy pulled out his fully capable smartphone and searched for the squad. He shook his head.

'Three goals and three assists in four games and he leaves me out! *On okhuyennyy trus!*'

'I know it's hard to take, but we knew this may happen. Breathe. There's only one way to respond.'

Dmitriy grappled with his tension for a moment, then took a deep breath and nodded briskly, looking towards the players' entrance. 'And here's the best place to do it.'

COWBOY
God be with Team Ezemonye today.
Enjoy the game x

Victor powered his phone down and unenthusiastically nodded to the camera crew as they entered the dressing room. As Dmitriy came in immediately behind them, Victor leaned down to put his phone into his bag, removing himself from the exchange of greetings.

A few moments later, McGlynn entered with a large kitbag slung over his shoulder. 'Afternoon, gents,' he said with gusto.

'Afternoon,' they echoed back. He sought out Dmitriy and shot him a thumbs up, to which Dmitriy nodded back.

'Nice afternoon to set some wrongs right, isn't it?' he said.

'Too fucking right,' yelled Finney over the other claps and shouts as he stood up and walked over to McGlynn, offering his hand for a shake.

'Language, Ian,' muttered McGlynn through his broad smile as he shook his hand whilst subtly nodding towards the camera.

'We ready to show the world what our football stands for?' asked McGlynn, raising a cheer from the players.

The door opened. The players who could see it hushed. In walked Cas, his mousey locks gone, given way to a blade one all over. Steve's expression sagged.

'Oh my days!' said Victor as he caught sight of him. 'Boss man's ready for war!'

'Good afternoon, guys,' said Cas, his expression steely. The players swarmed over to shake their manager's hand. Eventually, the bodies parted for McGlynn to meet him.

'Looking a little . . .' McGlynn bobbed his head side to side as he searched for the word he wanted, '. . . sterner there, my friend.'

He nodded as his mouth curved down in impressed surprise. 'I have an announcement for you and the fellas. Take a seat, gents.'

The players sat as Cas joined Steve and the rest of his staff standing off to the side. The camera crew situated themselves in the corner to get a good view of McGlynn and the three large, covered easels he stood in front of.

'Weavers. Last season we kicked this club into a new stratosphere. We went from surviving to thriving. From humble beginnings, over the last few years we have woven a footballing tapestry fit for football fans from all over the world to admire. We stand for our brand of beautiful football, we stand for the beauty of football itself, and I want to make sure that our stand is clear for all to see. I want to consolidate our position in this new stratosphere and give us a solid footing to push ourselves completely out of this world.

Today, for the first time this season, we welcome our fans home. The Cooperative has been our home for over seventy years. Our past is here. Our heart is here. But it's not in the walls or in that turf out there. It's in you, the players. And it's in our amazing fans out there. That's our home and that's where our heart is. These stands are just where our start is. Our future, like our football, belongs where the art is.'

McGlynn pulled the cover off the easels unveiling a tryptic of rendered images of a gargantuan modern stadium full of white and sky-blue seats, its stands covered with a rim of the same colours.

'I give you The MCG Cooperative. A sixty-thousand-seater stadium for the modern era that will welcome people from the world over to come and witness our well-woven football.'

The players' eyes widened. A round of applause began.

'Come take a look at your new home-to-be,' said McGlynn, beckoning the players and staff over. The camera panned to follow their rush.

'Sixty thou, Big McG?' said Victor at the front of the crowd.

'Sixty thousand, week in, week out, screaming your name as you bang in the goals.'

'S'pretty sick, you know.'

McGlynn grinned from ear to ear.

The players buzzed as they inspected the sleek images. Cas and Steve took a closer look.

'You see this?' whispered Cas, pointing to the structure on one side of the stadium. Steve peered closer. The concrete pillars and facade were cleverly shaped into the letters M-C-G. Steve's head need not shake; his eyes did all his disapproving for him.

'When he dies,' whispered Steve, 'they can bury him under the bloody thing like a pharaoh.'

A hand landed on each of their shoulders. 'What do you think, guys?' asked McGlynn.

'Very nice pictures, Andy,' said Cas. 'Very nice. Maybe we can talk very soon about our strategy going forward, so we can make the plans together?'

'Of course, Cas, of course. We're in this together. This is a starting vision. An inspiration for us all on a big day!'

Cas cordially smiled.

'I've put the pics in the matchday programme. I can't wait to see what the fans make of them.' He double tapped both their shoulders. 'Let's book in a chat soon.' As he slid off to mingle further, Charlie called his way.

'Mr McGlynn,' he said as the camera pulled up next to them.

'Andy, please, Charlie.'

'Andy, sorry. Unreal that stadium.'

'Thanks. It will be.'

'I was looking at the surroundings,' said Charlie. 'You changing loads of the surroundings here?'

'Ha. Wouldn't that be something? No, we're hoping this'll be over in the Traders' Quarter. Put our art where the art is.'

'Oh . . . across the city?' asked Charlie.

'Well, yes. Like I was saying, home is where we are. Where the fans are. We can't develop this here so we're going to have to move to grow.'

Charlie nodded earnestly. 'Most of our fans are from around here. It's a bit of a trek and it's expensive over that way. Isn't there somewhere a bit closer we can move to?'

McGlynn's eyes narrowed for an instant until he spotted the camera out of his peripheral vision and found a smile again. 'The fans are everything to us and we're everything to them. It'll heavy their hearts for a time, just like it has mine, but they'll understand. They'll follow us into our future, I'm sure. They're good people.'

'The best,' said Charlie, rubbing the back of his head as McGlynn broke away and headed over to the kit man, Dom, for a brief chat.

'By the way, guys,' McGlynn announced to the team, 'Dom and I have another little surprise for you.'

As they entered the pitch to warm up to the cheers of the slowly filling stadium, Victor knelt to tie his lace. His eyes fixated on the badge on his shorts. The lattice-like woven pattern emblem in its centre was not its usual Weavers' sky blue. Each strand had been recoloured a hue of the rainbow.

Shortly after the Weavers began limbering up, the Warriors made their way out to a chorus of boos and whistles. As Lawler jogged out, he scanned around his old home ground, occasionally catching eyes with a Weaver. A few uncomfortable stares later, he put his head down and carried on loosening up. The next person he looked at other than his teammates was a pitch-side camera operator as he went to retrieve a stray ball from next to him. The operator saved him a few yards of his journey, side-footing the ball to Lawler all whilst keeping the camera on him.

'Ta,' called Lawler as he chopped the ball back towards his teammates, only for another ball from behind to tangle between his feet. He rolled the intruding ball around with his studs and turned.

Dmitriy jogged his way to collect it. He cushioned a pass his old teammate's way.

'Thanks, Bry.'

Lawler stolidly nodded at him, then headed back to his black-and-gold clad troop.

As the Warriors' warm-up concluded and they left the pitch, their assistant manager, Tony, pulled Lawler aside in the entrance to the dressing room. 'Bry, the chief just phoned me,' he said quietly. 'You're out.'

'What you mean?'

'You're out of the line-up. He said I have to report you injured to the officials so we can swap you out.'

'What are you on about, Tone? I'm not injured,' Lawler said disbelievingly, his volume climbing.

Tony shrugged. 'Keep it quiet. What do you want me to do? He sounded livid. I dunno what you did, but I'm just the messenger so you'll have to take it up with him.'

'You're not leaving me out of that team, Tone,' grumbled Lawler, squaring up to the assistant manager.

'Listen here, Bry. I know you're fucked off. *This wasn't me.* And Gunnar said if you cause the slightest bit of bother here, you won't want to see what's coming so *calm yourself now.*'

Lawler stayed in the assistant's face for a few more seconds before stepping back.

'Now get an icepack from the physio and support the team.' Tony left the dressing room, leaving Lawler seething, his fists clenched into wrecking balls.

Steve showed the film crew out of the dressing room and re-entered. Cas took his place in front of the white board and rubbed his hand up the back of his freshly shaved nape. The players hushed.

'You know what they took from us,' said Cas, his eyes meeting those of many of his players as he paused. 'You know what we deserve.

Today, he can't take it again. Today, we make him watch at home as we dominate his team worse than before. We make him sit there helpless, watching the fight drain from them.

We have started strong. You know what to do. We strangle them with our game. *Hala,* Weavers!'

The team exploded, echoing their boss's rallying cry back at him.

CHAPTER 10

'Fucking Traders' Quarter,' said Rory as he screwed up the programme and shoved it in his back pocket. 'Six fifty a pint over there. On top of whatever the season ticket price 'ike is in those new posh seats. When did this all get so soft?'

'Soft seats for soft arses now, Roar,' sneered the guy stood next to him, over the building background music.

'Sounds about right. Travel costs too. The cunts'll price 'alf of us proper fans out for the fucking smoked salmon brigade.' Something caught Rory's attention a few rows in front. ''Ere. Get a load of fucking Munnar Gagnusson down there.'

His mates all looked down to see a Gunnar doppelganger – tall and with the same hair – in a long black dress jacket squeezing along a row of fans, all standing to let him through. 'Fucking 'ell. Uncanny that,' said Rory's neighbour. 'Oi!' he shouted towards the doppelganger, drawing his attention. 'Aren't you fucking barred?'

The doppelganger smiled back, carrying on along the row, as a few of the rows around Rory jeered and laughed like hyenas. The stadium announcer interrupted them as the music neared its crescendo, imploring the fans to get behind their team as the sides walked out. The chant of 'We love you Weavers, we do' rang around the stands. Rory and his friends cheered as he waved a large flag of the Weavers' badge overhead. A friend of his a few seats along boomed a hefty drum.

As the Weavers in their white kits lined up alongside the black-clad Warriors in the centre of the pitch and the sound climaxed, Rory squinted and shook the friend next to him. 'Are you fucking seeing that? You see the badges?!'

His friend strained to see too. ''Ave they . . .? You've got to be havin' a fuckin' laugh?'

'You seen this?' Rory asked around all those near him as he set his flag down. 'They've rainbowed the fucking badge. *Our* badge. It's one thing pissing around with the third kit. How far are they gonna take this?'

His mates blustered amongst themselves, indignant, spreading word of what they had noticed. Rory stuck his fingers in his mouth and let rip an ear-piercing whistle. When his breath ran out, he sucked in another and whistled again. He yanked his fingers out of his mouth and grabbed the badge on his home replica shirt, displaying it to those around him. 'BRING OUR BADGE BACK!' he bellowed before clapping five times rhythmically, then spreading his arms wide overhead. 'FUCK YOUR RAINBOW!' *Clap-clap-cla-cla-clap.*

'BRING OUR BADGE BACK!' Around a dozen of his mates joined in with the chant and clap. 'FUCK YOUR RAINBOW!' The drum beat along with the next claps as Rory thrust his flag back overhead. The chant picked up momentum on each successive round until six rounds in, around a quarter of The Hartington Stand or 'The Old Mill', as it was more commonly known – the most fanatical stand at The Cooperative – was on their feet, amplifying the chant.

Down on the pitch, as the dead-eyed Warriors passed the Weavers, shaking their hands, the noise drew Dmitriy's attention. The black cluster of away fans in the top of the northernmost end of the East Stand were relatively muted. It was the home fans adjacent to them. They were yelling down at the pitch, not their black-shirted rivals. As the volume rose, he finally made out what they bawled. He looked down at his badge in horror.

COLIN

Gunnar Magnusson must be up off his sofa willing his team to make it through the next two minutes after what has been forty-five minutes of Weavers' onslaught.

PETE
Look at Velasquez on the sideline, urging his team on like a man possessed to press until that half-time whistle.

COLIN
And again, Xavier picks Arkles's pocket – what a wretched time he's had filling in last minute. He finds Lebedev, who bursts towards the box. There goes Ezemonye – he's got across his centre back and he's begging for the slide-rule pass. Lebedev shapes to make it . . . no, he carries it further. He hits it left-footed. It whizzes past the near post to the relief of Clausewitz, who's hoping his second half is much quieter than his first.

PETE
The ball was on there for Ezemonye and he knows it. It's not the first time today that Lebedev hasn't found him at the right moment. If they can find their chemistry for the second half, you'd imagine this Warriors' back-line won't be able to hold on.

COLIN
And there's the half-time whistle that ends an action-packed yet somehow goalless first half. It'll be interesting to see if the Warriors' number two

can rally his troops for a better second-half performance in the same way his senior did on a few occasions last season.

PETE
It's not just the Warriors' players who need a talking to. We've just watched a dominant first half from the home side, yet some of the crowd have been at them from the off, whistling, aiming vitriol at the Director's Box. This is not the sort of thing we want to be seeing.

COLIN
It certainly isn't. The temperature is hot as we go in for half-time. Join us after the ads for the OmniSports half-time breakdown. It's Weavers nil, Warriors nil.

'Yo, man,' Victor said to the back of Dmitriy as they entered the dressing room, drawing a look over the shoulder from him. 'Stop hoggin' the ball. *Pass* de ting.'

Dmitriy gave a solitary apathetic upwards nod.

'Yo. You hear me right, fam?' asked Victor, louder than before, pulling in the attention of the surrounding players.

'I hear you very right, *fam*,' snarked Dmitriy. 'I didn't see you. I pass when I see you.'

'Bull-shit, fam! You see shit with your two eyes *and* that one in your bell-end. You see me, fam. I fucking see you too.'

Finney, the only of the players in his casual clothes, stepped towards them. 'Woah woah woah, lads. What's up?'

Dmitriy ignored Finney and fired his response at Victor. 'What you see from other side of the dressing room?'

'I see plenty, fam.'

'What you see?' asked Dmitriy, more forcefully this time.

'Apart from McGlynn sucking you off and giving you the fuckin' reach-around?' replied Victor. Everybody fell silent.

Dmitriy's expression dropped as he looked long and hard at Victor, then to Finney. 'You hear this?'

'You can't be saying shit like that, Vic,' said Finney.

'Are you fuckin' kiddin' me, big man? He gonna cry about that?' Victor's gestures grew more animated. 'We fuckin' grown men spittin' grown-men truth at each other. Andy might be right up McGl-in him but can't have man tinkin' he's special now.'

Everybody watched on as Finney stepped into Victor's space and put an arm around him. 'Easy – take is easy. You can't be saying that. Shit sounds a bit . . . well, you know.'

'What, big man?' snapped Victor.

'Homophobic, Vic.'

'Homo*phobic*?' He sneered Dmitriy's way. 'You think I'm scared of this fa—' He stopped dead, spotting Cas and Steve staring his way from the doorway. Everybody froze, waiting for Cas's icy stare to break. When it did, he looked at his shoes for a moment, shaking his head then looked past Victor and Dmitriy.

'Chris.' Everybody's head swung round to the far end of the dressing room where the team doctor stood. 'Take Victor to another room. Check his head. He needs a rest.'

'Umm . . . on it.' Chris scuttled across the room to grab a medical bag.

Cas walked over to Victor, put a hand on each of his shoulders, and shook his head. Victor averted his gaze and screwed his mouth shut. 'I won't make this conversation now,' said Cas. 'Go.'

Chris arrived with his bag and a tracksuit top for Victor and shepherded him away. Cas turned to Dmitriy. 'Are you OK?'

Wide-eyed, Dmitriy nodded.

'OK.' He addressed the group. 'Everybody sit. Is over. Give me one minute.'

As the players sat and got fluids onboard in the muted room, Cas pulled Steve aside.

'The daft fuck,' said Steve. 'We had them right where we wanted them.'

'We still do,' replied Cas.

'Who're we going with now up top? This would have been tailor made for Tezza to fight for scraps in the box, but for Raf . . . this is deeper than the deep end. Aren't we best off shuffling things around, maybe using some of the more experienced lads out of position? Dimmy could probably do a job higher up.'

Cas scrubbed his hands on the back of his scalp, interlaced his fingers, and set his eyes on the wall, eventually lowering them to find one of his players face down on the floor, legs spread, and motionless. Suddenly awash with nausea, his vision began to fade to black, only stopping as the player moved and retrieved the tape that had rolled under the bench.

'What do you reckon, guv?' asked Steve, snapping him back to the decision at hand. 'Shuffle the system?'

Cas's sunken eyes turned to him. 'Our system at *fifty* percent would beat their excuse for the football. We are not scared of them. We play Raf, we play *our* game.'

COLIN
Look at those Warriors as the referee blows the final whistle, pumping their fists in the air to their boss at home, after rescuing a point that will feel like three. One shot on target, one goal.

PETE
What a toothless second half from the home side. It was always going to be difficult losing the ever-dangerous Ezemonye at the interval but after that

Lebedev free kick, I thought they would put the game to bed.

It just proved too big a game to drop Rafaels into and without that dual threat of Ezemonye and Lebedev, it was easy for the Warriors to target the Russian and really limit the home side. Velasquez had the full half to change the shape and maybe bring on some more experienced personnel but without a plan B, they left the door open for the absent Magnusson's side to steal a draw at the death.

COLIN
Yes. And despite it being the manager's call not to shuffle his pack more, some of the fans are directing their frustrations at Lebedev, the man who tried to carry the attacking fight single-handedly at times, as he leaves the pitch. With Xavier limping badly next to him after that heavy tackle at the death, we leave this on a sad, strange scene all evens here at The Cooperative.

In the frame's reflection, Cas could see his much larger face hovering beside Amber's. He held the photo in his hands for a long while before closing it away, face down, in his bottom drawer. His face resting on one hand, eventually he reached across his desk for the remote.

'Can't even beat me when I'm not here.' The holler from outside the office door jolted Cas upright. It was Gunnar's voice. 'But then again, I'm never far away, am I?'

Cas shot up out of his seat as footsteps ran away along the hall. He flung his door open and looked right, seeing the back of a tall man in black disappear through the double doors. His heart raced as his bulging eyes jerked down to spot a black envelope on the floor, which he picked up and opened.

> *Attack him where he is not prepared,*
> *appear where you are not expected.*

He scrunched the note up, slammed the door as he re-entered his office, stormed back over to his desk, and dialled his office phone. 'Hi Bill, can you check who is fucking about up here please? Somebody just shouted outside my door, left some paper for me, and ran away.' He waited as Bill spoke back. 'Now? How long was he there with you?' He looked at the crumpled note in his hand. 'OK. Bring him here.' After tearing up the note, he sat back in his chair, squared himself to his desk, and evened out his breathing as he watched the door like a hawk. After a minute or so, the knock came. 'Come in.'

The security man, Bill, opened the door. 'Here he is, boss. I'll get on the other thing.' He stepped away, allowing Magnus to enter.

'Are you sure this is a convenient time for you?' asked Magnus.

'Is fine. Come in,' replied Cas, still on edge as he rose to greet his guest, his eyes studying the gigantic man, who he entered carrying a boxed bottle of his native *Brennivín*.

'A pleasure to meet you,' said Magnus before they shook hands. Although Magnus's hand was enormous, he did not wield it like his son did.

'Just a little thank-you for you.' He passed Cas the gift.

'For what?'

'For letting me in,' replied Magnus. 'And not judging the father for the sins of his son.'

Cas eyed his guest intently as he put the box on his table and invited him to take a seat.

'You come to watch for him today?' asked Cas.

'No no, for me. We'll all be playing one another soon enough so it's best I see everything live. I'm very much a fan of what you do here,' said Magnus.

'Thank you,' replied Cas stand-offishly.

'You were very unlucky today. It's a big loss, your boy Ezemonye at half-time. Is he OK?' asked Magnus.

Cas nodded. 'Should be fine soon.'

'Football crowds are fickle bunches,' said Magnus. 'You've developed a young team with a very specific, lauded brand of football and then they complain when you stick to your guns and bring in a young player to work in your generally winning system.'

Cas shrugged.

'They can't have it both ways. And your man Lebedev.' Magnus shook his head disapprovingly. 'These people . . . honestly. What he put into that game. How close he was to breaking them down. People don't understand how so many aspects of these results rest on knife edges. I saw how close he was, you were, to it paying off today. Their lack of appreciation annoys me to no end, so I wanted to come and pass on some of my own.'

'Thanks.' Cas sat back and folded his arms.

'You know, I came to England having heard tales of managers getting together after games and sharing war stories over a drink. Maybe we can't do that given my relation.' He examined Cas's poker face. 'I wouldn't blame you. I saw what he did last season. I guess you must know him fairly well from your season together. Even I struggle with him. I move half the way around the world so I can be near to my first grandson and I practically have to beg to see him. Anyway . . . I wanted, at the very least, to come shake your hand and let you know how much I admire what you do here. This is a lonely, harsh profession where all we hear is criticism from the ill-informed.'

Cas's expression softened. 'Thank you. It's nice of you to come. And thank you for the gift.'

Magnus groaned as he pushed himself up out of his chair. 'You're welcome. If you run out of that, I have plenty in my office.'

'I'm not much of the spirit drinker,' replied Cas.

'Oh well. For when you're in the mood,' said Magnus. 'Anyway, that was my way of extending you an invitation. You're welcome any time to the training ground . . . maybe except for the week before we play each other. I can make sure I have some softer bottles in stock.'

Cas grinned at him sceptically.

'You think I jest,' said Magnus. 'You must understand, before I got involved in football, information sharing was the professional norm. Cross-pollination brought about many breakthroughs. A rising tide lifts all boats. Surely, we want to win as the best of a brilliant bunch rather than the best of a mediocre one?'

Cas contemplated his guest's words.

'Anyway, those two weeks per season aside, my door is always open. My card is in the box.' Magnus walked away from the table, stooped under the doorway, and turned back. 'Keep doing what you're doing here. It truly is fantastic. Like I said, my door's always open,' he said in Spanish.

As he closed the door behind him, Cas's eyes narrowed. 'What was that?' he muttered to himself.

CHAPTER 11

Words emerged out of the shrieks, but he could not make them out yet. He turned to the referees next to him. Still as statues, their faces were devoid of eyes. Past them, the opposition players wore Weavers' white. He examined their faces; they were his teammates. He turned back to his team. They were there too.

The stands were full of white and blue Weavers' shirts, cloaked in shadow by the gloomy pregnant clouds above. The wind whipped at him, its whistling layering on top of the sharpening shrieks.

Dead ahead of him next to the pitch-black tunnel opening, a fan jumped over the electronic advertising boards. Then another. And another. They began to pour over en masse and sprint at him. The words finally emerged from the shrieks, like knives glimmering out of shadows. 'Fuck your rainbow.'

He went to spin but could not. His teammates tangled his every limb like a web of hands. The more he struggled, the tighter they held. The tidal wave of white shirts washed his way, their chant loudening. Through the gaps between them, the electronic boards all along the stand glared the modified spectrum of seven colours.

'It wasn't me!' he screamed at them as he tried to wrestle himself free but the more he struggled, the tighter the human web wove itself. With hands clasping all around his torso and his heart pounding so ferociously, it felt as if one could claw it right out of his chest.

As the stampede closed in, a figure in the centre stood out. She wore a skimpy white summer dress with blue polka dots. Her glossy hair tore around in the gale as her featureless face began ripping apart at the mouth, squealing in agony. She raised her hands aloft, clasped together. An axe sprouted from them, glinting in the floodlights.

He heaved to break free one last time, absolutely paralysed by the web, as the blade bore down.

Ripping the soaking sheet off him, he leapt out of bed. As he gasped in a few breaths and his racing heart slowed from sprint to canter, he noticed Andriy had not stirred. He crept around the bed to Andriy's bedside table, reached for the drawer handle but stopped short of it and instead light-footed out of the room.

He leaned against a wall in the living room, still catching his breath, looking out at the moon's reflection bouncing off the glassy lake. His eyes wandered over to the bridge that he had contemplated stepping off a few months ago. He yanked his attention away from it, ending up with his eyes on Andriy's laptop on the table.

He had not been on the internet since the final day of last season. If he wanted to focus on being the best player he could be, being exposed to a slew of online abuse from strangers across the globe was not going to be productive, Andriy had said. He would act as a filter for a while. He had given Dmitriy important email and messages to respond to with the laptop in offline mode. That was all that was necessary. Until now.

He fired up the laptop, logged into Twitter, and scrolled down the digital ream of direct messages. He had not disabled the ability to restrict messages from unknowns before his internet break and it showed. Every time he scrolled to the bottom of the scroll bar, it kept expanding. He clicked a few random messages.

You and your fag agent fuck off home

The cunt that ruined football

HIV player of the year

He kept going, stewing away. Many of the messages came from accounts which no longer existed or had profile pictures of 'The Egg', cartoon characters, or plain panels. Eventually he found one with a different tone from somebody with a profile picture of a person.

> You are the bravest man. Where I live I cant be so brave as you. Not yet... Thanks for showin us HOPE

He remained on this message for a moment and sighed before carrying on going through more messages and comments. Forty minutes evaporated before he heard unsocked footsteps patter along the hallway. Andriy arrived in the doorway, rubbing his eyes.

'I had to,' said Dmitriy.

Andriy reluctantly nodded as he walked over. 'You don't need to look for her. I'll know if she posts anything.'

'I know,' replied Dmitriy. 'I needed to know what everyone says.' He tapped restlessly on the keyboard. 'Tomorrow, I say something back.'

'Fuck sake, girl. Will you shut up?' said Lawler as he fastened his jeans.

Tara and Katrina stopped their chatter as they carried on dressing themselves on the end of the bed. Katrina slid herself across the sheets and clutched Lawler's hand. 'What's up with you, babes?'

He reached under the bed for one of his shoes, uninterested in replying.

She tugged his hand and lightened her tone. 'It's only a game, you know.'

He snatched his hand away to tie his laces and shook his head. 'Only a fuckin' game.' He muttered his next line under his breath. 'Better than *the game*.'

'There any need for that? I'm just trying to be nice, you twat.' She retreated over towards Tara.

'I dunno why you're so mardy. I like it when you don't play,' said Tara, a naughty grin across her face. She began to crawl across the covers towards him, her spine slinking like a lioness on the prowl as her space buns bobbed up and down. She pawed at his jeans fly. 'More petrol in the tank to take us where we wanna go.'

Lawler slapped her hand away with a loud clap. 'Shut up, you fuckin' tit.'

Tara recoiled. 'Oy! Wha'dya think you're doing, you shithead?' She clutched her hand. The skin was reddened.

Lawler yanked his second shoe on, stormed over to a nearby chair, and grabbed a fat wad of twenties out of his jacket hung over it.

'Don't just fucking ignore me,' she asserted, louder this time.

Six hundred into his cashier-speed count, he abandoned it, turned back their way, and stepped towards them. He saw her step back. Momentarily, the whites of her eyes bulged. He stopped and raised his hands.

'Look, I'm sorry. I didn't mean to. I shouldn't have. Can we just draw a line under it?' He jiggled the full wad at her then set it on the dressing table.

'That's more than fine, Bry, isn't it, hun?' Katrina said, looking to Tara. 'He didn't mean to catch you like that.'

'You know what? It isn't. That's assault,' said Tara, standing taller.

'Piss off. He just clipped your hand away,' replied Katrina.

'You think cos you pay us, that gives you the right to hit us?' asked Tara, louder again.

Lawler softened his voice, his palms still raised to her. 'No. I shouldn't have. I'm sorry. I just wanna make it right.'

'It's fine, Bry,' cooed Katrina. 'Leave it, Tara.'

'Piss off. He didn't hit you,' said Tara.

'He barely touched you!' strained Katrina.

Lawler removed his watch and dangled it by his thumb and index finger. 'That's worth three times that,' he said, nodding to the money. 'We sound?'

Tara dead-eyed him, eventually nodding.

He put the watch next to the cash, picked up his jacket, and backed away towards the hotel room's mini-hallway. Katrina bounced off the bed and headed after him.

'I'm done with her, Bry. She's being hysterical. Just me and you next time, yeh, while I find someone new if you want?'

He grabbed his nape and raked his hand around. 'Kat – I can't do this anymore. Me career's gonna go down the shitter if I'm not careful. I've gotta get me head straight.'

She gazed at him with genuine affection, stepped close, and kissed his cheek. 'Alright. You know where I am if you want me.'

'Get a good split of that cash. Take it easy.' He left, easing the door closed behind him.

'Jesus, fellas – no offence, Vic,' said Charlie, sat waiting for his turn. 'Is this a treatment room or a morgue?' A few of the masseuses lifted their gazes and smiled meekly before continuing to work on the half dozen players laid face down in front of them. 'Easy?'

Victor flailed a wave his way without taking his face out of the table's face-hole or saying anything. Nobody said a word.

'We absolutely twatted them. They got spawny. End of. Line under it. New day,' said Charlie.

Still no response came.

Charlie got up, strolled over to the sound system, and turned it on. The chatter of sports radio began. 'No, no.' He flicked through a few channels until he found music and turned it up. Sensual sighs overlaid the Vogue-esque instrumentals. 'This'll have to do.' He began to strut like a catwalk model along the aisle between the treatment tables, each step directly in front of the other, hips swinging side to side. At the end of the room, he swivelled and pouted before launching back into an even more flamboyant sashay with a full-on vogue hand performance. As the masseuses snickered, some of the players lifted their heads, shaking them and smiling.

'Don't judge, lads. I just go where the music takes me.' He stopped in the centre, everybody except Victor watching on, smirking and giggling, as the song's whispery female French vocals kicked in. He pirouetted and shimmied as the singer built towards a mid-song climax, at which point he dropped in a twirling split to the floor and rolled under Victor's treatment table to carry on his performance. His teammates and the masseuses creased in laughter as Charlie writhed around as if at the base of a stripper's pole.

'Charlie. Please, fam. It's too early for this shit.' Victor removed his dreary face from the table's face-hole and grumpily rested it on his forearm.

Finney walked into the room as Charlie grabbed the sides of Victor's table with his hands and heels then tried to hump its face-hole to the beat. 'What the fuck have I walked into here?!' laughed the club captain as the song built to its finish and his ears pricked up.

As Victor's masseuse backed off in a fit of laughter, the player jumped off the table and headed for the exit. Charlie rolled out from under the table, jumped to his feet, and minced after him.

'Lemme rub it better, EasyHoney,' called Charlie as his teammate disappeared out of the door. He turned back to his audience and resumed full-force vogueing as the song ended on the lyric, 'Ménage à trois trois trois.' Upon hitting his final shape, the remaining teammates burst into applause and wolf-whistles, many with tears streaming down their faces.

'And that's 'Trois Trois Trois', the steamy new track from—' Finney switched the channel and turned the music down.

'Don't let the boss see you dancing while it's so fresh,' said Finney to Charlie.

'I was just trying to pull the stick out of his miserable arse,' said Charlie. 'You heard him last night. He's out of order. Not been right all season.'

'I know, Chaz . . . I know.' He squeezed the right back's shoulder. 'I know everyone needed a lift, just don't let Cas see you dancing today.'

As Charlie nodded, the assistant physio and Xavier entered the room, with Xavier hobbling on a pair of crutches, one leg held off the floor. All the smiles soured.

'Fucking hell, mate,' said Finney. 'That looks worse than it looked last night.'

'Yeh, mate,' replied the dejected Xavier in his mellifluous Portuguese accent. 'Woke up this morning and can't put any weight on it. Had to get a taxi in.'

'Fingers crossed it feels worse than it actually is.' Finney nodded towards the physio. 'Let him work his magic.' As Charlie and him stepped aside to let them through, he looked over to Neil's open office door at the end of the room.

'Come in,' said Neil to the rattle on the door.

'Morning, Doc.' Finney opened the door fully as he came in and tipped his head back towards it. 'You seen Professor X?'

Neil leaned to look past Finney. 'Bastard.'

'Yep,' said Finney as he closed the door behind him. 'Bastard. Leaves us threadbare.' He sat across from Neil. After a few moments of silence, he started to tap on the table in rhythm with the tick of the wall-clock.

'What can I do for you, Ian?' said Neil, leaning back into his seat and folding his arms.

'I dunno, healer of men,' replied Finney as he leaned his forearms on the desk. 'What *can* you do for me?'

Neil adjusted his glasses as he contemplated his answer. 'You have to tell me you want it.'

'I *need* it. Not just for me.'

Neil raised his hands to his mouth and stroked his stubble. 'You understand the risks of operating in such a grey area?'

'Ha.' Finney combed his fingers through the front of his hair. 'No stranger to the grey, Neil.'

'Come in,' called Cas.

Victor entered, gave his manager a quick upwards nod, and then flitted his gaze around the office floor as he walked over, hands lodged deep into his pockets, and took a seat beside Finney.

'How are you?' asked Cas.

Victor shrugged, his gaze ever moving. 'Yeh . . . a'ight.'

Cas observed his striker's restlessness. 'Are you sure? Since we come back from the summer, you maybe seem less happy for something?'

'I'm a'ight, boss. I mean, obviously I'd prefer to be baggin', but it'll come. EasyMoney, you know?'

Cas nodded with a half-grin.

'The man upstairs works in mysterious ways,' said Victor.

'Yes . . . he does. How's Chuka?'

'Yeh, man. He's good. Doin' his ting, you know?'

'Good. Bring him in sometimes. It's been too long,' said Cas.

'Yeh, man. I will.' Victor fidgeted like a pupil waiting for a telling-off from his headmaster.

Cas drummed his fingers on the table. 'OK. Victor – you are a good boy. You are all my boys here. We are a family. We need to be good with each other because we are a family and it helps to make the football flow. We need the respect amongst us. You understand?'

Victor nodded, his eyes avoiding direct contact with Cas.

Cas tilted his head to attract Victor's gaze. 'You make it OK with Dmitriy? Shake his hand?'

'Yeh,' muttered Victor.

'Good. I want us good; together.' Cas blew a sigh of relief, dropping his shoulders.

Finney watched Victor nod half-heartedly. 'You know you can't say shit like that, Vic?'

Victor perked up. 'Shit like what, big man?'

'C'mon. Don't play games,' replied Finney.

'I ain't playin'. What I say?'

'You know what you said,' said Finney incredulously. 'What you called him.'

'I didn't call him nothin'. You spouted that shit about homophobia, big man.'

'Boys, let's leave this.' Cas gestured to Victor, directing his next comment to Finney. 'He said he'll make it good with Dmitriy.'

'Two minutes please, boss man,' replied Victor. 'Big man, I said McGlynn's givin' him special treatment cos he's . . . you know . . . and I said I ain't scared of gays, but I didn't call him nothin'. I just told man to pass me the fuckin' rock when he sees man stood in bare grassland.'

'Vic – we all heard what you were about to call him,' said Finney.

'Can't man call man a fuckface now?'

'*C'mooon, Vic,*' replied Finney, twisting his face in distrust. 'We were there. That wasn't what you were gonna say.'

Victor looked over to Cas. 'I dunno what to say. Big man's Minority Reported me. Mind's made up.'

'All that stuff about McGlynn sucking him off and fucking him,' said Finney.

'So? McGlynn be creepin'. People be talkin' about fuckin' and gettin' fucked all the time. If we can't talk about men bangin' men, ain't that homophobic?'

Finney sat confounded for a moment. 'Vic – come on. Be honest.'

Cas interjected, 'Boys, let's draw the line under this, shake the hands, and move on.'

'Wait there, boss,' said Finney. 'Best we air this stuff out, eh? Speak like grown men.'

'Oh, you want the grown-man-honest truth, yeh?' asked Victor.

'Yeh, go on,' replied Finney as Cas shook his head and sat back.

'Truth is Dimmy *is* getting special treatment. Where was all this for Chuks, eh?'

Finney's and Cas's heads sank.

'Exactly,' scoffed Victor. 'Man throwin' fruit down at him. No change of kit for him, was there?'

'Victor,' crooned Cas, 'You know I try to speak to him. He makes his mind up. He wouldn't listen.'

'I know you did, but I didn't see the club changin' no badge or shirt for him. A little press release, that's it. Boom. I ain't even sayin' they should have, but the difference vexes me, man.'

The duo stayed quiet.

'And now we gonna change how we chat shit in the dressin' room for one man? What . . . we gonna put a swear jar in the middle?'

No answer came for a long while. 'I want harmony, Victor. I want us to win,' said Cas.

Victor looked Cas straight in his eyes. 'So do I, boss man. Look, I'll squash the beef with Dimmy, but I ain't cool wid all the double standards. You get me?'

Cas nodded solemnly. 'I do.'

'You gonna make this good with Dimmy now, yeh?' asked Finney.

'Yeh, big man. Whenever,' said Victor as he got up.

'Do me a favour, Victor,' said Cas.

'Go on,' replied Victor.

'Sit back next to Dmitriy for me.'

Victor halted. 'Fo' real?' he asked, his half an octave higher than usual.

'Please. Closeness helps the closeness,' replied Cas.

Victor rattled his fingers against the desk as his eyes wandered again. 'A'ight, boss.'

'Thank you,' said Cas before standing. 'I come to the dressing room with you.'

The trio made their way to the dressing room where everybody had just began getting ready for training. Victor walked over towards Dmitriy, who had just taken off his top ready to put his training shirt on. 'Yo, Dim. We a'ight to put a fork in yesterday? Like done? Was more about McGlynn than anythin'.'

Dmitriy examined Victor's stoic face; his chin slightly tilted up. In his periphery, he noticed his teammates and coaches watching on hopefully. The room had quietened. Motion had all but ceased. He cautiously nodded and put out a fist for Victor to pound.

Victor bumped it and returned a likewise nod. 'Yes.' He turned his attention to the rest of the room. 'We a'ight. Nothing to see here, bredrin. Don't pull them jock straps on too tight.' A relieved collective laugh came back at him, giving the entire room subconscious permission for chatter and movement to begin again. 'Am I a'ight to get in my old spot again?' asked Victor sheepishly.

'Go for it,' said Dmitriy as he began to put his shirt on.

'Woah, Easy,' said Charlie. 'I quite like my new spot. I think I'm absorbing some of Dimmy's Chernobyl power. How much is this prime bit of real estate worth to you?'

An impatient look flashed across Victor's face before he found a smile. 'Tell you what, fam. I promise I won't meg you today.'

'Ha. You promise you won't meg me,' scoffed Charlie. 'Like that's a thing.'

'Five sessions on the bizounce and countin',' replied Victor. 'Reclaim some self-respect, fam. Take it or leave it.'

'Mate. This is a team sport,' said Charlie. 'What would God say about your obsession with individual showboating?'

Victor put his hands together in prayer, peeled them back apart, spread his five digits, and pushed them towards Charlie's face.

'Five?' asked Charlie, losing his attempt to divert the topic. *'Really?'*

Victor nodded with a cool smirk lacking some of its regular vibrance spanning his face.

'Throw in tomorrow?' asked Charlie.

Victor shook his head. 'Today.'

'I like it better a bit further along anyway,' said Charlie as he edged along to make space for the striker. After they swapped their training gear over, Victor took off his tracksuit top and hung it up. 'Yo, Dimmy,' he whispered, nodding for him to come closer.

The trouserless Dmitriy stepped in close.

Victor smiled widely as he sized up the teammates in their vicinity, then leaned in. 'Pass . . . the . . . fucking . . . rock, *fam*.'

Dmitriy pulled away to see Victor's winning smile juxtaposed against his stony eyes. They stared at each other for just a moment before Victor turned away and carried on undressing.

CHAPTER 12

'Two,' called Polly.

Lawler swiftly adjusted his body angle and side-footed his next volley against the centre of the square labelled '2'. The three-by-four grid taped onto the side of his house was numbered '1' to '12'. His next few shots all hit two, with him switching to his left foot for one of them.

'Eight,' called Polly, immediately shoving her box drink straw back into her mouth and slurping away as her dad aimed his next volley halfway between '2' and '8' – three squares along and one down – and then his next at '8'. 'Ey, that's cheating!'

Lawler laughed as he tried to keep his concentration on hitting his target. 'Naaah. I can't just go from one end to the other like that. Look.' He played the ball back at '2' and scurried across to make the rebound off the wall before it hit the floor. Just getting there with his left foot, he volleyed the ball back at the '2' only to have to scramble again for the return. His next volley went high and wide of the two. 'See?' he asked, turning to his daughter. 'Can't do it without the little cheat so it's not really cheating, is it?'

Polly pondered on the question and offered him her juice box.

'He's got his own,' called Lawler's wife, Suze, as she appeared from round the corner and lobbed him a sports bottle as she carried on over in her Ugg boots and hair rollers.

'Ta,' he said as he caught it. After taking a swig, she arrived by his side and wrapped an arm around him. 'You off somewhere?' he asked as he nodded towards the rollers in her hair.

'No, just wanted to look nice for you with you home early on a recovery day, babe,' she said, squeezing him. 'Obviously, they've got to come out and I've got to put me face on. Work in progress.'

'You look boss, hun,' said Lawler, kissing her on the cheek as Polly came over and made the embrace into a group hug. Lawler snatched her up and tossed her high in the air to her delight, before catching her for a higher hug. 'How about we go out for tea? Somewhere nice?'

'Do they do ice cream?' asked Polly.

'I'm sure they'll do somethin' sweet *if* you're good,' said Suze to her daughter before looking at her husband. 'Yeh. I'd really like that,' she said, her voice teeming with joy. 'It's been a while.'

'Yeh, I know,' he said, his eyes lowered whilst tightening his hold of Polly. 'They've changed a bit of stuff at the club – less two-a-days, less stopovers – so I reckon I'll be here more now, under your feet.'

'Don't be daft,' said Suze.

He aimed his next words at Polly. 'It alright if I'm here a bit more, darl?'

She took the straw out of her mouth. 'Does it mean more ice cream?'

Andriy stopped his Aston at the red light. The OmniSports head office and its blazing white neon sign dominated the skyline to the left a hundred yards ahead. 'Are you sure you want to do this?'

Dmitriy nodded, grating his hands against his jeans.

'We can reschedule. Give you some time to calm down, perhaps?'

'I am calm,' replied Dmitriy tersely.

'I know. I meant settled. With some more time to process and draw conclusions,' said Andriy.

'It's been a few months we've been back. I know my conclusions.'

'Very well,' said Andriy as the light turned green and he drove on. The left turn for the OmniSports office came and went in silence. 'Then talk you shall.'

Five minutes later, they pulled into the car park of a much smaller, unbranded office building, entered, and approached the reception desk in the small lobby.

'Hello,' said Andriy. 'My client and I are here for an appointment with a Mr Paul Hollace.'

On hearing this, the multitasking receptionist – in his mid-twenties with an angular hairstyle – snapped his attention away from the email he was writing. A wide grin appeared as he recognised Andriy and looked beyond him to confirm his suspicions. 'Mr Romanov,' he said in a high, lispy voice as he jumped to his feet and thrust a hand towards Andriy to shake, startling him a little before he shook it. 'Mr Lebedev.' He waved over excitedly with both hands to Dmitriy, who nodded back his way. 'Oh my God, oh my God, oh my Goooood. It's such a pleasure to meet you both.' He dashed out from behind the reception desk and cast a quick glance outside to search for any more incoming guests. 'They'll manage without me for a jiffle. I'll take you to Paul. Follow me, guys.' He took off like a Mentos-fuelled Coke bottle towards a set of double doors, swiping his staff card and leading them through into a long, wide corridor. 'My God, you guys. I can't believe you're here!'

'Thank you for inviting us,' said Dmitriy, casting an amused sideways glance at Andriy as the receptionist stormed along the hallway lined with framed magazine covers.

'You're too sweet. Honestly, guys, you're heroes here. Like, I'd ask you for a selfie right now if I wasn't on duty.' As they passed a few guys, Dmitriy and Andriy were warmly smiled and nodded towards.

'When we done, how about we come back to do selfie with you? I ask, you not get in trouble,' said Dmitriy.

'You're tooooo sweet!' squealed the receptionist.

Dmitriy and Andriy grinned and glanced at each other again, not quite knowing how to deal with the receptionist's brand of enthusiasm. A few more friendly faces passed by before they arrived at an open office door. 'Paul. Your guests are here.'

The bearded, nose-ringed man stopped typing and rose to his feet, beaming with his arms wide open. 'Guys. Welcome! Come in.' He heartily shook their hands. 'It's such a pleasure to meet you both. Thank you so much for coming to speak with us. I don't think you have any idea how much this'll mean to our followers.'

'Thank you for invitation and the warm welcome,' said Dmitriy.

'Please, take a seat,' said Paul, gesturing towards his office sofas. 'Water, tea, coffee, or something stronger?'

'Not for me, thanks,' said Dmitriy.

'I wouldn't turn down a long black,' said Andriy.

'On it!' blurted out the receptionist as he vanished from the doorway.

'Guys. Thank you,' said Paul, his words brimming with gratitude, as he settled onto the sofa opposite them.

'You say this already. It's OK,' replied Dmitriy.

'No, not just for coming here. Thank you for what you've done. Coming out like you did, so early in your career, on a televised interview . . . it was like Roger Bannister breaking the four-minute mile barrier, not just for some sport but for peoples' lives. You made the impossible possible for a generation of young boys and men worldwide. I hear from enough of them here. *Thank you*. Both of you.'

Dmitriy felt the precursors to welling up and looked away to stop them triggering teary eyes as he nodded gratefully back. Andriy squeezed his hand, recognising the swell of emotion.

Paul spoke on. 'I can't imagine how challenging the last few months have been. There'll be no challenge here. We want this to be as easy for you as you want. We want nothing that feels too revealing. Here, you're amongst friends who've boated similar journeys to you, except we've been down canals whereas you're going over Niagara Falls. You have a new team here to help you now.'

Dmitriy turned to Andriy as he laid his free hand on top of their already-linked hands and nodded. 'Let's talk.'

Joki gurgled away as his chubby little hand reached out and grabbed the adult nose hovering over him. Gunnar walked into the living room and halted at the sight of Magnus leaning over his son on the changing mat, opening his nappy.

'*Afi,*' said Magnus, tapping his grandson's hand. '*Afi.*'

As Joki smiled, Penelope turned to see Gunnar, his face like thunder. She mouthed to him, 'he just turned up,' and beckoned him over with her hand.

'Here, I'll do the dirty work,' she said to Magnus, encouraging him to move aside for her to change the nappy. 'You can be my helper. Still more use than he is,' she said, directing his attention towards the dawdling Gunnar. 'The bag's just over there.'

'My boy. How are you?' Magnus asked Gunnar as he crawled across to retrieve the changing bag.

'Fine.'

'Not a bad result the other day,' said Magnus, trying to keep the conversation going.

'You're going soft, old man,' replied Gunnar, deadpan.

Magnus smiled pridefully back his way. 'Maybe a touch.'

'You need a Viagra to get it up these days?'

'Gunnar!' gasped Penelope.

'It's OK, dear,' assured Magnus as she shook her head at her husband.

'I'm so sorry about him. Would you be kind enough to pass me those wipes please?' said Penelope, putting her hand out. The old Icelander passed her the pack and pulled the other items – talcum powder, baby lotion, and a nappy – out of the bag. As she wiped Joki's bottom, he inspected the ingredients on the back of the talc and lotion, then nodded and passed them her way. Penelope chuckled bemusedly. 'They meet your approval?'

'Yes. You just have to check for parabens and phthalates and suchlike. We want our little man to be big and strong.'

'Don't you worry, *Afi*. I'm quite mindful of all that stuff,' she said pridefully as pulled out the dirty nappy from under Joki, bundled the dirty wipes into it, and took the talc. 'No formula for this little one for as long as I can keep feeding him. I know how good it is for him.'

'Excellent. He'll be made of strong stuff indeed!' replied Magnus before turning to his son. 'You've struck gold with this woman, my boy.'

'What're you doing here?' asked Gunnar in an acidic tone.

'*Gunnar*,' scolded Penelope.

'It's OK,' Magnus assured her. 'I came to see my boys.'

'Job done,' said Gunnar.

'Can we speak? Just you and I?' asked Magnus.

'Why?' asked Gunnar.

Penelope interjected. 'Look. He's staying for dinner,' she said to her husband. 'Which I have to go see to. Make the effort.' She turned back to Magnus. 'The hard bit's done here. Could you finish up – bit of lotion, new nappy?'

'It would be my pleasure,' replied Magnus.

Penelope stood and walked over to Gunnar. 'Be nice,' she murmured into his ear before planting a kiss on his cheek and leaving.

Magnus's joints creaked as he crawled back round his grandson. As Gunnar sat on the sofa nearby, Magnus squirted a blob of baby lotion onto his hand, spread it from palm to palm, and smiled at Joki. 'Not that you need to be any silkier smooth, do you?'

Joki cooed and smiled as the lotion went on.

'What do you want?' asked Gunnar. 'Apart from to keep using her to get into my house?'

'My boy – I just want this to stop and for us to be good. I appreciate you letting me see him and I want him to see us well with each other as he grows.'

'You think you can use him to try to clean the slate between us?' said Gunnar, keeping his volume steady as his voice jangled with intensity.

'No, son. There's no cleaning any slates. I can't change the past. But I am changed now. You said it yourself . . . I've gone soft. All I want to do is be there for my family. It's all I ever wanted really but now I see how to go about it.' He rubbed the lotion into Joki's legs. 'I lacked finesse. I lacked warmth. I lacked the human touch with my own blood. For that, I'm eternally sorry.'

'You think I believe a word of this?' said Gunnar. 'You can run this show all you want for these two, but you will never fool me.'

Magnus hung his head as he grabbed the fresh nappy. 'Would the old me have ever said sorry? Could the old me have ever even faked niceties?'

Gunnar stared at his father, who began putting the nappy on Joki.

'Would the old me give you advice on how to beat me?' asked Magnus.

'P-ha! You think *I* need advice on how to beat you?'

Magnus fastened one side of the nappy. 'To be honest, yes and no. I think you know where your team is weak, but I think you're easily distracted by your feelings and don't understand the damage taking your eye off the ball for a few games while you calm down can do. You need Lawler in there, you need a better link between the midfield and the attack, and I think you know it. The question is why you do nothing of it.'

'Shut the fuck up,' seethed Gunnar with utter disdain.

'That anger will do you no favours, my boy. Let me help you get out of your own way.'

Gunnar's volume rose. 'Are you delusional? Eleven league titles and I'm in my way?'

'Son, you've done very well, but you can do much better. I've always seen it. You shouldn't be burgling titles on the last day of the season.'

'Burgling?! *You* taught me a win is a win and now you want to make out like you're holier than thou?!'

Joki began sobbing at Gunnar's ferocity.

Magnus scooped the little one up and rocked him back and forth. 'Son. Please.'

Gunnar breathed deeply, bringing himself down a little.

Magnus continued. 'I want your team as strong as possible, as I do mine. I want us to push each other on to even greater things. I don't care which of us takes this league, I just want it to be one of *us*. Come spend some time with me. We can learn from each other.'

'Pass my son here,' said Gunnar, getting up and walking over to his father, who handed Joki over. 'You might have weaselled your way in here, but I will never willingly spend a moment with you outside of these little *family* get-togethers. You do your thing and I'll do mine. I'll play son here for them, that's it. You got it or do you need another PhD to get that through your thick skull?'

Full of sadness, Magnus nodded as Joki began crying again in his father's arms.

'Gunnar, Magnus. It's ready,' came Penelope's call from the kitchen.

Gunnar locked his eyes on his father, waiting for him to go first then watching him every step of the way out.

Cas yanked the ends of his belt, tying his gi jacket tightly.

'It looks good on you, but you really didn't need to buy one yet. Sometimes we train without it too,' said the instructor in his lilting accent, himself in black gi pants and a skin-tight black rash guard with his long, dark hair top-knotted.

'I start like I mean to go on,' replied Cas.

'OK. Very good. Come over here. We warm up.'

As Cas walked across the empty dojo to join him on the mats, the instructor voice commanded his smartspeaker to play Sepultura, flooding the gym with heavy metal music.

'This isn't samba,' said Cas, looking around amusedly as if trying to see the surprising airwaves.

'No. I leave that for the capoeiristas to dance to,' replied the instructor with a wry smile. 'After BJJ, this is my country's finest export.'

After various forms of shrimping – shuffling in various directions off the back – rolling, cartwheeling, crawling like different animals, long lunges, and breakdance-esque floorwork on the hands and feet, Cas had a light sweat on. The instructor remarked on how well he had done, noting that most who played football at even amateur level were too tight to move with the multidirectional ease required for a Brazilian jiu-jitsu warm-up.

'As somebody with a short reach, it's important you learn how to manage distance,' said the instructor. He explained and demonstrated to Cas that if a larger adversary started to fling punches his way, the worst thing to do is to exclusively try to block them. 'You either get completely out of range or get so close there is no range.' After demonstrating, he had Cas dart to meet his torso as quickly as possible, bending at the knees and clamping both arms around his body above his waist. Body tightly against body, there was no space for blows to generate much power. Next, the instructor showed him how to take this double-underhand clamped position to lift somebody and throw them to the floor. Cas could not contain his smile the first time he tossed his instructor to the mat. The rush of adrenaline practically pushed it out of him.

The instructor then showed Cas how to mount a thrown assailant and place an Americana arm-lock on them, wrenching their shoulder to a point where they would either submit or suffer severe injury. 'Very good,' said the instructor after a succession of better repetitions. 'You're a natural. The short reach disadvantage for exchanging punches becomes an advantage down here on the ground. Shorter limbs can lock tighter.'

Even though Cas was kneeling, he felt inches taller.

'Now I'll show you one of the best ways to deal if you get mounted. Get on your back.'

Cas got off and obliged. The instructor knelt over Cas's midsection. 'From here, a street-fight will go one of two ways. The attacker will try to rain down punches on you,' he said, feigning punches over Cas's squinting face. 'Again, the natural instinct is to cover up, but I showed you the problem with that when standing. What do you think we do down here?'

'Get close?' asked Cas.

'Excellent! We call it *climbing the tree*. Wrap your arms around me just like when we were standing and glue your head to my chest.' Cas obeyed and then used his legs, as instructed, to help him climb the instructor almost like a koala would a tree, catching a close-up glimpse of the instructor's cauliflower ears. After a few reps, the instructor showed him how to make the position even more secure and then how to roll out of it to reverse the mount. A few minutes into drilling the new skill, the instructor called a drinks break.

'I'm OK,' said Cas.

'OK,' said the instructor, seeing Cas looked untaxed. 'This is incredible for a first session. Your bodily skill is a big asset. Now back down.'

Cas rolled to his back.

'Way number two.' The instructor climbed on him and placed his hands lightly on Cas's throat. 'They try to strangle you.' He leaned forward, placing a little more pressure on Cas's windpipe.

Cas's entire body flooded with white-hot panic. After blinking, his eyes opened to see Gunnar over him, sneering and trembling, hands latched down around his throat. In a flash, he was on his side and could feel Gunnar's arms tightening around his neck like a boa constrictor.

'There's only one little bitch here,' said Gunnar, the air of his words wisping against Cas's ear as he gasped for breath, his body disobeying his mind's commands to fight his way out of the ever-tightening grip.

'Cas. CAS!'

Cas snapped back to the dojo with the shout of his instructor ringing in his ears. He laid on his side in the recovery position, his instructor's hand supporting the underside of his head.

'Are you OK?' asked the instructor.

Cas sprung up to sitting. 'Yes, yes, I'm OK.'

'You just fainted. I put my hands on your neck and you just cut out,' said the instructor. 'Do you have a history of passing out?'

'No, no,' said Cas, scrambling to his feet.

'Take it easy, my friend,' said the instructor. 'You were here, fine, and then you were gone.'

Cas shook his head as he reoriented himself. 'I'm OK. But maybe we stop for today?'

'Definitely,' said the instructor. 'We have people put to sleep all the time in here, but this wasn't that. You might want to go to your doctor to get checked out before we train next.'

'Yes, definitely,' said Cas as he strode off the mat. 'I go to the doctor before I come back.'

'Yes. Get checked out and we can get back to work. You have great potential to pick this up very quickly. Right now, let me drive you home,' the instructor said, following Cas as he rushed towards his bag by the lockers.

'No, is OK,' said Cas, flustered. 'I have my car.'

'I can't let you drive. You just lost consciousness for no reason.'

'I'm OK. I call a taxi.'

'Cas,' pleaded the instructor.

'You go home to your family, please. I wait in my car for the taxi.'

The instructor reluctantly agreed before they both gathered their belongings and he locked up. He made sure Cas called a cab before heading off. As his car disappeared out of sight, tears streamed down Cas's face as he ragged at his steering wheel, trying to rip it from its column.

CHAPTER 13

The unpredictable ginger winger Nixon was in a world of his own, shaking his arse by the common-room's sound system. 'Trois Trois Trois' vanished from the airwaves and was replaced by a '90s Verve song.

'You dancing or having a seizure there, Tricky Nicky?' asked Finney, having changed the radio channel.

'Where the music takes me, I must go,' answered Nixon.

'Riiiiight,' replied Finney with a bemused raised eyebrow.

'It's an absolute banger that, Clooney,' said Nixon. 'Number one all over it.' He paused. 'It's not true what they're—'

'In a bit, Trixon,' said Finney, cutting the winger off and leaving him confusedly hanging, as he dashed over to head off Neil, who was passing through the common room. 'Howdy!'

'Alright,' replied Neil, lowering his volume and non-verbally encouraging his patient to do the same.

'Sorry,' said Finney. 'A bit on edge. Any news?'

'Thunderbirds are go,' replied Neil. 'One new yellow will be in your supplement stack and I'll get the others to you. You need three a day, after food preferably.'

'Career-saver,' whispered Finney. 'Thanks, Nee.'

Neil stoically nodded. 'I'll find you with your course later. Not another word on it, yes?'

Finney nodded before they parted ways and he headed over to the sofas, where Charlie was goading Victor.

'One game, you pussy.'

'Nah, Chaz,' replied Victor as he tried to manipulate the TV remote between his fingers like a casino chip.

'C'mon, man. Don't be a square,' said Charlie. 'You lose one big one and what, you're never gonna touch a deck again?'

'Fam, I just don't fancy it right now. That OK wid you?'

'What's this – a lover's tiff?' laughed Finney.

Charlie put on a woman's voice. 'Ian. He doesn't take me out anymore. He won't *play* with me anymore.' He raised a hand to hide his mouth from Victor but increased his volume. 'I think he got one of those soaps lodged up his battyhole and he hasn't been his effervescent self ever since.'

Victor side-eyed him and leaned back into his side of the sofa. As Finney sat down, the OmniSports BREAKING NEWS banner appeared across the bottom of the screen.

LEBEDEV SPEAKS OUT AGAINST ABUSE

Victor turned the TV up.

'Since coming out on the final day of last season, Dmitriy Lebedev has not spoken publicly. Today, he has broken his silence in an interview with leading gay magazine 'Nothing But Pride' in which he has talked of the trials and tribulations he has faced during his first few months back in the game.'

Dmitriy appeared on screen. 'I try to stay away from everyone, everything outside of my home, my training, but eventually it gets in. The other day, I check my social media for first time since summer. Many people, they message, comment saying beautiful things, but I also have many comments wishing me hurt, to get diseases, to die. Me, my partner, my family.

I know it's easy from behind keyboard to forget real person at the other end but here I am. I don't know if these people think how they deal with this, strangers wishing you to die.'

'And how have things been in-person?' asked the interviewer, Paul.

'I tried to stay away from many people. Not do the interviews. You not see the press with me on the evening after I make the interview at the end of last season. Then there was what happened at the airport when I came back for the preseason. I didn't talk to the fans so much since then. Mostly when I have seen the people, they have been very nice. I expect sometimes the away fans they boo me, they whistle. They always did. Now, they're louder but it's OK. I expect this. The big disappointment is some of my fans, they whistle me, boo me. They boo me for the badge. I didn't make it like this, but they boo me.' He sighed. '*My own fans*. All I want is to play. Make good for the team. Please support me, support us. Be the real fans.'

The viewing crew, which consisted of half of the team by now, looked around at one another. They all knew what each other were thinking. *Be the real fans.*

'And have your teammates and coaches been supportive through all of this?' asked Paul.

'Yes,' replied Dmitriy. 'Nearly all of them.'

The players became deathly still. Some eyes flickered Victor's way as he shoved himself more upright on the sofa.

'Nearly all?' followed up Paul.

'Yes. The guys, the boss, they've been very good with me. You see the club makes the big gesture to show I am welcome, other people like me are welcome.'

'But not everybody?'

Dmitriy paused. Victor raised his hands to cover his mouth.

'No.'

'And how does that make you feel – not to be fully accepted by those who should be on your side; who are literally on your team?'

Dmitriy shrugged and scrunched his nose up, trying to stop himself welling up. He went to say something then stopped himself and shook his head, bringing his own hands up to cover his mouth.

The camera stayed on his sad face for a few moments before the screen cut back to the OmniSports anchor.

'Difficult stuff to listen to there from one of the league's best. You can catch more of this intimate interview over at the Nothing But Pride website.'

Victor lowered his gaze and grated his lower jaw's teeth against his top lip. When he lifted his gaze, he scanned around his teammates, checking for direct eye-contact. Many sat rigidly, their eyes avoiding his. He tossed Charlie the remote, rose to his feet, and ambled towards the exit. A few metres from it, Dmitriy appeared in the corridor coming towards him.

'Morning,' Dmitriy said, nodding Victor's way.

Victor eyeballed him vacantly and carried on past him silently.

Baffled by the cold treatment, he continued in and looked around his stifled teammates. He nodded towards Charlie and Finney over on the sofas, who returned the greeting and waved him over, finding the best smiles they could. OmniSports played in front of them. The penny dropped.

The training session that followed was intense yet awkwardly quiet in between drills. Cas had not yet seen Dmitriy's interview and still attributed the sombre atmosphere to the late dropped points at the weekend. He fervently encouraged Dmitriy to slip Victor in during the game at the end, but Victor was on his heels, only moving expectantly for the ball when the wide players had it.

After a media-less day, Cas got to his still-sparse apartment, watched some impressive Surgeons' footage, and whilst tearing through a treadmill session, he saw the interview. It swirled around his mind until he finally fell asleep, when it was ejected by a dream of Amber with another man. A series of unsettling dreams – memories of which disappeared into the ether – followed until a nightmare snapped him wide awake with just a few of its details seared into his consciousness: the blackness, the panicked sleep paralysis, and the feeling of his ankles being yanked apart from each other.

After splashing his face with cold water and looking out over the river and the docklands for twenty minutes with his phone in his hand, open on his one-way message thread with Amber the entire time, he threw a bag together, readied himself, took Magnus's business card out of the gift box, and dashed off to the training ground to get on the team bus, where he and all the players and staff gave in their passports as they climbed aboard. A short journey later, they rolled up towards an airstrip. The hush of the previous day was long gone. The bus rocked as many of the players jumped up and down in their seats, singing at the tops of their lungs. As the bus pulled up next to a Rolls Royce Phantom and the TaloVision crew, Cas stood and addressed the team, shouting over the unruly bunch until they quietened.

'GUYS. Guys. For one hundred twenty years, the club, we competed on English pitches. Because of how we play last season, we make the honour of being the first Weavers to compete in other countries.'

The team cheered his way, Finney starting the chant, *'Hala, Weavers!'* which quickly led to a chorus of singing and stamping.

After smiling along, Cas hushed his audience again. 'Guys. Be proud, enjoy the journey together. Let's enjoy our game, work hard for each other, and most important, make our fans, who make the big journey with us up through the leagues and now over the seas, enjoy it too.'

The team applauded his words and he applauded them back, then wafted his hands in the air like a conductor, encouraging another verse of their song. As they alighted the bus, McGlynn climbed out of the back of the Rolls, wearing aviator shades, a white linen suit and matching Panama hat.

Finney nudged Victor and Charlie, gesturing McGlynn's way. 'Bet he says yes.'

The duo looked at him blankly.

'The man from Del Monte?'

Blank.

Finney shook his head and carried on.

After the flight took off and the seatbelt sign went off, Cas made his way down the aisle to McGlynn, who sat opposite the TaloVision guys. 'Can we speak?'

'Yes, of course,' replied McGlynn.

'Can you give us a minute please, guys?' Cas asked the crew.

'Yeh, no problem. Mike,' said Adam, reminding McGlynn to switch off his microphone before he and Michael made themselves scarce.

'Talk to me,' said McGlynn.

Cas leaned in and lowered his voice. 'After this trip, the crew, they can't come with us on the road. There's too much going on around the squad, in the team.'

McGlynn forced a smile and leaned towards Cas. 'They need to film something. The documentary's going to help put this club on the map, attract us a larger audience, increase the money you have to play with in the market.'

'They can still film around the outsides, but they can't be in the private spaces with us. Is not good for the players or the club.'

McGlynn lowered his voice further to a quiet growl. 'Who's the problem? Who's giving Dmitriy bother?'

'Let me deal with it,' said Cas. 'Is complicated. Delicate.'

'Who?' demanded McGlynn.

'I'm taking care of it,' reassured Cas.

'You'd better. If any details go public, they're gonna be gone faster than a pint in The Old Mill. I will purge this club of anybody against our progress. Careful you don't end up a casualty by association.'

Cas nodded and stood. 'How long do we keep the new colour badge?'

'As long as it takes. We won't let a small pocket of narrow-minded idiots dictate the direction of this club,' stated McGlynn.

Cas could see he would not budge. 'No more on the road with us.'

'We'll speak again when this *thing* is sorted,' said McGlynn.

Reluctantly nodding, Cas headed back along the aisle towards the toilet, where he could hear the tap running inside. A moment later, Finney opened the door, jumping at the sight of his manager.

'Gaffer!' he blurted out as he stepped out, wiping his mouth dry.

'You OK, Ian?' asked Cas.

'Yeh, yeh,' he said, his voice almost at double speed. 'Just didn't hear anyone outside is all.'

'You sure you're OK? You look a bit pale,' said Cas. 'I have some travel sickness tablets if you like them?'

'No, no. I'm grand, thanks,' said Finney, edging past his manager.

'Ian.'

Finney looked back.

'Fantastic to see you back in the full training. I know it was a tough journey. Nearly there now.'

Finney appreciatively nodded, not knowing where to look, and headed back to his seat.

After a chunk of mingling with his coaches and players, Cas called for Dmitriy to come sit with him near the front of the cabin. 'How is the flying now since you do the work with Brygg?'

'Fine, thanks.' Dmitriy paused. 'It was always fine.'

'What do you me—' Cas halted. His eyes darted round as he pieced together a realisation. 'Oh. Shit.'

'I'm sorry you pay for the expert to help me.'

'No, no. Don't be sorry.' Cas blew out a deep breath, still processing the situation. 'Is all so much. So much. How are you?'

'Ahh,' said Dmitriy, shrugging as he failed to find better words.

Cas screwed his mouth up, taking a moment to pick his next tack. 'You see my statement to the fans?'

'Yes. Thank you.'

'No thanks. You are one of mine. They need to be behind you. You didn't make the badge.' Cas paused. 'I see your interview.'

'Uhuh.'

'I see the training yesterday too,' said Cas.

Dmitriy folded his arms.

'Can I be doing more for you?' asked the manager.

Dmitriy shook his head. 'You can't change what is in the people's hearts, in their minds.'

'No, but they can watch or play somewhere else.' Cas paused. 'You feel a problem here with the team?'

'You saw the problem,' replied Dmitriy.

Cas frowned. 'He apologised, yes?'

'Kind of,' replied Dmitriy.

'OK. I speak with him again. Look, I can't imagine how hard this is for you. All the things. I see the national team selection. I don't know all the things. I will try my best for you. I only ask you one thing. Any problems, we speak about them *here*,' said Cas, circling his finger to signal the team.

'The fans, your teammates; they love to hear the nice things in the press about themselves. You say anything not so nice, they do not like,' said Cas.

'They shouldn't do the things then,' said Dmitriy without skipping a beat.

'They shouldn't. Give me some time and they won't. But call them in the public is like the fuel on the fire. We don't want the fire or the war. We want peace for you, for everyone. The press, they want the fires. Just speak with the people who love you - me, your teammates, Andriy, your family.' Cas noticed Dmitriy's expression drop at his last word. 'Your family?'

Dmitriy's eyes shifted away as he shook his head.

Cas lowered his head for a moment. 'I'm sorry. I hope their minds change. I know how important family is. I know I'm not the same, but I'm here all the time.'

'Thank you,' said Dmitriy, only meeting his manager's eyes briefly.

'Are you good to play tomorrow?' asked Cas.

Dmitriy nodded stolidly.

Cas clasped Dmitriy's hand. 'Good. Keep showing them what you're about.' He looked deeply into his playmaker's eyes. 'Hey. Anything. Anytime.'

In the evening, the team trained on the pitch they would play on the following day. After the light, lively session, Cas introduced the players to two special guests – his mother and father, María Pilar and Alberto. María Pilar stood at just five foot and was sparrow-like in her build. Her mousey shoulder-length hair resembled Cas's before his harsh restyling. The soft contours of her face clearly gave rise to those of her son's. The stocky Alberto, aside from being a similar height, bore no resemblance to his son. His hair retained much of its natural blackness and his skin was much darker and more weathered than his fresh-faced son. His gnarled hands enthusiastically shook the players' hands as he greeted them in quick-fire Spanish that few of them understood. María Pilar gave hugs all round, welcoming the players to Spain in broken English, apologising it was not more fluent.

Cas and his parents dined at the hotel afterwards.

'We were hoping you'd bring Amber,' said his mother, complaining that they had not seen her in the summer either. Cas explained that after a summer working at the women's World Cup, she was now run off her feet in her new role. He assured them that if they came at the end of the season, hopefully to see his team lift the league trophy, that they could all enjoy the start of a victorious summer together.

'And finally, a trophy,' said Alberto, his eyes shining joyfully.

'Yes. Finally,' said Cas, stroking his wedding ring.

'Nah. It's disgraceful, really. Look at the shift he put in over there. First game in Europe, bagged two and an assist. Got more on the slate than Easy so far this season. He bleeds for this shirt and yet you've got a bunch of bigoted morons – his own ruddy fans – screeching at him. They should turf them out,' said the caller on the football phone-in.

'I couldn't agree more that it's an ugly situation but there are a number of people we've heard from – lifetime fans, people with season tickets – who've called in and told us that there was nothing bigoted or homophobic about booing the recoloured badge,' said the host of the OmniSports FansSay show. 'They just don't believe that one player and what he represents is bigger than their club.'

'They're a bunch of homophobes hiding behind technicalities is what they are. They don't like his kind because they're a bunch of ruddy cavemen.'

Dmitriy's radio was interrupted by the ringing of his phone through the car's sound system. 'Papa,' showed on the display. He scrambled to accept that call. 'Papa?'

'Dima!' screeched his distressed mother. 'Dima!'

'I'm here, Mama,' he assured her in Russian, trying to keep a lid on his panic. 'What's wrong?'

'We're coming! We're coming!' she shrieked. 'The next flight. Please meet us at the airport.'

He slowed the car and pulled towards the hard shoulder of the empty road. 'Of course. What's wrong, Mama?!'

'The batte—' The line cut.

He dialled the number back. Voicemail. Again. Voicemail. He tried his mother's phone five times. It kept ringing out. He clasped his face as his heart drumrolled in his chest.

In the early hours of the next morning, the tannoy announcement stirred Dmitriy. He peeled his eyes open beneath his shades and cap and picked his head off Andriy's shoulder. 'Is that for us?'

'I think so,' said Andriy, also hidden beneath shades and a cap, before the two stretched out their uncomfortable limbs and used the wall to heave themselves up off the floor. They hobbled towards the Arrivals gate.

Twenty minutes later as the couple took their shades off, Dmitry's mother, Iryna, appeared through the one-way doors. Everything about her screamed exhaustion. 'Dima,' she cried before jogging over and throwing her arms around her son. Alexei, Dmitriy's father, emerged through the doors pushing four large suitcases on a trolley.

'Mama. Are you OK?' he asked.

'It's so good to see you,' she said before smacking a kiss on each cheek and peeling away to look Andriy's way.

'Mrs Lebedev. It's a pleasure to meet you,' said Andriy, offering his hand to shake. Her depleted eyes examined him for a moment.

'Nice to meet you too,' she said, eventually shaking his hand.

Alexei arrived at them with the luggage, staying behind it.

After a long moment, Dmitriy finally spoke his way. 'Papa.'

Alexei lowered his gaze down to the trolley's wheels, barely acknowledging him as he did.

'Mr Lebedev. It's good to meet you,' said Andriy, offering his hand again.

Alexei surveyed their surroundings, looking everywhere but at Andriy, and began wheeling the trolley towards the exit. Dmitriy offered Andriy an apologetic look to which Andriy nodded. Before the exit, Alexei stopped suddenly, left his trolley, and turned a hard left into an airport convenience shop. The trio waited outside, Iryna cuddled up against her son.

'Iryna!' came Alexei's call from inside the store. 'They won't take my card or money. Get me some of their Monopoly money,' he barked in Russian. Andriy handed her a twenty-pound note and she dashed in.

Dmitriy looked apologetically at Andriy again.

'It's OK,' said Andriy. 'It's OK.'

Having complained under his breath of their inferiority to his usual brand, Alexei puffed away on his cigarettes silently as Iryna breathlessly relayed their story. Over the past few weeks, Alexei had been ordered to work from home after a skirmish with a colleague.

'Thirty-two fucking years and they send *me* home,' he seethed before shutting up again.

'What were you fighting about in an architect's office?' asked Dmitriy. Alexei rolled down his window to flick some ash out.

Iryna said he would not say, but that trouble had escalated since. Cars lurked outside their house on numerous occasions. Their rubbish collections were vandalised, with bags split open and waste scattered and smeared all over their lawn and driveway. Windows were smashed. Then yesterday, she came back from the local supermarket to see inside the house on fire. The fire service arrived swiftly and put out the blaze, with the hall, living room, and dining room suffering the damage. The firefighters concluded that a dowsed rag through the letterbox had caused the fire. By the time Alexei got home from his phoneless long walk, the police were leaving and Iryna had packed as much as she could. They could not stay there one more night, she declared. After suggesting hotels could tide them over while the police investigated and they thought about what to do longer term, Iryna demanded they go to England to see their son. After a heated row which culminated in a divorce ultimatum, here they were.

Dmitriy peered over his shoulder towards his father, who gazed out of the open window at the foreign scenery.

'You can stay here as long as you like,' he said to his mother. 'I have plenty of space. You can practically have a wing to yourselves.'

Alexei spat out of the window. The awkward atmosphere thickened.

Eventually, they passed through the gates and over the bridge that led to Dmitriy's house.

'Wow. That's quite the view,' said his mother as she got out of the car and admired the lake.

'Yes. It's a lovely walk around it too,' replied Dmitriy.

Andriy opened the boot and went to lift the first case out.

'No,' grumbled Alexei, eyes fixed on the floor as he walked around the car.

Andriy took his hands off the case and stepped back, leaving Alexei to unload the cases himself, before walking over to Dmitriy and his mother. 'I'll leave you all to settle.'

Dmitriy sadly looked his way. Both restrained themselves from reaching out to each other.

'Where do you live?' asked Iryna.

'I have a place just down the road,' replied Andriy.

'Oh,' said Iryna, glancing over at her husband, who was heaving two bags towards the house. 'Thank you for driving us. It was nice meeting you.'

'A pleasure,' said Andriy, bowing a little before turning away. As he drove away from the house he had practically lived at since returning from their summer holiday, he watched in his rear-view mirror as Dmitriy let his parents in.

CHAPTER 14

The last two young teens remained, trying to appear nonchalant as they waited to be picked between. The picking captain hovered his finger between his two options, eventually picking one and condemning the other to the default role of last pick.

'Any room for two little ones?' called Victor as he emerged in view of the court with Charlie.

The boys gasped with exhilaration as their four teams swarmed into a single cluster and they ran to greet the players at the court's gate. After Victor marked himself with the sign of the cross – Charlie followed in suit behind him out of politeness – the two entered the court and greeted the youths with fist bumps and handshakes, eventually getting to Chuka, who wore a black tracksuit and some astroturf trainers.

'Bit of room for the famdem?' asked Victor.

'Bit tight this pitch for six-a-side, isn't it, lads?' Chuka asked the boys as a wind-up. He failed to keep a straight face as they begged and pleaded for the two professionals to be involved. 'Alright, alright. The mob have spoken. Chaz, you can be on mine.'

'Can't have all the Easy on one team,' said Victor. 'Shit is nuclear.'

'Victor,' said Chuka, shaking his head, gesturing to the boys.

'Sorry. Sorry. Sorry,' said Victor to his brother, the boys, and the sky. He gathered the ball on the blindside of Chuka and rolled it through his legs to the amusement of all the boys.

Chuka smiled along. 'Best enjoy a free one while you can.'

The kickabout started. The two non-playing teams bubbled with excitement as they watched on from pitchside. Chuka marshalled the space in front of his team's box as Victor dropped deep for his team, getting as many tricks and flicks in as he could while circulating the ball with his teammates. Eventually, Victor played a one-two around Charlie and was through against Chuka two-against-one. He dribbled, closing the space between himself and his brother, and shaped to square the ball across to his teen teammate. Like the ball was tethered with elastic to his foot, he turned his simple side-foot pass across into a flip-flap for a right-footed shooting position for himself. The observers squealed gleefully. Just before Victor's swinging foot hit the ball, Chuka toe-poked the ball into the boards, leaving his brother to kick fresh air as he collected the ball off the rebound and carried it forward. The observer's roared as Victor spun and tried to win possession back from his brother but just as he tried, Chuka slotted a through ball forward that one of his younger teammates finished. One-nil.

'Best enjoy a free one while you can,' called Victor, a big, competitive smile spanning his face towards his brother as the goalkeeper fished the ball out of his net.

After his team kicked off again, Victor jogged straight forward to stand in front of his brother. 'Yes, little man,' he called, pointing to his feet. The pass came from his youthful teammate, narrowly missing an interception from Charlie. He backed into Chuka, putting his forearm against his brother's body, and controlled the ball with his sole, rolling it rapidly back and forth. 'You want some, Chuks?' taunted Victor. 'Come get s—' Before the word left his mouth, Chuka buffeted his brother and pickpocketed the ball in one fell swoop, immediately sending a long pass forward. The boys whooped again from pitchside. Victor tried to catch Chuka up but failed to get to him before he received a return-ball and laid it into a teammate's path for a shot. Two-nil. Chuka fist bumped a few of the boys and trotted back towards his half, crossing Victor on his way.

'What you on, man? Somethin' in dat holy water?' asked Victor.

'Just playing for the team,' said Chuka with a slight edge and his own winning smile.

'A'ight, bro. We'll see how dat goes.'

Over the next half hour of games when the brothers were both on the pitch, the teens marvelled at a battle of the Ezemonyes. Victor made it his mission to humiliate his brother but with all his trying, tricks, and flicks, he mostly failed. Chuka was like a shadow that was somehow slightly ahead of him when it mattered. Body-to-body, he was also stronger than his little brother, much to Victor's exasperation.

Chuka called time on the session. 'Well played, everyone. What do we do?'

'Shake hands,' came the collective response as the boys all shook hands and fist bumped each other.

'I wish somebody'd have filmed that so I could show the lads,' said Charlie as he shook Chuka's hand. 'Absolute throwback. Easy C and Chaz Dogg shutting fools out!'

Chuka smiled. 'Those were the days.'

Crowded by the boys asking for their T-shirts to be signed and for selfies when they got their phones back, Victor obliged.

'Any handshakes for us, little brother?' asked Chuka after infiltrating the cluster of youths with Charlie.

Victor slung a limp hand their way, intentionally keeping most of his attention on the boys.

'He calls this a handshake,' said Chuka, shaking his head towards Charlie and some of the boys.

'Victor? Victor?' asked one of the boys, eventually engaging his attention.

'Shoot, little man.'

'Did Chuka always merk you so bad?' asked the boy.

Victor's smile morphed into a sneer. 'Little man. First of all, I don't know what game you was watchin'. Stay in school. Second of all, I thought the church,' he looked round to his brother, 'is meant to teach you some manners. *Merked*. Respect your elders, little man, innit?'

The boys laughed at their friend's chastisement and Victor's clear irritation.

'Don't listen to my brother, boys. When pride comes, then comes disgrace, but with the humble is wisdom. Gather your stuff and we'll head back.' Chuka turned and smiled disapprovingly at his brother before shepherding the boys off the court.

Charlie wrapped his arm around Victor. 'It's alright, man. Now you remember how it feels.'

Victor sucked his teeth and nudged Charlie off. 'You're contagious, fam. Megged three times today. Wide open like *yo mudda*.'

'Yo mudda. Yo mudda,' said Charlie, imitating his mock accent. 'Maybe if you stop trying to showboat and remember you have other teammates who can do damage too, you won't leave yourself so open to getting *merked,'* he said, playfully shoving the striker as they left the court and caught up to the group.

'Brother,' said Chuka, 'I've just seen the time. Zack's parents needed him done promptly. They'll be waiting. Can you bring up the rear?'

'Dunno about that,' replied Victor, 'but I'll bring them across, no biggie.'

Chuka beckoned one of the boys over and they both jogged off. As the remaining group sauntered along turned the corner, a camera crew and interviewer, all donning white and sky-blue T-shirts branded 'Weaver Pitch TV', approached. The boys buzzed amongst themselves as the interviewer reached them.

'Are you here to film us?' asked the boy who had asked Victor about being merked.

'Not today, unfortunately,' said the interviewer. 'We need all sorts of permissions and forms filled in by parents for young ones.

We're here to try and get a word with these two gentlemen if they'd be kind enough,' he said, gesturing to Victor and Charlie.

The boys looked back towards Victor, who raised a sly eyebrow back his way.

'Anything for the Weaver Pitch fam, man,' said Victor. 'Where's Normzy and what's his name and the gang?'

'The main men are on their holidays. They send their best. They heard the Ezemonye brothers were kicking about in the community and got straight on the line to us to get here pronto for some footage and interviews if possible.'

'How long you been here?' asked Victor, slightly panicked.

'Literally just pulled up now,' answered the interviewer.

'Seen, seen,' said Victor, his tone settling. 'What's your name, man?'

'Dave,' replied the interviewer.

'I know you. I seen you on some vids, yeh?' asked Victor.

'Yeh, yeh. Mostly in the background. Season ticket holder twenty-odd years.'

'Good man,' replied Victor, bumping fists with him.

'You game then, fellas? You'll make a lot of subscribers very happy, especially seeing you out here.'

Charlie checked his watch. 'I can do something really quick before I shoot off.'

'Perfect! We can chat then get Victor after.'

'Saving the best for last, fam,' he said nudging Charlie.

'Can we watch the interviews?' asked one of the boys.

'It's fine by us along as you're out of shot,' said the interviewer before looking to Victor for his opinion.

'Easy all the way, little bredrin,' Victor said to the boys. 'Long as he can't see you.'

'Like you didn't see them balls goin' through your legs?' asked Merk Boy, to the amusement of his friends and the crew.

Victor shot him a look. 'Disregard little man,' he said to the interviewer. 'I think he sniffs PVA,' he whispered.

The boys moved behind the crew as the cameraman and sound man readied themselves.

'Ready, Charlie?' asked the interviewer.

'Fire away.'

The interviewer stepped into frame, straightened out his beard and black Weavers' cap, tightened the camouflage jacket tied around his waist, and took the microphone off the guy with the boom mic. 'We set, boys? Action.'

Cas pulled open one of the double doors by its custom sculpted metal door handle – half of a scalpel with half a snake wrapped round it – and walked through the blood red lobby up to the reception desk. 'I have an appointment with Magnus. My name is Cas Velasquez.'

'I know who you are, sir. Take a seat. He'll be with you shortly,' said the receptionist, pointing him towards a hyper-sleek, contoured leather chair that his body melted into.

A few minutes later, Magnus greeted Cas and brought him though the entrance from reception, which had a facial recognition lock. 'I'm so glad you took me up on my invitation. Today, I am not in this alone. Let me give you the grand tour before we get settled.'

Just from the style of the lobby, Cas knew that this training facility was on a different level from his own. Even the quality of the finish of the blood red corridor and the lighting was far superior. The place looked more like a high-end hotel than a leisure centre. The first major space they came to was the gym. A huge glass wall looked out onto the club's training pitches, making the space feel united with the outside. Brushed stainless steel beams formed the skeleton of the rest of the room. Around ten of the squad were in training at the far end of the room but it was so spacious they were nowhere near them. One wall was almost fully lined by custom squat racks and power cages, each containing a monitor on the wall that allowed players to watch multi-angle video replays of their exercises back and provided real-time feedback of rep speed and power to the players as they exercised. Away from these racks, the large floor was covered in a multitude of surfaces. The majority was new generation astroturf lined with electronic timing gates, at one end of which were several high-tech speed training resistance harnesses. Some of the floor was sprung gymnastics training floor, some was more highly sprung inflatable gymnastics tumble track, and some was matted like a dojo. There was a large sand pit in a corner of the room, as well as multiple trampolines and a foam pit. Around the space were hurdles, obstacles, and plyometric boxes galore. It was like a playground for athletes.

At the last squat rack, beside the massive custom monkey bar rig and dumbbell section, two players trained – one squatting and another performing a variation of a single arm dumbbell press. Cas noticed a whir coming from their respective barbell and dumbbell, which the players seemed to be having problems stabilising. 'What's that noise? Like a buzz and a rattle?'

'Ah, they're our Controlled Chaos bars. It's like stability training on steroids, so to speak,' said Magnus. 'The bars contain elements that vibrate at frequencies and magnitudes that we control, allowing a programmable random-seeming training stimulus. They can constantly tremor or quite violently kick out of nowhere, challenging the athletes to make themselves extra stable. You want to try?'

Cas watched the players struggle with their loads. 'Maybe later.'

They carried on over to a group of players watching a demonstration from a top-knot wearing coach crawling gracefully along the floor, resembling a balletic lizard. The coach kicked up into a sort of spinning cartwheel and swivelled into the standing position. It was Vasily Kalashnikov, the world-renowned movement coach who led a session for the Weavers last season.

'Your turn, gentlemen. The floor awaits you,' said Vasily, setting the players off crawling. He spotted Cas and bounded over, offering a sturdy handshake. 'Mr Velasquez. What brings you behind enemy lines?'

'Ha. Not enemies . . . not today, anyway,' replied Cas, grinning at his host. 'Magnus invites me to see the set-up, talk about the football.'

'Superb. There's no place like this!' said Vasily, scanning around the gym in awe. 'Please excuse me. I must get back to the guys. Great seeing you.'

After Vasily trotted away, Cas turned to Magnus. 'Is he just here for today?'

'Vasily? No, he's with us full-time. Slotted in alongside our head of S and C a few weeks into the season. We're very fortunate.'

'Oh wow. Very good for you.' Cas contained most of his surprise. When the Weavers enquired about his recurring consultancy or hiring him for a part-time role last season, he said he was booked up for eighteen months solid so this would be impossible.

The pair left the gym and Magnus continued to show Cas around the comparatively space-aged training centre. The pitches, almost double in number to those the Weavers had, were immaculate. Cameras were dotted around the sides and corners of the ones in use that day.

'Are they drones?' asked Cas, pointing to some objects by the far side of the training pitch.

'Yes. We film lots of the training games from above for pattern analysis,' said Magnus.

Cas's mind still boggled minutes later as they entered the analysis room. '¡*Dios mío!*' he muttered under his breath. The room was like a miniature NASA control centre. Nine analysts typed away furiously at computer terminals, each with a minimum of two screens, ahead of a giant monitor that took up an entire wall. A video of what looked like that day's training played on the giant screen from four different angles, with what looked like pattern-recognition software tracing dynamic patterns over the aerial angle. White boards and tactics boards lined the other walls.

As they left the technological hub, Cas thought he spotted a familiar face cross the end of the corridor. 'That guy who passed at the end. Is this Brygg McMullin, the phobia coach?'

'It was, yes. How do you know Brygg?' asked Magnus.

'He did some work for us last season.'

'Ha. Small world,' replied Magnus.

'And for you today?' asked Cas.

'Brygg is our psychologist. He mentioned he had worked in the league but not who with.'

'Small world,' said Cas, again hiding his surprise. Brygg, like Vasily, was booked up the rest of last season and unavailable for the foreseeable future. To Cas's knowledge, he was also a phobia specialist rather than a general psychologist or a specific sports psychologist.

Their next port of call was a laboratory, which they observed through its window onto the corridor. Cas noticed the lock on the door was different, with a keypad and swipe slot in addition to the facial-rec screen. Three lab technicians beavered away: one filling a sample tray's cavities with liquid, one looking through a microscope, and the other at a computer.

'You do the analysis here?' Cas could not help his shock escape him this time.

'Oh yes. Call it my empirically justified nostalgia,' said Magnus like a kid showing a friend his gleaming new bike. 'Using the external analysis companies is fine for occasional tracking but I want day-to-day data on blood, urine, and saliva to inform the training loads, the nutrition, and the hydration of the guys. We don't sign superstars here. We build them percentage point by percentage point through marginal gains.'

'I can see,' said Cas, shaking his head.

'I know I'm very fortunate here. I've fought tooth and nail for all this stuff at my previous clubs and finally, now the stress of it all has turned my hair white, someone backs me. Better late than never, as they say, yes?'

'Yes,' replied Cas, marvelling in through the window.

As they carried on along the corridor, one of Magnus's players nodded their way. Magnus broke out into fluent German. The player chuckled and responded in kind as he carried on.

'Wow. You have German as well as the Spanish and your English,' said Cas.

'Ah, just a tiny bit of Spanish,' said Magnus.

'And the Icelandic,' continued Cas. 'Any others?'

'Bits and pieces,' replied Magnus. 'It passes the time.'

Cas raised his eyebrows and puffed out a sigh. 'I been here nearly ten years and my English . . . how they say . . . is fresh off the boat.'

'The secret is to learn the swear words and insults first and go from there,' said Magnus with a grin. 'They have lovely memorable rings to them.'

'I have the swear words OK,' replied Cas, 'but my other words, they aren't too good and I don't have too many of them.'

Magnus smiled his way. 'You don't need many if the ones you have work just fine. And you seem to be managing better than fine. Besides, trust me when I tell you you should be happy you haven't had *my* time on *your* hands.' The big Icelander had a moment of melancholy before snapping himself back into tour-guide mode. 'Anyway, before we retreat to my office, the last major department.' Magnus opened the double doors and led Cas into the newly kitted-out, spacious communal treatment room, where multiple players laid on treatment tables being rubbed down, stretched, and electrostimulated. 'Good afternoon, everybody.'

'Good afternoon, Magnus,' was the chorus that came back as everybody waved and nodded his way, double taking as they noticed his guest. One double take was on a different scale to all the others:

Amber's. Her sunny smile instantly clouded over upon seeing Cas wave her way. He lowered his hand.

'I'm sure Amber has told you a little about the renovation, but she can fill you in on the details better than I,' Magnus said as he took a step forward. Cas gently grabbed Magnus's sleeve. 'Is OK. Is very busy now here. She works with the player. Maybe I speak with her on my way out.'

'It's no problem,' said Magnus.

'Thanks, but I do later. I don't want to interrupt her work.'

'Very well,' said Magnus, turning back to the door and waving over his shoulder.

Amber's cold stare followed her husband out of the room.

'Too early?' asked Magnus as he pulled a bottle of *Brennivín* from his middle drawer. 'I think I've got something a little softer, maybe some red, if that'd be more to your liking?'

Cas batted away his softer suggestion. 'Is OK. When in Rome . . . or Reykjavik,' he said with a raised eyebrow and a playful grin.

'Indeed,' replied Magnus, pulling a pair of glasses out of the drawer too before pouring them both a generous measure and sliding Cas's across to him. '*¡Salud!*'

'No,' smiled Cas. 'Your house, yours cheers. How you say in your language?'

Magnus grinned and lifted his glass. '*Skál!*'

'*Skál!*' replied Cas, clinking glasses with him before squinting at a sip of the fiery schnapps.

Magnus's office was the least impressive part of the training ground. It was large but bare and unstyled. Apart from a white board and a large TV, the walls held nothing. The only personal flourish was a solitary framed photo of a baby on his desk. 'Who is this?' asked Cas.

'This is Joki, my first grandson,' replied Magnus.

'Aww. Very nice. How old?'

'Three and a half, maybe four months.'

Cas smiled warmly. 'Does he live in Iceland or somewhere else?' he asked as he raised his glass for a second sip.

'No no,' replied Magnus. 'He's Gunnar son.'

Cas's drink went down the wrong way. He tried not to splutter it out, managing to gulp it down awkwardly before coughing a few times.

'Are you alright there?' asked Magnus.

Cas banged his chest a few times. 'Yes yes. Is just strong.'

'Yes. Back home they say it puts hairs on your balls. Somewhat vulgar but possibly true.' He chuckled.

'Maybe I need the bigger glass then,' said Cas, raising his glass again jokingly before taking a gulp.

Magnus downed his. 'I think you have plenty on them. Nobody is as committed to their footballing principles as you. They justify their means by their ends. I see with you that the means are equally important.' He reopened the bottle and poured himself another shot. 'People who don't understand how commendable that is, process on par with product, stability of vision and strategy . . . well, they operate on another plane. They will always struggle to understand and aren't worth your mental space.'

'Cheers to that,' said Cas, lifting the little drink he had left, then taking another sip.

'Top you up?' asked Magnus, jiggling the bottle in his hand.

Cas considered it for a moment before offering his glass towards the bottle.

'To sticking to your principles,' said Magnus, clinking glasses with his guest.

As the familiar tapping pattern sounded at her door, Amber rolled her eyes its way. 'Come in.'

Cas crept in and faced the back of the door as he eased it closed.

'What are you doing here?' she seethed.

Cas took a moment, then turned and admired the office before moving his gaze to her, his smile wide. *'Hola.'*

'Don't *hola* me. Showing up here for no good reason,' she said.

'Magnus invites me. I would come whether you are here or not,' he responded.

'And you didn't think to warn me?'

'Warn you? Warn you what?' asked Cas. 'Like I'm a scary thing?'

Amber examined his face. 'Have you been drinking?'

'How can I warn you when you don't speak to me?' he replied.

'You're pissed. Cas, go home.' She lowered her voice. 'This isn't the time or the place.'

'Ahh. Is OK,' he whispered. 'Is empty out there. But when is the time or place?'

'Not at my place of work!' she said, straining to stay quiet.

'Look at you. This. It suits you. You look good. The boss. Making the decisions.'

'Get out, Cas. I made myself crystal clear. You could have spoken to me properly any time over the last few months, but instead of acting like a grown man you come in here like a child. If you want to speak to me, we do it properly, somewhere appropriate, not here.'

'Mi amor,' he pleaded.

'Go,' she flatly ordered him.

He lowered his head then looked at her again. She stared back unflinchingly. He turned and headed out of the office, closing the door soundlessly behind him.

After ambling through the maze of corridors, he reached the double doors to the lobby. They required a facial scan to open. Through the windows, he could see no receptionist at the desk. He wandered back down the corridor until he found the first office with somebody inside and knocked on its door. 'Come in.'

Cas opened the door. 'Excuse me. Can you let me out of the main doors, please?'

The man at the computer wheeled himself out from behind it and stood. 'No problem.'

Cas looked at him curiously. As he walked over, he seemed familiar. They stepped out into the corridor, walked to the double doors, and the man pointed his face towards the facial-rec screen. 'Enjoy your evening,' said the man as he pushed one of the doors open, holding it open for Cas.

'You too,' said Cas as he stepped out. As the door closed behind him, he glanced back through its window and noticed the man's cauliflowered ear. *'¡Gillipollas!'* he muttered to himself.

CHAPTER 15

Dmitriy checked his messages, scrolling to Emily's thread, as he entered the kitchen to find his mother rummaging through the fridge.

'Do you have anything normal people would eat for breakfast?' she asked.

'There should be eggs. There are always eggs,' he said. 'Porridge too.'

'I see no eggs. Don't you have any oladyi or syrniki?'

'I have to go, Mama. There will definitely be eggs somewhere.'

'What do you mean somewhere?' she asked.

'I mean they're always here. I don't sort the food. I can call Andriy when I get in the car to check, then call you.'

'No, it's OK. I'll carry on looking,' she said.

'If you'd like,' he said, pulling her shoulder round to kiss her cheek as she continued searching, 'I'm going to call my friend Barry to take you to the Polish supermarket later this morning.'

'Can we go later? With you?' she asked.

'I don't know. Maybe.' He glanced at the clock as he trotted towards the door. 'Where's Papa?'

She shrugged. 'Still in bed. Jetlagged, probably.'

'OK. Make yourselves at home,' he said as he dashed out of the door. As he ran to his car, Andriy's came down the drive, pulled up next to him, and rolled down its window.

'Have you seen it yet?' rattled off Andriy, his eyes wide.

'Seen what?'

'Get in,' said Andriy. As Dmitriy jogged round the car, Andriy pulled his phone from his pocket. It began ringing. After a quick glance at the caller ID which read 'Oleg', he declined the call, and searched YouTube for 'boys will be boys victor.'

As Andriy turned into the training ground twenty minutes later, they sat in a queue of four cars at the gate. Victor's car waited at the front. Eventually the gate opened, allowing them all in. As they parked up, Dmitriy gripped his thighs as he eyeballed Victor's car nearby. The moment the engine stopped, Andriy flung his door open, jumped out and ran over towards Victor as he climbed out of his car.

'You narrow-minded piece of shit!' he yelled as he launched himself towards Victor, hands out to shove him.

Victor dropped a shoulder and sprang aside, leaving Andriy to crash into his car. 'Fuck off, Andriy. They messed wid it. Don't start somethin'.'

'Don't start something?! DON'T START SOMETHING?!' He pounced again, shoving fresh air.

'Check yo' man before I wreck yo' man, Dimmy' called Victor in what sounded like a hollow threat. Dmitriy grabbed hold of his partner and pulled him back. Finney, Charlie, and a few others arrived, having galloped over from their cars, and positioned themselves in the middle of the scuffle.

'I didn't say it like they made it look, I swear,' said Victor.

'You're a fucking bling-bit simpleton,' hissed Andriy as Dmitriy stopped him wriggling free.

'Chaz, tell 'em. Where'd the man say he was from?'

'Weaver Pitch TV,' said Charlie to the couple. 'Swear down.'

'You were there?' asked Andriy.

'Yeh, I spoke to them before he did then rushed off. It seemed legit, to be fair to Vic. Proper camera, branded up 'n that,' said Charlie.

'Did you spout any of the same drivel as him?' asked Andriy.

'Course not,' said Charlie.

'See, he had no hate-riddled words for them to twist,' said Andriy. 'I've seen your disdain for me since day one, heard your little snickers, and now the world sees it for him too,' he said, gesturing towards Dmitriy. 'You need to pray for more than goals at that church of yours, you toothless vile cretin.'

Victor lunged towards Andriy, only for the other players to restrain him.

'What the hell goes on out here?!'

Everybody turned to see Cas at the training ground doors.

Cas scrolled down the YouTube page displayed on the big screen on his wall. The top few versions of the video had millions of views and the next few were in the hundreds of thousands. He shook his head and sighed. 'This is a fucking circus, all over the news, the papers. Worst, you make the circus here.'

'I'm sorry, boss. I didn't say anythin' bad, I swear. They twisted it, took it outta context.'

'Victor. You make the interview. You criticise the rainbow badge,' said Cas.

'Nah, man. I said I love our badge,' said the striker, 'but if we're gonna change it every time someone has an issue, I was just aksin' where was the all-black badge?'

'Just coincidence you changed your profile pic last night then?' snarked Andriy.

'What, man? Can't I hold the club's badge after I just talked about it?' replied Victor.

'Well, you could just support a teammate, but we know why that's not happening, don't we?' said Andriy. Dmitriy nudged him, signalling him to stop. 'Boys will be fucking boys. The irony,' Andriy muttered, earning him a sharper nudge from Dmitriy.

'Yo. It was just a shout-out,' protested Victor. 'I didn't know.'

'You want to shout-out the National Front too?' snapped Andriy.

'Andriy, please,' said Cas. 'I understand the anger, but we need to control the conversation. Dmitriy – you've been very quiet. Do you want to say something?'

He side-eyed Victor and paused. 'Why?' he asked, his voice laden with apathy.

'Why?' echoed Cas, concerned by Dmitriy's demeanour. 'So we know how you feel. To help make the things better for you.'

'I let you all know how I feel the other day. Look at all this.' He thought for a moment. 'My words don't make these people feel better to me.'

Cas rubbed his nape. 'They don't work all the time but the words, they do matter. And the actions, they matter too. I'll speak to McGlynn about this Rory Johnson and this group.' He turned an expectant look towards Victor.

'Yo, Dimmy man,' Victor rose from his seat. 'I really am sorry, man. I didn't mean for any of this, God's honest.' He offered his hand to shake.

Dmitriy stared at him coldly, staying as still as a statue. Cas watched on in horror.

'No,' said Dmitriy, keeping his hands on his lap. 'I know how you feel. You know how I feel. I play with you properly while we're both here, but no pretending from me.' He turned to Cas as Victor retracted his hand and leaned back. 'Can we go, boss?' he asked, climbing out of his seat and signalling for Andriy to do likewise.

'Uh, yes,' said the shell-shocked Cas. 'We speak again later, yes?'

Dmitriy barely nodded as he turned away and they headed towards the door.

'Victor, you stay. We need to speak about what to do with you,' he said, his eyes wandering to watch Dmitriy and Andriy disappear out of the door.

In the dressing room later that morning, Dmitriy swapped spaces with Charlie. He only spoke when spoken to, keeping most of his answers monosyllabic.

'He's just a fucking div, Dimmy. He won't have meant anything by it,' said Charlie, his sentiments echoing those of his teammates. The arms around Dmitriy and the stand-offishness of his teammates towards Victor that morning did little to thaw his mood or stop the early rooting of the seed that had planted itself in his mind.

Dmitriy was consistently one of the team's best trainers. That morning, his focus and intensity were dialled up even higher than usual. Every action was crisp; precise. During the games, his running with the ball was even more bullish than usual. He sliced through the lines like a hot machete through butter. And he sought Victor out with pinpoint passes time and time again. Victor was not on his heels like during sessions of late. He was his old, mercurial self, flashing into pockets of space and lasering balls into the corners of the net. But neither celebrated any of their contributions in the slightest.

Later that day, Victor faced a dressing down from McGlynn. The club had already released an official statement on Victor's viral video, citing Victor's lapse of judgement in giving an interview to an unofficial source, who edited the interview "in bad faith to serve a divisive agenda". The statement reiterated the club's stance towards inclusivity, their support for Dmitriy, and their commitment towards all those who felt empowered by the rainbow symbolism. McGlynn oversaw Victor's official club video apology to Dmitriy, the club, the fans, and anybody affected or offended by his poor judgement, and arranged for Victor to make a hefty donation to and a number of appearances for the 'Weave Got You' initiative over the next few weeks.

The club's statement also noted that those singing songs or holding banners denigrating the rainbow-coloured badge or third kit could face stadium bans from this point forward. They were also set to investigate those directly responsible for the "dishonestly motivated" interview with Victor.

'Do you like it here?' Dmitriy asked Andriy as they pulled up past the lake after training.

'I like it very much,' replied Andriy. 'Look at that,' he said, turning the car around so the water laid before them. 'What's not to like?'

Dmitriy's eyes wandered over to the bridge; his mind to being stood there with Cas, his weighted vest on under his big red jacket.

'Why do you ask?' asked Andriy.

Dmitriy hesitated. 'No reason.' He unclipped his seatbelt.

Andriy knew there was something but did not dig for it. 'I had the reflex to ask if you're OK. How silly. Let me be more specific. Will you be OK with these tonight,' he said, nodding to the house, 'or do you want to come stay with me?'

'It's OK. Maybe in a few days,' replied Dmitriy.

Andriy squeezed and said goodbye to him before he left.

On walking through his front door, his mother shouted him before the door had even closed. 'Cherry or apple?'

'What?' he yelled back. 'Give me a minute.' Upon arriving at the kitchen, his mother was holding up two pirozhki. 'Cherry or apple?'

He hesitated as the last time he had pirozhki in the house popped into his mind. 'Neither thanks, Mama.' He kissed her cheek as he patted his stomach. 'They can't call me fat too.'

Iryna let his comment slide past her. 'That supermarket's not bad, you know. Did you say this man Barry is your friend?'

'Yeh. Why?'

'He has tattoos right up to here,' she said, pointing at her throat. 'And a gold tooth.'

'Was he nice to you?' asked Dmitriy.

'I think so. He kept trying to talk to me. I have no idea what he was jabbering on about though.'

'Here, they call that *being friendly*,' replied Dmitriy.

'Cheeky so and so,' she said with a chuckle.

'Anyway, I'm glad you liked it. No more egg-hunting. What did Papa think?'

'He didn't come. I've barely seen him.'

'Is he in?' asked Dmitriy.

'Yes. He's probably still in our room.'

'OK,' he said. 'I'll go speak him and sort out some bits. I'll be down in an hour or so.'

'OK. I'll leave some pirozhki for you in case you find the appetite,' she replied.

The words rang in his ears as he left the room, causing him to check his messages as he headed upstairs. Emily's thread remained unchanged. He reached his parents' room and knocked. Silence. As he turned the door handle, a gruff call came. 'Leave me sleep.'

Dmitriy let go of the handle and stepped back. He knew from checking his phone it was only just after four thirty. He stood there mentally rehearsing all the things he could say for a few minutes before going downstairs to his gym and gloving up.

As the waiter, Winnie, loaded one of the side plates onto his lower arm, one of the prep chefs shouted at him. 'Come back for it. We don't need more droppage. Table twelve, yeh?'

Winnie set it down and nodded, picked up the other main plate, and headed out onto the restaurant floor. His eyes locked onto one of the pair sat at his destination table. She was roughly his age with voluminous extension-enhanced hair, shiny full lips, feline-esque dark eye make-up, and ample cleavage on show. He felt his greasy skin frazzle as he arrived near her. 'The salad?' he asked.

Giggling at her conversation, she did not acknowledge him.

'That's hers, thanks.'

Winnie did not look at the source of the male voice, his eyes staying fixed on the woman as he set her plate in front of her as she carried on talking as if he was not there. 'There you go.' She kept talking straight ahead.

'And the Ragazzi Special,' said Winnie as he finally tore his eyes away from her and passed the steak-filled spaghetti dish to her companion, who had almost as much cleavage on show as his date.

The man's T-shirt neckline dipped below the bottom of his sternum, showing his artificially brown muscular chest, which contrasted sharply against his unnaturally white teeth. His hair looked like it had taken longer to do than his date's, his eyebrows were even more preened than hers, and he may have been wearing eyeliner. 'Can I get you anything else?' he said, aiming his words back at the woman.

'I'll have some parmesan and black pepper please,' said the man as his date continued to talk.

'And you?' Winnie asked her.

'No thanks,' she replied, her eyes not travelling his way.

Winnie gathered the side dishes and extras and headed back to the table to find the woman gone. After setting the side plates down, he asked the man to tell him when to stop and began to grind pepper onto his food, all the time, his eyes wandering to the woman's empty seat. 'And the parmesan,' he said as he began spooning pre-grated cheese onto the pasta, his eyes still magnetically drawn back to the empty seat. The man snickered at him, causing him to fix his eyes down. 'Would she like any?' asked Winnie.

The man grinned his way. 'Definitely not.'

Winnie made his way back to the kitchen, his eyes searching for waiting food as another waiter came in behind him.

'I think we're past the rush now,' the manager called over. 'Thanks, you two. You can call it a night.'

'But it's rammed out there,' said Winnie.

'That was the last major round of bookings,' said the manager, taking out his phone. 'We can take it from here, thanks.'

Winnie and the other waiter looked across at each other and darted for the cloakroom while taking their aprons off. As they got there, they rummaged through their coat pockets and pulled out their phones, tapping and swiping at their screens frantically. As Winnie opened the servU app and straightened his glasses, the other waiter called across to him. 'Sorry, mate.'

Winnie tapped the solitary green shift at the top of the screen, but it turned grey on touch, indicating it was no longer available.

'Hopefully another one comes up for you soon.'

After they both left the restaurant, said their goodbyes, and the other waiter headed to their next shift, Winnie sat in his car, constantly refreshing the app, hoping for a new green shift to appear. Instead, the next notification he got was from YouTube. He tapped it immediately.

'Welcome everyone,' said Rory Johnson to camera. 'It's been a mad week. Thanks for all the support, the subscribers, all the people who joined the group. It's nice to know plenty of you feel the same as I do about what's 'appening.' He raised a printed letter up to the camera. 'It's only getting madder from 'ere on out.' He held it closer, making the Weavers' letterhead clear. 'They gonna say I twisted this too? In my 'and 'ere is a letter that landed today, special delivery – the season ticket renewals don't even come special – giving me an official club warning for my *conduct*. "Dear Mr Johnson" . . . blah blah blah . . . I'll skip to the good bit . . . "any further videos that you create negatively portraying the club's use of the" . . . I don't think I'm allowed to say that word . . . I'll go with *colour scheme* . . . " – a symbol celebrating diversity of sexual orientation, love, tolerance, and hope – in our kits, promotional materials, or any other materials will lead to immediate termination of your season ticket and a lifetime stadium ban." *Lifetime.* 'Ow's that for tolerance? Oh, and check out this lovely little flourish.' He pushed the letter back close to the camera, this time showing its rainbow-coloured footer and web details for 'Weave Got You'. 'Even the stationary isn't just blue and white anymore.' He read from the letter again. '"We hope that you take this opportunity to reflect on your views and chose to support the team and the wider culture in a way more in keeping with the club's values."

The club's values. I've loved this club for thirty years like loads of you watching. 'Ow's it valuing me? 'Ow's it valuing *us*? I'm being told by an owner who ain't even a fan, who's happy to rip the club away from its roots and price 'alf of us out in the process so he can make an even taller stack of money, what the club values. If someone came and offered 'im top dollar tomorrow, he'd be out the door. Those players – I love what they do for us but most of 'em are the same. A bigger payday and out. There's no amount of money you could give one of us to stop supporting this club. I reckon you could give most of us ten million quid tomorrow to never to watch or listen to this team again and we'd end up 'aving to pay it back. And even those of us who could keep ourselves from it, we'd still be curious. Our ears would prick up every time we passed a radio with a game on. Our eyes couldn't 'elp but flicker to a back-page 'eadline or a TV showing the footy in a shop window. This team is in our 'earts, in our blood for life. *Values.* We value this club. We have a say in what it stands for. And I've seen since my first vid, I've 'eard you in the stands, and I've 'eard from plenty of you over the last few days that you agree with me that there're people at the club trying to twist and turn it against its die-'ard fans and drive a culture we're not part of. Fuck that!

They're threatening to ban me for talking. Not inciting violence, not even for being abusive and saying some of those words they call *hateful* now. For talking about the colour of our kit. Are they banning Easy? Selling 'im? Are they fuck. You 'eard 'im. Just like us, he agrees the club is bigger than any political issue and that badge of ours is sacred and what do they do? Stick a camera in 'is face like a bloody Al-Qaeda 'ostage vid, forcing him to denounce what he said the day before. Easy come, easy go. I get it, he's on big money. They've got 'im by the balls.

Where they've muzzled 'im, some of us 'ave to show our teeth. We can't let 'em weaken us and keep shoving this agenda down our throat. This is our club, our culture, and they will never take it from us. 'Ere's what I think of your fucking gag order.'

Rory picked up the camera, made his way out of a door onto a strip of concrete by the river, and set the phone on something waist-height for a moment as he crumpled the letter up into a long, thin strip. He took out a lighter and lit its end before picking his phone back up to show himself bending down to light a fuse attached to a box. A few moments after stepping back, the box's top exploded into a white shower of fireworks overhead. Above the rain of white sparks, deafening rockets exploded into bursts of sky blue. As the bangs and crackles of white and blue sparks filled the night sky, Rory got himself back in frame with the show behind him. 'Fuck your rainbow. Bring our badge back. White and blue till I die, no matter 'ow much you try to shut me up. And to the jokers who sent me this . . . we all know who you are . . . don't you ever forget, we *are* the value.'

Winnie hit pause and gazed at the compelling face on his screen for a while. He then checked back into the servU app. A green shift sat at the top of his feed for a restaurant six miles away. He screwed up his mouth and glared at it for a moment before accepting it, setting his phone down, and starting his journey across the city.

The clock ticked to 1:27. The home office was lit only by the light from the laptop and the TV. Gunnar pinged a finger repeatedly against the glass of his tumbler as he watched a montage of the Warriors defending against transitions on his laptop. He scrolled back along the video's play-bar to some clips where Lawler occupied the central midfield last season. After a minute, he skipped forward to some Lawlerless clips from the current campaign. He took a swig of *Khrabryy* as he watched on, then downed the rest as he stopped the montage. Lifting the remote, unpaused the TV. The blood red Surgeons stole the ball on the edge of their area and within two sharp passes – the second cutting across the centre circle – were forty yards up the pitch with players streaming forward in support. A few similar clips followed. Gunnar placed his head in his hands then looked up at the clock before his eyes meandered to the open newspaper on the desk. 'Scalpel Meets Silk: An unlikely footballing friendship' read the headline and subtitle above a blurry, distant photo of Cas shaking hands with Magnus in the Surgeons training ground lobby. The big Icelander ground his teeth.

The titanium of Lawler's phone buzzed against his bedside table. Lawler stirred and moaned but remained asleep. The next buzz roused Suze to semi-consciousness. She shoved Lawler, waking him enough to reach for his phone. 'Piss off, Tara,' she said in his dream state, swiping the decline button then rolling back over.

A minute later, a noise bled into Lawler's awareness – the house phone. Suze shoved him hard. 'Go get that before it wakes Pol.'

He sprang out of bed and tiptoed downstairs as fast as he could. 'Yeh?!' he hissed down the receiver.

'You're in the squad tomorrow.'

'Gunnar?' asked Lawler, squinting confusedly.

'Well, I'm not your fucking tart, am I? Be there for midday.' The line cut.

Lawler checked his watch, baffled.

'What the bloody hell was that about at this hour?' asked Suze, half-asleep, as Lawler climbed under the covers.

He puffed up his pillow before dropping his head onto it. 'I'm in the squad for tomorrow . . . I think.'

'Sup, Cloons?' asked Victor as he bro-hugged Finney, both having just parked up.

Finney patted Victor's backpack, feeling its solidity. 'Jesus. You carrying some fat stacks in there, Walter White style?'

'Haha, not quite,' replied Victor nervously before changing the subject. 'Feeling strong there, big man. Granite body. Not long now.'

'You know it,' replied Finney.

'You done your homework, fam?'

'Yeh. Read it to Lulu last night.'

'Oh yeh?' said Victor, his voice climbing an octave higher than usual. 'You think it's . . . appropriate?'

'Don't start.'

'What?' asked Victor. 'Can't I aks you a question now?'

'Vic. It's a children's story. It obviously has a purpose. Just leave it.'

'A'ight, man.' Victor slotted his hands into his pockets and spotted a stone on the tarmac, which he kicked through Finney's legs. 'Boom. You want it promoted to your daughter though?'

Finney shook his head. 'Did it turn you?'

'Ha, dickhead. Nah, fam, but I ain't got a mind like a sponge or a piece of plasticine, you get me?'

'That's very fucking debatable. Anyway, keep your curious, simple thoughts to yourself.' He nodded past Victor, one of his eyes involuntarily clasping shut for a second.

'You gonna be winkin' at me like dat, maybe it did turn you, Cloons.'

Finney rubbed his eye. 'Shut up. He's here.'

As Victor turned to see McGlynn's Rolls Royce enter the car park, he noticed a blacked-out Vauxhall Vectra parked just outside the school gates.

The Rolls pulled up next to them and McGlynn climbed out with the recording TaloVision crew. 'Gentlemen,' he said, shaking hands with Victor and Finney. 'Let's open some young minds.' As he marched forth and the players followed, Victor could not help but look back over his shoulder. The Vectra lurked.

"What was the score?' asked David as they picked the ball up.

'Did you enjoy the game?' said Callum.

'I loved it,' said David.

'That's all that matters. We don't keep the score around here,' said Callum as he took hold of Ravel's hand.

The rain shower stopped. 'Look at that,' said Nicole as they walked off the pitch. 'Isn't that better than any scoreboard?"

Victor lifted the book and showed the assembly the final image of the book – the row of friends, in their white and sky-blue kits, walking towards the sunset and the dazzling rainbow-embellished sky.

'The end.'

The primary-school audience filled the hall with applause, led by their teachers. Victor took a bow while Finney and McGlynn clapped the audience.

'Can we give Victor, Ian, and Andy a big school thanks for reading to us on three?' asked the school's head teacher, receiving a hall full of nods. 'One, two, three.'

An enthusiastic yet muddled 'thank you' came, with the kids mixing up the order of their guests' names.

'Now, if you've got any questions for our Weavers, put those hands up high in the sky,' said the teacher, triggering a horde of hands to shoot up. The teacher picked the first questioner.

'What's it like to score a goal in front of all those people?'

'You remember or you want me to take this?' Victor asked Finney for all to hear.

Finney smiled disbelievingly and nodded as he stepped forward. 'It's been a while, I'll admit, but it's something you never forget. Looking up at all those happy faces, knowing you made their day and their week better by doing something that made yourself incredibly happy. It's the best. I hope I have a few more in me yet. Vic?'

'You know like when you ask Father Christmas for somethin' and you really don't know if you're gettin' it and then BOOM, you tear the wrappin' paper off it?'

The kids nodded gleefully.

'Imagine that with chocolate sauce and a flake on the top.'

The audience laughed and the headteacher selected the next questioner. 'What does a chairman do?'

'What an excellent question,' said Andy, wiggling forward like a peacock who had fanned his tail feathers as Victor and Finney exchanged a look. 'Well, technically I'm actually an owner, which means the club is mine and so I have to look after everything off the pitch to make sure the team wins games and that the fans are happy. I help with buying and selling players, making sure the fans at home can see us on *the tele*,' he said, trying to sound common for a moment. 'For those of you who can come, I want to make it the best football to come to in the world. I want everybody to feel welcome, like we're one big family. I want us to have an amazing, comfortable stadium for you all so I'm trying to get us an even better one of those.'

'I like the Co-op,' said the questioner.

'So do I,' replied McGlynn, 'and I promise you'll like the new one even better.'

'My Daddy said it's too far away,' said the kid.

'You can tell your Dad we'll have buses that can bring him and you and his friends straight there. You think that'll work?'

The kid nodded and smiled.

'Next one,' said the headteacher, pointing at her pick.

'Did you ever get bullied like Ravel when you were at school?'

'Not quite like Ravel,' answered McGlynn, 'but I went to a school where we all lived together and the boys could be very cruel to each other there so yes, I've experienced a bit of it. We don't tolerate that at my football club, do we guys?'

Finney and Victor shook their heads.

'I don't think I ever got properly bullied growing up – got called "Fifty Foot Finney" and a few other bits – but nothing too bad. I've seen it though. If you see it, trying to help is good. How about you?' Finney asked Victor as his eye twitched again.

'Not like yo' boy Ravel, but yeh, people said bits to me through my life cos I'm black. Black players get horrible people in the crowds shouting things sometimes. My brother stopped playing cos of it.'

'Why do people shout at you?' asked the kid.

'I'm not sure. Cos I look different from them.'

'Like Ravel?'

'Nah, that's cos he acts different,' said Victor.

'Next question,' said McGlynn, pointing to a kid in the back corner near the TaloVision crew.

'Is there going to be another Weaverinhos book?'

'Aren't you an inquisitive little bunch?' said McGlynn. 'Indeed there is. We've got a whole series to follow this first one. Hopefully they'll be in your school library soon. Tell your mums and dads to buy some for home too as with every copy we sell, the profits go towards helping kids like the ones in the book play football without having to worry about being bullied.'

The headteacher began a round of applause.

'Can I ask as well,' shouted up the kid, 'what's your favourite book?'

'I'm a little bit biased. I love this Weaverinhos book,' said McGlynn. 'I wish it'd have been out when I was your age.'

'I like this book a lot too. My daughter, she's the same age as some of you,' said Finney. 'She enjoyed it loads. She was a big Gruffalo fan. Now she likes all of the spells and potions in Harry Potter.' He turned to Victor.

'Shout out the Bible. You do R.E. here?'

A ripple of nods went through the audience.

'Tell 'em to read you dat. Blueprint for right living. Brought some from my brother's church,' he said, pointing to his backpack at the back of the stage, 'you can take with the Weaverinhos books.'

'That's very kind of you, Victor,' said the headteacher, starting another round of applause as McGlynn painted on a smile and glared through the back of Victor's skull.

CHAPTER 16

'He'll have dissected us over and over,' said Gunnar. **'**He'll think he knows every soft spot, every weakness. He'll have ordered his players to poke at them again and again, from every angle, until they draw blood. They play for death by a thousand cuts. He thinks he knows us. But all that *knowledge* will mean fuck all when they realise you're not made from what any of these other fuckers they've faced are made from. Prodding with their little semi-ons works on all those soft cunts. We are fucking Kevlar. We are *impenetrable*. Make them feel it, make them remember it, and make them realise they knew fuck all about the Warriors!'

His black-and-gold clad players leapt to their feet in uproar, ready for battle. As they filed out of the dressing room, Gunnar signalled to Lawler and his attacking midfielder, Massingham, to hang back.

'You've been good these last two games, Bry. Today, good doesn't do it. We need bulletproof. From both of you. They're gonna prod and poke and probe at you from the first minute to the ninety-fifth. No . . . fucking . . . weakness.'

'Yes, chief,' they replied in tandem.

'Go,' said Gunnar. 'Go.'

As the Surgeons and Warriors walked onto the pitch side by side and broke off to line up, the corporate box was still three-quarters full, with many at their tables showing no sign of going to their match seats.

'Any chance we can get that round in before half-time?' shouted a pink-tied suited man from one of the tables, sloshed and sneering.

'It's coming, sir. Just a minute,' strained the bartender, Winnie, wiping the condensation off the inside of his thick glasses lenses on his uniform waistcoat. He mopped the sweat from his reddened forehead as the pump spluttered the final centimetre of foam into the top of the pint he was pulling. Imperfect but acceptable, he loaded it onto the tray with the other nine pints, dashed round the bar, precariously ran it over to the waiting table, and passed out the pints, the last one going to the suit who had hassled him.

'What do you call this?' he asked, pointing to the flat foam at the top of his pint.

'That's the IPA, sir.'

'I mean the head,' said Mr Pink Tie. 'It's shite, that.'

'It looks alright to me,' replied the bartender, peering closer.

'You sure you're looking at the right one?' laughed the suit, referring to the bartender's slightly crooked eyes. A few of his mates snickered. 'We're not at Wetherspoons here, drinking dregs. A few of these are bottom of the barrel. Do us some new ones, yeh?'

'Yes, sir,' replied Winnie, loading the offending pints back onto his tray.

'Chop chop,' said Mr Pink Tie. 'Kicking off any minute.'

Winnie grabbed his tray and took off. Halfway to the bar, he tripped on the untied lace of his cheap, oversized dress shoe and crashed to the floor, drenching himself in ale. As he grabbed his fallen glasses and rolled to his back, the table of suits jeered him and began a chorus of 'She fell over!'

Mr Pink Tie, shaking his head through his laughter, tapped his watch at Winnie, who scrambled to his feet and scurried into the storeroom behind the bar. 'Fucking puff cunt,' he mumbled to himself as he changed the keg.

Five minutes later, having served everybody with most of them taken to their seats in the stands, Winnie was back in the storeroom, stood on top of the slightly unstable spare keg at the end closest to the pitch, watching the match out of the high, narrow window.

'Winnie!'

He startled and jumped off the keg at the gruff woman's voice.

'Get out front. You need to be out here, plus you can watch it better from out there anyway,' she said.

'Yes, Chrissy,' he said as he scuttled towards her. Taller and more strongly set than him with half of her hair shaved short and sporting a nose ring, she barely edged aside to let his meagre frame past her and out of the narrow space.

'Have you soaked yourself again?' she asked, catching a whiff of him as he passed.

'I got a bit on me,' he replied.

'Winnie – much more spillage and I'm gonna have to note it on the app,' she said.

'Please don't. Please. I need this,' he begged. 'It's not just my shifts here I get through that. I'll do better. I promise.'

'Last chance,' she said.

'Thank you. Thanks.'

'Just keep the drinks in the glasses,' she said before leaving.

He watched her every step out, his redness rising.

COLIN

And Lawler cuts it out again and carries the ball forward, giving his team a breather and a chance to make some progress up the pitch. He's not spoiled for choice with forward options, but he threads a lovely pass to Massingham, who sees the space and drives into it. The red wall reassembles and directs him wide. He throws his weight at Clyde to try to give himself a yard, but Clyde stays with him, breathing down his neck. Look at those red shirts closing that space around him.

PETE
It's unbelievable work rate and organisation from Rúnarsson's side yet again.

COLIN
And again, Massingham is pressed and harried out of possession and the Surgeons break. The ball goes wide to Anderson. First time back in-field towards Jesé. Look at the reds swarm across and upfield. Jesé finds the third man runner out wide. He zips the ball back to the edge of the area. Lawler gets the block in and wins the second ball. He feeds Massingham. Clyde is like his shadow so far. He's trying to make half a yard to play forward to Ayissi, but he sprays it out of play.

PETE
Magnusson's down there on the sideline going ape, telling his side to pick up the pace. Midway through the first half and some of them are blowing. At half-time he might have to ask his dad to cut them some slack.

The Warriors sat silently waiting. Lawler scanned around his teammates. None of them met his gaze as they drank and peered at their boots. The dressing room door swung open, smashing against the wall. Gunnar stormed into the centre of the floor, his scowl roving for a solid thirty seconds. 'Look at you. Most of you daren't look at me.'

A few of the players lifted their eyes, including Massingham.

'Here,' said Gunnar, waving to the creative midfielder, beckoning him to come up to join him. 'Come on.'

Massingham tentatively stood up and traipsed over to him.

Gunnar held his shoulders and positioned him to face out to the group, then took position beside him. 'Most of you daren't look at me and you shouldn't. You make a mockery of this shirt for forty-five minutes then come and try to eyeball me like you're fucking El Chapo or something. You should be a-fucking-shamed of that shower of shit of a first half. We're lucky to only be one down. They've outthought you, they've outworked you, and fucking worst of all, they've outfought you. How dare you wear this fucking shirt and let anybody outfight you. Then have the gall to come in here and front me. Especially you,' he said, turning to look at Massingham next to him. 'You told me no weakness and then all you go and do is sweat it all over my shirt. Take it off.'

Massingham's eyes flickered towards his manager, not looking at him directly, as he remained otherwise still.

'You waiting for me to stuff a tenner in your fucking G-string? TAKE IT OFF!' Gunnar put his hand out.

Massingham kept his eyes down as he peeled his shirt off, handed it to Gunnar, and made a move back towards his seat.

'No,' said Gunnar. 'You stay here.' He turned his attention back to the rest of the players. 'He was scared of them and they sniffed it out. The only thing any of you should be scared of is me dragging you if you play like this piece of shit just did. You go out there, you tighten it up, and you fucking bludgeon your way back into this.' He dropped the shirt on the floor and stormed out of the dressing room.

PETE
These two couldn't be any more different in their demeanours. Gunnar is screaming instructions at his players, willing every ounce of fight out of them. To be fair, it's working so far in this second half.

Then you have Magnus stood there with his little notepad, occasionally waving a player over for a quiet word in their favoured language.

COLIN
Yes, in some ways, it seems the apple has fallen quite far from the tree, but things couldn't be closer here. The Warriors have created some moments during the second half after being dominated during the first. Can they finally make one pay here and get level with just over ten minutes to go? Botterill swings the ball at pace towards the mass of bodies jostling around the penalty spot. Hardison wins the header under pressure but it goes straight up in the air. The goalkeeper punches the ball away. Sweeney's going to retrieve that and . . . he's slipped. Juliansen's off. It's two against one. Black shirts haring back. Can he pick the pass? He can. Goldwasser is through. Lawler's hurtling back. Can he get there? He slides in just outside the area. Goldwasser's gone down, but it looks as if he got a toe to the ball. The ref blows. PENALTY! He's running over to Lawler. It's red!

PETE
That looks incredibly harsh. I think the ref's got that completely wrong.

COLIN
I'm inclined to agree. Let's see the replay.

* *

SURGEONS 4-0 WARRIORS
FT
(HT 1-0)

Li (34', 91')   Lawler (78' ■)
Goldwasser (81')
Juliansen (84')

The Warriors lumbered past Gunnar up the golden steps onto their team bus. None of them directly looked his way but all had noticed, during the period of abject silence since the end of the match, that his pale Nordic flesh was rosier than usual and he had an almost imperceptible tremble to him.

Lawler's twenty metre path from the stadium exit to the coach felt like the walk from death row to the electric chair. He approached Gunnar with his eyes fixed on the steps, but fully aware of his boss in his periphery. His left hand pulled his bag and his right fist sat cocked in this pocket. He stepped within arm's length of Gunnar. Nothing. He stepped level. Nothing. He stepped past him, losing sight. Was it coming? Nothing. He continued up the steps, strode along the aisle to the back seat, and plonked himself down. Chunky headphones on and hood up, he slid down, relaxed his fist, and disappeared into his music.

As the last few Warriors made their way onto the bus, Gunnar remained statuesque by its door in a world of his own.

'My boy,' said Magnus, proudly emerging from the players' exit. 'You ran us close there!'

'Go to hell,' said Gunnar in Icelandic, turning his blank eyes to his father.

Magnus's smile diminished. 'Son,' he said in their language, 'I mean it. You can take a lot of positives from today. The referee killed the game for you.'

Gunnar turned to the bus, as if looking through it with X-ray vision. 'I know who killed the game for us.'

'Gunnar – he was your best player.'

'He destroyed our chances of getting back into it.'

Magnus shook his head. 'No. The guy who you subbed – he destroyed your first half. Like I said, you need better there. Lawler was excellent. He had to make that tackle. He *did* make that tackle.'

'What the fuck is this? You want to manage my team too?' snapped Gunnar.

'No,' sighed Magnus, edging back. 'Sorry. I just want to help.'

'Then stay out of my fucking business.'

'Very well,' said Magnus. 'You won't hear another word on it from me unless you want it.'

Gunnar blankly looked through him.

'Come have a drink with me,' said Magnus earnestly. 'We won't talk about the game. Just drink with me to the two of us here, together in the league. It's special. It deserves a toast.'

The last of the Warriors wandered past them onto the bus.

'Oh. We have to go. How dreadful,' said Gunnar in a deadpan monotone. He swivelled and began climbing the bus's steps. 'Maybe you can have another with your little boyfriend. Best pop a little blue pill now. Give it some time to kick in.'

Magnus restrained his impulse to answer immediately and lowered his head. 'Son. It really was a great effort today. You can't ask more than that.' Before he had finished his sentence, Gunnar turned and trotted up the steps. The doors closed, leaving Magnus looking down at his shoes.

Gunnar sat in the closest free seat. As the bus started, his father's final words looped in his mind.

*

'Five, six,' **chanted a pack of the boys in Icelandic as the quiet Gunnar watched Jónsson juggle the ball from shoulder to shoulder, popping his next touch up in the air for him to comfortably head twice.** 'Seven, eight.' The chant grew louder as Jónsson brought the ball back down to a shoulder and then the other. Some jeered, trying to put him off. Left knee, right knee. Louder still. Jónsson hoofed touch thirteen high in the air. Most of his teammates gasped. Jónsson calmly looked up at the ball, took a step backwards, then did a forward roll, taking a perfect touch on his right foot from his sitting position on the count of fourteen before smashing the ball into the distance. The huddle of cheering lads piled onto him. After a moment, Gunnar cracked a smile and joined them, jumping on top with his limbs akimbo like a starfish.

After the hullabaloo died down, Jónsson, grinning ear to ear, picked up a drinks bottle and tapped a nearby ball to Gunnar. 'Go on then.'

Gunnar stopped the ball with his studs. 'It's pointless.'

'Only cos you can't do it,' replied Jónsson.

'No.' Gunnar rolled the ball away behind him. 'When are you gonna use that seal shit during a game?'

'This *is* a game.'

'You know what I mean,' said Gunnar.

Jónsson gathered another ball at his feet and looked around his other teammates. 'All work and no play makes Gunni a dull boy. It's alright. If you don't want to play our silly little game, we'll leave you to your serious preparations.' He tossed Gunnar his drinks bottle and began to turn away with the ball.

Gunnar took a long look at the bottle. 'Pass it here,' he said to Jónsson.

Jónsson and the pack stopped and turned towards Gunnar. 'That's more like it!' said Jónsson, his smile returning as he walked the ball towards Gunnar and the pack assembled around them. 'You right-handed?'

Gunnar nodded as Jónsson set the ball just in front of his right foot.

'Start with your right then. Easiest that way when you get up to the shoulders. One more thing.'

Gunnar set his studs on the ball, ready to drag it back and flick it up, waiting for his friend's final tip.

'The shoulders.' Jónsson reached up and laid both hands on the front of Gunnar's shoulders. They looked each other in the eyes for a moment, Jónsson's smile eventually drawing one from Gunnar. Then Jónsson shoved him, causing him to topple back over somebody crouched in a ball directly behind his standing leg. The pack of lads howled as Gunnar scrambled to his feet, red in the face, and sprinted after the impish perpetrator. After flat-out chasing and failing to catch his agile teammate for a solid twenty seconds, much to the amusement of his teammates, Gunnar slowed. Jónsson turned, still cheekily smiling. 'Truce?'

Gunnar drew in a few deep breaths, smiled, and nodded.

Jónsson jogged over, breathing easily, his palms open to communicate no more trickery, and patted Gunnar's shoulder. 'Games don't all have to be so serious, mate.'

Gunnar playfully shoved him.

'Boys. Over this way, please,' shouted the coach from the other side of the pitch. As they all turned and set off his way, Gunnar spotted his father amongst a cluster of parents pitchside. Magnus's scowl burrowed into him.

Half an hour later, the coach blew the final whistle. The players from the training teams circulated around each other, shaking hands with their opposition for the day. After a few shakes, Gunnar beelined for Jónsson. They bro-hugged and walked off the pitch laughing as Gunnar peeled off his training bib. After his head finally emerged from the fluorescent tangle, his father stood directly ahead of him on the sideline. His laughing dampened.

The team's coach emerged through the bodies behind the duo. 'Outstanding, Jóno! Some superb breakaways there.'

Jónsson turned and grinned the coach's way. A few metres from the touchline now, he turned back to Gunnar. 'See you tomorrow, Gunni.'

'See you,' replied Gunnar as he watched his friend peel away. His eyes snapped back to his father instinctively, helping him catch a sports bottle Magnus had flung his way.

'Great effort, Gunnar,' said the coach, patting Gunnar's shoulder before turning his attention towards Magnus. 'I can't ask more than that. See you tomorrow, guys.'

Gunnar peered straight ahead and guzzled his drink during the drive home, his dread growing with each extra silent minute that passed. As they pulled into their drive and Magnus cut the engine, Gunnar realised his fingers were clawing into his empty bottle. They climbed out of the car and Gunnar walked round it towards the house's front door.

'No,' grunted Magnus. 'In there.'

They entered the garage. Bright strip lighting illuminated the breeze-block walled space. In one corner stood a squat rack and a weights bench with dumbbells and plates. The walls were decorated with posters showing a variety of subjects: professional footballers, anatomy charts, Olympic judokas, nutritional infographics, quotes and figures from ancient wars. A chalkboard and a whiteboard displaying tactical drawings took up some wall space. Two footballs hung from the ceiling on adjustable pulleys. Half of the concrete floor was covered with judo mats.

'Pass that here,' said Magnus, gesturing to Gunnar's sports bottle.

Gunnar handed it his way. Magnus's hand latched around his wrist. Gunnar's eyes lit up with panic as he saw his father's expression change. In an instant, Magnus yanked his arm up while stepping in tight to Gunnar's body and wrapping his free arm around his son's head. He wedged his pelvis under Gunnar's, then bent forward, wrenching Gunnar's head and hand down with him, pulling him up in the air and tossing his onto the concrete with a dull thud, minimised by Gunnar's break fall. Magnus scrambled round to pin his son and examined his grimacing face. 'So you *do* know how to fall?'

'Get off me!' yelled Gunnar, only for Magnus to lean more weight on his torso, crushing his final word quieter.

'You let that little shit push you over and all of them laugh at you,' seethed Magnus.

'They're just messing about, Dad,' wheezed Gunnar.

'And what about you? Are you fucking messing about?' asked Magnus, his face screwed up in disdain.

'No, Dad!'

'Then why do you let him run rings around you in the fucking game too?'

'I couldn't help it,' spluttered Gunnar.

'You're on the fucking reserve team and you let him do that to you. You let him leave you in the mud. You want to let him fuck you down there too?'

'No!' strained Gunnar.

'Couldn't fucking help it. You listen to me and you listen to me well, boy. No son of mine is going to lose out to a bunch of little pricks like those. Do you understand?'

'Yes!'

'If I hear "great effort, can't ask more than that" from your coach one more time, this concrete will feel soft compared to what I do next time. Do you understand?'

'Yes,' panted Gunnar.

Magnus studied his son's expression, waiting for eye contact until he got it. 'Good.' He eased his pressure on his son's torso, stood up, and walked over to fetch the sports bottle from across the room.

Gunnar sat himself up, gasping and holding round his ribs. 'I'll sort your dinner while you stretch. Fish or chicken?'

Gunnar brooded as he ran a hand along the rough patch of cold concrete beneath it. 'Fish.'

Magnus nodded and left the garage. Gunnar balled his hand into a fist and screwed it against the rough concrete, imagining it to be his father's face. Eventually, he used his knuckles to help push himself up to his feet and walked over to the mats to start stretching.

*

CHAPTER 17

Lawler expected to face the wrath of Gunnar the week following their drubbing at The Theatre, but it never came. Gunnar addressed him as part of the group but never individually. The midfield enforcer trained ferociously, looking to earn his place in the starting line-up back for the midweek European tie after his league suspension. When the squad was announced two days before the match, he was not in it. When they travelled, he remained and trained with the U23s. Upon returning after a convincing two-goal away win, he rejoined them. After dominating the middle in training for two days, he was selected for the weekend's squad. Come game day, he made the bench and never left it. The following week, he kept his mouth shut, his head up, and his feet moving. He tackled everything that moved and threaded even more passes than usual through the black and gold mesh of players ahead of him. Teammates quietly assured him he had done enough to win his place back.

'Have you seen this?' asked Suze when he arrived home that Friday afternoon. She played him a clip from Gunnar's end-of-week press conference. Lawler had not made the squad. When pushed by the press for a reason why, Gunnar cited a 'disciplinary issue' that the club was dealing with 'internally'. Gunnar never divulged any behind-the-scenes issues to the press and it was a cardinal rule of his that the players did not either. Warriors' business was Warriors' business.

Lawler assured Suze that he had not done anything beyond the recent sending-off that constituted any sort of disciplinary issue. His exclusion stemmed from a vendetta from the final day of last season and this public fabrication was a declaration of war.

Over the coming weeks, as Lawler was frozen out of the Warriors' squad, Finney's medicated recovery heated up, first with him playing for the U23s a couple of times before his first-team return as a substitute. It had been ten months since last ran out at The Cooperative. The hairs on the back of his neck rose like a Mexican wave as the fans sang his name. His knee did not feel perfect. Scans showed that the ligaments still needed to hypertrophy more, which should come over time with the increased load of playing, but even if they thickened to their pre-injury girths, there was no guarantee that the limb would ever feel as good as new after such a trauma. Given his contract situation, his age, Xavier's absence, and copious consultations with the rehab staff, he decided it was worth the gamble. One thing he neglected to mention to the single member of the rehab staff that had full knowledge of his situation was that he seemed to be suffering side-effects from his *secret supplement*. His eyes occasionally ticked, mostly in the evenings. He often felt nauseous after hard training sessions but had only vomited a little once. Twice in the night, he woke himself with writhing, automatic movements of his arms and legs. On giving him the course of medication, Neil had implored him to declare any odd sensations or symptoms, but they were so infrequent or minor that half the time he forgot them and half the time he did not think there was anything worth telling.

Even though he was a yard off the pace, his return to the team steadied the defensive ship that had tossed around on choppy waters since Xavier's injury.

At the other end, the team scored freely. Victor, although not as clinical as last season, was finding the net plenty from the glut of chances coming his way. Dmitriy was playing out of his skin as the side's creator, playing key pass after key pass to Victor, getting Nixon and the other wingers into dangerous positions, and scoring plenty of goals himself. After the final game of the calendar year, he was on nine goals, equalling his career-best tally for an entire season. Off the pitch however, all was not so harmonious.

After the first school visit, Victor was bollocked by McGlynn for his Bible giveaway. 'We're not bloody missionaries,' the owner said, drawing a snicker that Victor just about managed to hem in. McGlynn demanded that Victor keep the school talks purely to the 'Weave Got You' agenda and insinuated that any deviation from this would cost him dearly, as would him saying or doing anything remotely controversial in the media, mainstream or social. Victor's regular churchgoing drew larger and larger congregations, to his brother's mixed feelings. Jack had not showed his face inside the church again, but Victor had noticed the blacked-out Vectra near the church a few times and was certain he had seen his tormentor's hatted silhouette inside it. The striker prayed over and over again, secretly hoping that God himself would assure him of his family's safety.

Just as Victor did not hear from his heavenly Father, Dmitriy had not heard from his earthly one. When he was home, Alexei made himself scarce, going for walks around the lake or shutting himself in his bedroom, where he built architectural models – new model materials arrived by courier every few days – and sozzled himself with cheap vodka from the Polish supermarket. When they occasionally crossed paths, the most Dmitriy got from his dad was a recognitory nod devoid of eye contact. The longer this went on, the more Dmitriy only came home to speak with his mother and go a few rounds on the bag before leaving to stay at Andriy's house.

'Everything . . . my house, the club, this city . . . everything apart from here with you doesn't feel like home anymore,' Dmitriy said on the evening of December thirty-first. 'Maybe we take our home somewhere else.'

Andriy was not all that surprised to hear his partner had been thinking of moving for a while. He had noted a change in him since their office mediation with Cas and Victor. 'Where are you thinking?'

'I don't know. Just somewhere fresh, without the drama.'

'The drama will die down, you know,' replied Andriy.

'I know,' said Dmitriy, unconvinced.

'But I don't know that we'll be without it wherever we go, for a while at least,' said Andriy. 'Of the top football countries, we're in one of the most tolerant as it is.'

'I know but tell the fans that,' said the tired playmaker.

'It's only a small group of them,' said Andriy. 'You see how the vast majority are.'

'I know,' replied Dmitriy, 'but that small group whistles loudly. And it's not just them. *And* it's not just what's happening now. Sometimes I drive past that industrial estate where I dropped off the money last season. When I pass through town, I go the long way so I don't drive past where the premiere was. I avoid where her house was,' he said, sighing deeply. 'I know that as long as I play, this will follow me, but at least some fresh scenery might help.'

'Are you sure about this?' asked Andriy, examining his partner's expression.

Dmitriy nodded laboriously.

'Very well,' replied Andriy. 'I'll speak to McGlynn in a few days after the game. Hopefully he's amenable.'

'May as well get the ball rolling tomorrow,' said Dmitriy. 'I'll speak to Cas too. Give them as much time as possible to replace me.'

'Oh . . . OK. Tomorrow it is then.'

Dmitriy smiled bittersweetly.

'Get your passport and pool shorts ready,' said Andriy. 'The new year may bring us back nearer paradise.'

Dmitriy raised his glass of sparkling water. 'Cheers to that.'

Cas's headband did little to soak up the sweat that his lustrous hair used to absorb. His eyes stung as the perspiration streamed into them, but the burning muscles of his legs had most of his attention. As his feet pounded the treadmill belt, the bangs from outside drowned their noise out. He was in such a world of pain that the fireworks outside barely registered. The only externality penetrating his trance of suffering was the red figure distance display on the treadmill counting up. At nine thousand six hundred metres, his gliding gait began to drag, finally fitting with his pained expression. Over the next few steps, the treadmill took him backwards, centimetre by centimetre. Aware of this rearwards drift, he gritted his teeth and willed himself to find another gear, praying that the flickering display would help tow him forward. His stride buckled more with each step, like he had hit a resonant frequency that would cause his entire frame to pull itself apart. The explosions outside loudened. He closed his eyes, finding a pocket of peace in amongst the ear-piercing sound and suffering. *'Sigue adelante,'* he gasped, pulling his feet off the belt as quickly as he could in an effort to keep his speed. When eventually he opened his eyes and wiped them with his wristband, the display had already passed ten thousand metres. He grabbed the side support bars, used them to help him jump and land his feet either side of the spinning belt on the stationary frame, and flailed his hand at the stop button, only succeeding in switching off the treadmill with his third attempt. He stumbled off the machine, grabbed his drinks bottle, squatted down, and rolled his bare, sweaty back onto the floor. *'Puta madre,'* he panted as he unclipped his heart monitor chest strap before tossing it across the room in exhaustion. As he closed his eyes and sucked some deep breaths in, the crescendoing fireworks finally caught his attention. Between the bangs, he faintly heard people shouting out from their balconies below. 'Happy New Year'.

    He rolled towards the end of the treadmill, grabbed his phone, wiped his hand on his shorts, and checked his plentiful new messages. None were from Amber. As his breathing calmed, he typed one to her.

> Feliz Año Nuevo mi amor. Congratulations for what you achieve last year. I hope this one is even better for you x

After lying there for a while waiting for a response, the firework racket ceased, triggering him to get up, shower, and go to bed, checking his phone multiple times throughout the process.

He awoke in the pitch black with a startle, clawing his pillow away from underneath his neck before fully waking. He peeled his cover back and slowed his breathing as his gaze rested on the empty side of the bed. It dawned on him to go to the toilet to break himself fully out of his nightmare before trying to resume sleeping. He picked his phone up on his way. Amongst more Happy New Year messages was one from Amber.

AMBER
Happy New Year to you too. Can we meet up to chat after the game in a few days?

He responded immediately.

Of course. When is good with you?

He barely slept another wink that night and what sleep he managed was paper thin and dream laden. Rising early to no reply, he faffed around the barren flat for a while before going for a walk around the foggy, run-down docklands that surrounded the stunning hotel-apartment building he had lived in around five months. On arriving back and seeing he still had no reply, he looked through his last texts to her, scrutinising not what he had said but instead his poor English. A few minutes later, he bought some English grammar and introductory French and Russian language audio lessons he found online.

With it being a rare New Year's Day without a game for the Weavers, training was arranged for early afternoon to give the players and staff a lie-in and the morning with their loved ones after a potentially late but sober – for the players, at least – night. Cas headed in a few hours early to prepare for the following day's match and was surprised to find Dmitriy's Mercedes in the carpark. After making his way through most of training ground, Cas spotted Dmitriy out of a window on a training pitch, practising free kicks.

A minute or so later, Dmitriy set a new ball in place outside the penalty area, took three measured steps back, and heard a ball struck behind him. He paused his preparations and turned to see Cas had kicked it and was walking his way. The struck ball skidded past Dmitriy, knocking the ball he had just set for the free kick.

'Better than Magnusson,' Dmitriy called Cas's way.

After the momentary jar of hearing that name in this setting, Cas sardonically smiled his way.

'Too soon for this joke?' asked Dmitriy.

'No,' said Cas as he reached him, his voice thin. 'Happy New Year.'

'Happy New Year, boss.'

'Yes. Let's make it like this.' Cas ran up to the ball nearest by and bent it over the wall of free-kick mannequins, losing his casual-shoed footing. As the ball swished into the inner side-netting through the top-corner gap left by the target trainer, he hit the turf. The two burst out laughing and Dmitriy lent him a hand, pulling him to his feet.

'I think you need the boots for the next one,' said Dmitriy as his chuckling calmed.

'Is not a bad idea,' laughed Cas as he wiped some of the mud off his right side. 'What brings you so early today? You not want to enjoy the long morning with your parents and Andriy?'

'Maybe Andriy.'

'Ah,' replied Cas. 'You want to speak about it?'

'No.' Dmitriy paused a moment. 'But I want to speak to you about something else.'

'Please,' said Cas.

Dmitriy lowered his head. 'I not know how to say this in a good way . . . I think maybe it's best if I make a transfer somewhere else.'

Cas's brow furrowed as he looked his playmaker in the face. 'Oh.' His eyes flitted around as he searched for the right words. 'I know there have been some things going on, but I want you to know I want you here and I will do everything I can to make the things right.'

Dmitriy sighed and met Cas's gaze. 'I know you try but you can't make all this right. All I want to do is play football like everyone else. My teammates, the fans, they like me if I try, if I'm good; they not like me when I'm shit. But now some they not see me properly. They see through the lens, you know, the glass?'

'I understand,' said Cas.

'I play like a beast, some of them, they more impressed than they should be. *Wow. Look how the gay one plays. So good. Unbelievable.* Others, it not matter how good I play, they see shit. You can't take this lens away.'

Cas frowned. 'I know is hard. Nobody has been like this before. Give it some more time. The people, they will change. We will keep making the changes until we find the way to make it go fastest.'

'What can you really do?' asked Dmitriy. 'You ban the fan for saying the thing. I know too much about these sorts of thing where I'm from. Maybe the ban works to stop the people saying these sort of things but they get angrier. They still find the different way to let you know. Maybe they make the whistles instead. You can't ban them for whistles. It won't make it go away,' he said, growing more exasperated by the second. 'Maybe you have another player who doesn't like me. He never say why but you know why and I know why. What you do? Sell him? You can't do it. You can't tear the whole thing up because of me. Let me go somewhere else. They know what they get before I come, not like here where I change and they're all supposed to change without the choice.'

'Dmitriy. I know what you say and maybe you are right but maybe I am too,' replied Cas. 'I can make the team better. I can make the fans better. I just need the time. And I know what you say about it being better somewhere when they know you, know about you already, but unfortunately, I don't think there is a place without this problem. Maybe some places a bit less, a bit more but this is football right now. It won't always be.'

'Maybe,' said Dmitriy. 'But now I know that here is like this. Maybe a little bit less somewhere makes life a lot better.'

'Maybe.' Cas sighed and shook his head before searching his mind for something more solid. 'I know one thing definitely. You said you just want to play. I know you want more than just to play. I know you want to be at the very top.'

Dmitriy's eyes met his boss's, whose next words were bassy and solid. 'I know here I can help you become the player you want to be. This team, the way we play, where we all came from together. There is nowhere better and I think I can help you better than everyone. Me and you, we see with similar eyes. I walked the similar path to you. I can show you the way, the better way than I did it too.'

Dmitriy's eyes flickered down.

'I know I have the selfish reasons to want you here,' Cas continued, 'but I know that if you leave the best place for your football, for the player you want to become, early because of what the other people say and do - the crazy people, people who don't know you, don't matter to you, don't want the best for you – it will haunt your dreams always. I promise you, I don't say this to scare you. I *know*.'

Dmitriy's shoulders slumped before he retrieved a nearby ball and lined it up for a free kick. 'My sleep it's not so good, anyway.' He took his three measured strides back, eyed the goal, and whipped the ball into the far top corner. 'Andriy speaks with McGlynn today. We not put a request in. I loved it here for years, especially since you came, you make this special for me, but now it's not the same, not for me. There are too many other things. I give everything I can and I will for long as I have to. Just please don't make me have to.' He walked a few yards to gather a new ball and rolled in back with his studs.

Cas looked at the top corner Dmitriy bent the ball into. 'We see what McGlynn says and I think about it. Think about what I say too.' He gestured for Dmitriy to pass to him, which he did. First time, he spun the ball off his instep into the same top corner as Dmitriy. 'Please.'

CHAPTER 18

After a final tactical briefing and a short, sharp training session, the players showered and readied themselves to leave. On his way to see them all off in the dressing room, Cas checked his messages. Amber had seen the one he had sent in the early hours but had not replied. As he turned the corner, a holler drew his attention.

'Where are they?' called McGlynn, storming along the corridor with his film crew in tandem.

'Woah,' said Cas, shoving his phone in his pocket. 'What are you doing here?'

McGlynn reached him, grabbing his arm, and leaning in to whisper as he almost pulled him along. 'Has Dmitriy said anything to you?'

The crew trotted along to keep up.

'Yes, just before we train,' replied Cas.

'Fuck. I've just had Andriy in. I'm not having it. We're not having it. That little fucking rudeboy isn't ruining it for us.'

'Rudeboy?' asked Cas.

'Andy,' called Adam. 'Mic.'

McGlynn aimed a thumbs-up back his way and flipped his microphone power pack on before tearing through the dressing room door. 'Gentlemen, gentlemen, gentlemen. May I have your attention please?' he asked as he arrived with his crew in sight of the players. The dressing room din immediately died down. 'Take a seat, please. This won't take long.'

As the players sat and the crew positioned themselves, Cas propped himself against a wall, exchanging a miniscule shake of his head with Steve across the room.

'When I was a growing lad, my Mum and Dad used to insist that every evening in the holidays when we were home from school, whoever was in would sit and eat together at the dining table. No dinner on our laps or in our room. We ate together at the dining table because that's what the McGlynns did. The McGlynn dinner was sacred.

My brother and I, we got on like a house on fire when we were small but when we hit our teens, we became a little . . . mouthy, shall we say. It was like a light switched flipped us from serene kids one week to vicious reprobates the next. Mother McGlynn had always taught us that if you can't say anything nice, you shouldn't say anything at all, but I guess the changes that were going on for us at the time overrode what we knew.

My Dad got back from a stint working away after we had been giving Mother McGlynn a headache for a week or two at this point. We set the cutlery and sat down, she set our plates in front of us like a normal night but then my Dad got up and wandered around the table. Next to Jerry's fork he laid down a bar of sky-blue soap. He continued round to me and put one by my fork too. Didn't say a word. Just sat down, thanked my Mum for cooking a lovely meal, and tucked in. I remember Jerry and I just looking at each other. Anyway, after a few minutes, conversation started flowing and sure enough, Jerry and I got into it. I don't even remember what I called him, but I remember my Dad's gaze turning to me.

"What do us McGlynn's do if we've got nothing nice to say?" he said. "We don't say anything at all," I replied. "Was that nice, what you just called your brother?" he said. His stare was strongly inferring the answer, so I told him it wasn't. He told us that Mum had told him all about our dinner-time name-calling sessions. "We're McGlynn's," he said. "And McGlynn's can't be having filthy mouths like that." He got up, poured me a glass of water and set it by my soap. He made me wash my mouth out with the soap there and then at the table. Have any of you ever done that?'

The players looked amongst each other, most shaking their heads.

'It's definitely something to be smelled and not tasted, is soap. Anyway, that week, Jerry and I had a few mouth-washing sessions. After I'd been sick after one of them, despite all that hormonal madness, I managed to find a way to keep my mouth shut at the dinner table. The soap sat on a butter dish for a while in the middle of the table, but we never had to use it again.

Some things are sacred, guys. Ugliness should not taint them. The Cooperative is one of those things. Here we are sitting joint top and where the majority of our fans are celebrating this exciting time with us and spurring us onto glory, there is a loud minority that seem to have forgotten what they're here for. Instead of enjoying and appreciating and supporting, they're clearly fixated on a non-football issue, whistling at the tops of their lungs at a very specific target, exposing ugly sides to their natures.'

Dmitriy crossed his arms and looked down, his teammates straining not to look his way.

'That bigot who stirred them up, he's not welcome here, and neither are his sentiments. They've stopped their song and they think they can get away with their bigotry under a different guise.

This place is sacred, and I will no longer allow it to be contaminated by ignorance, narrow-mindedness, and hate. This isn't how Weavers act,' he said, looking towards Victor, drawing a tightening of the striker's face. 'Later today, the club will be announcing that excessive whistling towards any of our own players from our own supporters will be met with a one-match stadium ban.'

Dmitriy's stomach sank as if the floor plummeted from underneath him.

'Further infringements will be met bans of greater durations and from now on, we will have staff resource dedicated to monitoring behaviour in The Old Mill.'

A rustle sounded as many of the players shifted around on the benches. Dmitriy remained utterly still. He was overcome by an awareness of the clamminess of his skin.

'This minority, my hope is that most of them will choose to change. These bans will sit there like that bar of soap on the butter dish, encouraging them to think before they act. Most people are good. Given a reminder of who they are, they will remember what it is to be a Weaver,' he said, his gaze moving back to Victor as he paused. 'The others who don't, well . . . they aren't welcome at the table with us.' He clapped his hands together. 'Big game tomorrow, gents.' He looked quizzically towards Cas. 'What is it you say? *Hala, Weavers!*'

The players timidly applauded McGlynn's flat motivational call.

'I'm going to make it so that the only noise is to support you boys!' He nodded forcefully and clapped the players a few times before winking Dmitriy's way and marching out.

Cas caught up with him out of the door. 'Andy, Andy,' he said, jogging to meet McGlynn's pace.

McGlynn took his lapel microphone off as he pulled out his phone. 'Great stuff, eh?'

'I don't know. I never hear anything like this before,' replied Cas.

'We're making history this season, Cas,' said McGlynn. 'You, me, and them. Nobody said it'd be easy.'

'No. I guess not.'

'I've got a call I need to make. Is there something specific I can help you with?' asked McGlynn, scrolling through his contacts.

'Dmitriy. What you say with Andriy. Are we going to discuss letting him go?'

McGlynn chuckled. 'Are we bollocks. He has a contract. We're doing everything we can to protect him. End of. I've strung it out with Andriy. Said I'll give it some thought, talk with you.' He sped off and Cas halted, mulling over what to do next.

The film crew emerged out of the dressing room.

'Alright, Cas?' asked Adam.

'Yes, yes. You guys?'

'Very well, thanks,' said Adam as he spotted McGlynn down the corridor. 'See you later.'

'Yes, later,' said Cas. As the crew made it a few steps away from him, a realisation dawned on him. *Puta madre.* In the dressing room,' he muttered.

Down the corridor, the crew caught up with McGlynn as he exuberantly began his call. 'Jezza!'

After a light, somewhat muted training session that afternoon, Cas returned to his office and checked his phone. There was still no response from Amber, but a message awaited him.

MAGNUS
Best wishes for the game tomorrow. May the best team win.

A knock came at the door.

'Come in,' said Cas, inviting Steve into the room.

'Guv. What you doing for tea?'

Cas shrugged. 'Just making myself something at home.'

'No, you're not,' said Steve. 'Sheila told me you're coming to ours to see the year in with us.'

'No. I'm not good company at the moment.'

'Now she's got an empty house, any company that isn't my ugly mug is good company,' said Steve.

Cas smirked. 'It is quite the ugly mug.'

As Cas followed Steve's car towards his house, a myriad of roadworks diverted them way off the regular route. As a Motown song started on his radio, he realised that the route would go past his house. His heartbeat quickened. His eyes checked his phone again. Still no messages. For the next few minutes, his mind cartwheeled through various scenarios as his instincts drove the car. Finally, his house came into sight. He eased off the accelerator, turned his head, and sat up in his seat to peer through the gate's decorative railings. Amber's car was on the drive. A bloody warmth climbed his neck. He dialled Steve over the in-car phone system and turned off at the next turn.

'What are you doing?' asked Steve.

'Amber – she say she needs a quick word with me?'

'What, just now?' asked Steve.

'No, last night. I'm here now. I go see what she wants.'

'OK,' said Steve, his tone dubious. 'She said it'll be on the table in an hour, hour and a half. I'll have a glass of something waiting for you.'

'Thank you,' said Cas as he turned the car.

'Break a leg,' said Steve.

'*¿Qué?*' asked Cas.

'I mean good luck,' replied Steve.

'Oh yes. Thanks. *Adios.*' As he hung up, he rolled up towards his gate, stopping short so that the automatic opening sensor was not triggered by his car. He got out, walked over to the intercom, and dialled in, standing in front of the screen.

After a short while, Amber answered. 'Hey. What're you doing here?'

Cas pushed a pang of anger down. 'Hi. Happy New Year.'

'Happy New Year,' she replied bittersweetly.

'I was driving past to go to Steve's house and I saw your car so I thought I try you.' A long silence followed. 'Can you hear me?'

'Yes, I hear you,' replied Amber. 'Look, now's not a good time. Can we leave this until after tomorrow?'

'Why is not a good time?' he asked, striving to keep his tone neutral.

'It's just better we do this after tomorrow.'

Cas drummed his fingers on the wall, knowing she was watching him via the intercom's camera. 'You have plans?'

'No,' she insisted. 'Please . . . the day after tomorrow, I promise. Can we do that?'

He peered through the gate's railings at the lit-up house, which he could see no movement within. 'OK. We leave it a couple of days.'

'Thank you,' she said.

Wistfully, he stroked his hand down the straight section of one of the railings, stopping where the metal curved into a knot that looked similar to a figure eight. They had these custom made to Amber's design many years back, replacing wooden gates that blocked out streams of light. He stared at the knot for a few seconds – its beautiful curves looking to him, for the first time ever, like a noose – before conjuring his next words. 'Have a good evening.'

'And you,' she said. Just as he had turned away from the intercom, she said his name, prompting him to turn back to it.

'*¿Sí?*'

'Sorry for not getting back to you. I should have,' she said, her voice creaking with emotion.

'Is OK, *mi am*—' He stopped himself. *'Buenas noches.'*

'Goodnight,' she replied.

He climbed back into his car, took another look at the house through the railings separating him from it, and slowly eased the car backwards. Out of nowhere, a black Lamborghini ripped along the road just behind him at breakneck speed extremely close to hitting his car. *'¡Que cabrón!'* He pulled back towards the gate to loop out of the turn-in, only realising too late that he had gone close enough to the gate to set off the sensor. He winced as he turned out, anticipating it opening. It remained shut. He stopped the car and looked over his shoulder at it, puzzled, then reversed slowly towards it. He pulled a good metre past the point the sensor would detect his car and it stayed closed. Everything inside him sank.

Lawler adjusted his cardboard crown as he turned onto his home road. Suze pointed ahead. 'Isn't that thingy's car?'

Lawler saw the black Hummer along the road. 'Oh shit. I completely forgot.' He checked the car clock. 'Least I haven't kept him waiting too long.'

As they drove towards him, he flashed his lights repeatedly before manoeuvring round and following them into their gate and up their drive. After parking, Lawler walked around the car, opened a back door, unfastened his sleeping daughter's seatbelt, and scooped her up. Arnold jumped out of the Hummer, scattering the underfoot granite chippings as his pot belly jiggled, and slammed his door behind him. 'What time do you call this?' he asked, waving at Suze as an afterthought.

Lawler raised his finger to his lips and gestured to Polly, flat out in his arms. 'Sorry, Arnie lad,' he whispered. 'Does it take some of the heat off me if I tell you I watched one of them Terminator films?' he continued proudly as Suze walked off to open the front door.

'Finally!' proclaimed Arnold in a loud whisper. 'What did you think?'

'That bird from Game of Thrones is boss, lad.'

Arnold's expression dropped. 'You watched fucking Genisys?'

'Yeh, that's the one,' replied Lawler.

'Jesus Christ,' said Arnold, forgetting his volume and shaking his head. 'Do you put your rubbers on after you jizz too?'

Lawler glared at him, nodding down to Polly and shaking his head.

'She's asleep. It's OK,' whispered Arnold.

'Bet that's not the first time you've said that,' replied Lawler.

A few minutes later, after carrying Polly up to bed and leaving Suze to settle her in, Lawler joined Arnold in the living room, set a few different bottles of cold pressed juice on the table in front of him, and took his crown off as he sat down. Arnold picked the green one up, inspected the sediment in the bottom of it, shook the juice up, and watched the particles float through it. He screwed his mouth and nose up before setting it back on the table. 'I'm alright, thanks. I prefer our usual meeting spots and their libations.'

'Oh well,' said Lawler with a small shrug.

'How are the girls?' asked Arnold.

'Yeh. Sound, ta,' said Lawler with a warm smile. 'Polly enjoyed tonight. Had a nice Christmas. Don't think she's too keen on going back to school, but I'm sure Suze won't mind.'

'Good . . . good. I meant *the other girls*.'

'Keep your fucking voice down,' hissed Lawler. 'I dunno. Haven't bothered with 'em for a bit now. Kat messaged me once but not exactly gonna chit chat, am I?'

Arnold chuckled to himself. 'I guess not. So's The Animal been tamed?'

'Fuck you,' replied Lawler. 'You should be happy. All that stuff was an accident waiting to happen.'

'I am, I am,' assured Arnold with a smirk. 'I just thought of all my clients, you'd be the last one to hang it up. We had some fucking good times, Bry.'

'We still will,' said Lawler. 'Just not like that. It had to change.'

Arnold nodded quietly to himself. 'So, what can I do you for this evening?'

'Well, some other shit has to change too,' Lawler said, rubbing his bristly scalp. 'I need out of the Warriors.'

Arnold sat up straight. 'That big bastard breaking your balls?'

'Yeh. He wants blood for some reason,' replied Lawler. 'You heard him in the press, the arlarse. Absolutely full of shite. You've seen how I've played when I've had chance this season.'

'Yep. And yet he's had you in and out like you're doing the fucking Hokey Cokey.'

'Exactly,' said Lawler. 'You reckon you can do it?'

'Bry, you're speaking to *me* here,' said Arnold, puffing out his chest as he nudged his mirrored shades from off the top of his thinning, greased-back hair down over his eyes.

'That's exactly why I'm asking you point blank,' replied Lawler, half-amused by Arnold's bravado.

Arnold flipped his client two middle fingers. 'The market's up and open, you're the P-O-T-Y for the champions, and I . . . well, I'm the motherfucking, sistershagging, daughterdiddling T-800 of deal-makers, so do I reckon I can do it? I reckon it's as likely as your boss only being able to get off to torture porn.'

'Ey. Seriously. Have you spoken to 'im recently?' asked Lawler.

'No, but I probably won't have to, anyway.'

'Well, just be warned,' said Lawler. 'He's an absolute crank.'

'Bry,' he pointed at himself with both thumbs. 'Deal-making machine. Don't sweat it.'

The nearby trees' branches whipped to and fro in the whistling wind as Dmitriy drove through his gate. As he pulled up to his house and rain began to spatter his bonnet, on the drive was parked an unfamiliar black Lamborghini. Puzzled, he walked towards the house and checked his phone to find a text message.

PAUL HOLLACE NBP
Good luck for the big game tonight!

He typed a quick text back thanking Paul but telling him the game was tomorrow, then entered the house to find his father lurking in the hallway. He held a glass of what was probably vodka in his hand and was spying something through the living room door.

'Hey,' said Dmitriy hesitantly, breaking his father's attention away from its subject.

Alexei quickly averted his gaze to the floor, mumbled something, and turned for the stairs.

'What did you say?' Dmitriy called after him.

'I said *disgrace*,' replied Alexei, carrying on up the stairs without so much as a fraction of a turn.

As Dmitriy's eyes stopped following his ascending father, his mother appeared out of the living room, coming over to greet him.

'Hello, darling,' she said before kissing his cheek and cupping his face. 'I've set you up with some nibbles and drinks in there. I'll leave you two to it now.'

'Erm, thanks. Who's in there?' asked Dmitriy.

'Oh . . . his name's left me. Your football friend. Handsome fellow.' She walked him to the doorway and called back in English, 'It was nice meeting you.'

'The pleasure is all mine, Iryna.'

Dmitriy froze as the sight of the guest hit him. Stood looking out of his living room window was Gunnar.

'This is breathtaking,' said Gunnar, pointing out at the moonlit view as he looked back over his shoulder at Dmitriy. 'You move just that little bit further out of town and look what you get for your money. All of us living in the trendy areas are fools.'

'What are you doing here?' asked Dmitriy, still in the doorway.

'Come in, come in,' beckoned Gunnar. 'This is your home. If there's one of us to be heading for the door, it's me.'

Dmitriy edged into the room. 'You shouldn't be here,' he said flatly.

'That's true,' said Gunnar as he walked with a twinkle in his eye towards his unconsenting host, 'but then if we only did what we should do, not much would change in this world of ours, would it?' As the two approached each other, he offered his hand for Dmitriy to shake and was met with an icy stare. 'I'm sorry about the stunt. Please. I'm a huge admirer of your work, of you.'

Dmitriy examined his face and only found sincerity. 'No thank you.'

'Fair enough,' said Gunnar, lowering his hand and nodding. 'Can we?' he asked, gesturing to the sofas.

Dmitriy tightened his mouth. 'Two minutes.'

'Two minutes,' replied the Warriors' manager. The two sat across from each other. 'Firstly,' said Gunnar, 'it goes without saying that I won't tell if you don't about this little get together. Not that anything wrong is going on but I understand how things can look. The car outside is borrowed and my phone is off so there's nothing to say I was ever here.'

Dmitriy's poker face persisted.

'You are a supremely talented player. You could be one of the very best if left to build your game but there is a whirlwind of bullshit blowing around you at the moment and your employers think an umbrella is the answer. Their plan B is probably a kite.

Now, if you want to weather a storm, fine, but you weather it properly. This isn't the time for umbrellas or fucking kites. It's the time for nuclear bunkers.

I've watched you play over the last few years. I know what you are, how far you can go. You don't seem the type to weather storms. That seems like your current employers. You . . . you strike me more as a man who becomes the fucking storm.' He locked eyes with Dmitriy and leaned forward. 'Have you thought about how your life and your career would be under the care of somebody more like you? Somebody that can batten down the hatches around you when needs be and that can rain down like a natural fucking disaster and rip every distraction and obstacle out of your path when required?'

Dmitriy tilted his chin up a little, regarding his unwelcomed guest. 'Somebody who tears out his best midfielder for no good reason?'

Gunnar chuckled to himself as he leaned further forward to get a glass of water off the table. 'Oh, if it's a best midfielder, I'd imagine there's a pretty good reason. I don't have to tell you about how the media and the fans can blow a whole lot of bluster about what goes on behind closed doors, do I?' He sipped his water, never taking his eyes off Dmitriy. 'Besides, imagine that *best* midfielder, a future world-beater, coming into training one day to find an old pal, another worldy, next to him. Someone he came up with. Someone he has a telepathic understanding with. If that happened, I can see that good reason,' he swirled his water around its glass and then knocked it back, 'just . . .' he blew a puff of air, '. . . disappearing.' He set his glass down on the table, stood up, buttoned his impeccably fitted suit jacket, and checked his watch. 'Two minutes. Wouldn't it be nice if everybody did what they said they would?'

Dmitriy rose as Gunnar walked his way.

'Please thank your mother again for her hospitality and sorry again for ambushing you. Well, sorry*ish*. I had to meet you. Winners recognise winners and rules will never stop that.' Dmitriy shepherded Gunnar past him, out of the room and to the front door.

'Thanks for your time,' said Gunnar, offering his hand to shake again. 'You can turn this down a million times and if I want it, I'm still coming for the next.'

Dmitriy examined Gunnar's expression again. The moment was so quiet that the ticking of Gunnar's watch was audible to him. Eventually, he shook the rival boss' hand with a sturdy, singular motion.

Gunnar smiled, opened the door, and looked out. The rain sheared across the black night sky, pelting the cars on the drive. He looked back at Dmitriy. 'Think about what I said. No fucking umbrellas.' He marched out into the rain, outstretched his arms to the sides, and turned his palms and face skywards, savouring the now torrential downpour on the way to his car.

Dmitriy closed the door but watched him through the side window until he got in and drove off. In the distance, he could see the black mass of trees swaying all around the lake, its surface bombarded chaotically by bullets of rain. As he turned away from the window, he studied his right hand. It felt different. He rubbed it against his trouser leg, took his minimalist phone from his pocket, and dialled.

As Gunnar halted his car at the gate and waited for it to open, he closed his eyes, took his right hand off the wheel, and covered his cheek with it, recalling the sensation of Dmitriy's hand against it. A tingle surged up his spine.

CHAPTER 19

Dream-plagued sleep. 05:30 rise. Blow out the cobwebs with an eighteen-minute five thousand metre canter on the treadmill whilst watching game footage. Hydrate. Scrawl notes. Watch more Weavers' clips. Underwear-only check in the full-length mirror. Press-ups, jump squats, planks. Shower and trim hair. Shave face with a fresh blade. Eau de parfum *de* Amber. Crisp new outfit. *Café Bombón* whilst talking along with an English grammar lesson. Admire the docklands in the freezing mist. Breathe. Head out for the stadium eight hours before kick-off.

At the same time, Finney poured his daughter some cereal while she sorted out his morning supplement stack. 'Two of the droitins,' she said to herself, fishing a couple of capsules out of a big jar and placing it into a small paper cup, 'two of the ashwa's, a little fishy, and some knee magic.' She popped the cup by her dad's smoked salmon eggs Benedict at the table as he pulled out her chair and set her cereal down. *'Merci,'* she said as he pushed her in.

'Beacoup,' he replied before sitting down. A few bites into his breakfast, he broke off to take his capsules, washing them down with some fresh orange, then finishing with his *knee magic*. Before he began eating again, he turned over his silent phone to check for any messages. Fifty-four waited for him. His brow furrowed as he opened them. He read the most recent one from Victor, sighed deeply, and clicked the link it contained.

'Daddy. Your eye's doing that thing again.'

He rubbed his eye, trying to make the twitching stop.

'And no screens at the table.'

'Sorry, Princess. Just—'

'Together time,' she interjected.

'Together time,' he replied bittersweetly, turning his phone over and sliding it to the other end of the table. 'Where'd you learn to be so smart?'

She grinned, shrugged her shoulders, and downed a spoonful of cereal.

'It certainly wasn't from your fucking mother,' he murmured to himself.

Victor stared at the blue ticks on the message he had sent Finney as he piled bundles of fifty-pound notes into the holdall laid across his bedroom door.

'Victor. Chuka's here. I'm dishing out. Do you want the akara or the plantain and egg?' shouted his mother from downstairs.

'*Mudda*,' he shouted in his mocking accent, *'just leave mine. I can dish it out myself.'*

'Boy. While you live in my house, you will eat with your family,' she hollered back.

Victor sucked his teeth as he threw a few more bundles into the bag before standing. *'You de craze?'* he mumbled.

'What you say, boy?' she yelled back.

'Nothin', Mum,' he said as he lifted the holdall aside and placed it by his single bed next to two full ones.

Hair a mess and a few days without a shave, Alexei wandered into the kitchen. 'Good morning, darling,' he said to Iryna as she plated some breakfast items at the counter.

'Ah. He sees light outside of the room!' she said, kissing his cheek as he arrived at her. 'I was just about to bring it up for you.' She slid a plate his way. 'What do you want to drink?'

'Tea, please. The real stuff.'

'I'll bring it over.' She gestured for him to go sit down at the kitchen table. He picked up his plate and turned to see Dmitriy and Andriy sat eating over there.

'Good morning, Alexei,' said Andriy.

Dmitriy mutedly nodded his father's way.

Alexei turned back towards Iryna. 'I'll take it in the living room when it's ready, thanks,' he said and walked out of the kitchen.

Iryna called after him to no avail. Andriy resumed eating as Dmitriy glared over at the doorway.

'Leave him,' said Andriy, laying a hand over one of Dmitriy's. 'Eat. It's a big day.'

After a few breaths he nodded and turned back to his breakfast, hacking his eggs apart as if they were a gristly meat. After his mother joined them, the atmosphere at the table gradually thawed and small talk eventually flowed. Nobody brought up Alexei, but Andriy noticed Dmitriy occasionally glancing towards the door.

'What's this thing I keep hearing on English TV the last few days?' asked Iryna, only halfway through her breakfast as the guys finished theirs. 'It's in so many of the adverts. *New year, new me*. What do they mean?'

'It's tied into their resolutions for the coming year,' replied Andriy.

'Well yes, I thought it would be something like that,' she said. 'It just seems peculiar, a bit like they're wishing themselves away. I get wishing to be better at something, to lose some weight, to save more money but *new me*? It sounds like they want to change the very nature of who they are. What sort of wish is that?'

In a flash, Dmitriy swivelled out of his seat and made for the door. Andriy's and Iryna's eyes bulged.

'Dima!' she cried as they both leapt out of their seats and headed after him.

Dmitriy stormed into the living room where his father watched the Russian news. 'You old fuck. How dare you come here and disrespect me and my partner like you have!'

Alexei half-looked over his shoulder at his son. 'Watch how you speak to me, boy,' he grumbled before turning back to the TV as Andriy and Iryna arrived at the doorway.

'How I speak to you?! Are you kidding? At least I actually speak to you,' said Dmitriy. 'You're my father and you come to live in *my* house and give me the silent treatment like a child would, not just for a day or two. For weeks and weeks!'

Alexei stayed silently facing the screen, impelling Dmitriy to come further in.

'Hey! You can't act like this in my house. Do you understand?'

Alexei turned his way. 'Do you understand I don't want to be in your shitty house in this shitty country, but I have to be?'

'You don't have to be anything. You're a grown man!' raged Dmitriy.

'I *do* have to be because you have ruined our fucking lives back home. And I didn't have to tell you that. You knew it happened and you knew it would happen, but you did it anyway without so much as a word of warning, you selfish, confused little prick.'

Dmitriy piped down.

'Exactly,' said Alexei. 'You knew what would happen. It's one thing fucking over that nice girl you were seeing, but another thing to do it to us. We are your blood.'

'Shut up,' mumbled Dmitriy.

'We brought you into this world. We provided for you. We made sure you got educated. We drove hours a day out of our way, back and forth over the border like a yo-yo, to take you to gymnastics and boxing and futsal and football. We helped you make this life. And now I barely have a career and your mother is scared to live in her own home. And why? Because you want to tell the world how special you are?' said Alexei as he stood up, mockingly framing his face with his hands. 'Like everybody else in this bullshit country where people want to talk publicly about which hole they like to put it in? How dare *I?* How dare you!'

'Shut your fucking mouth, you horrible bastard,' said Dmitriy, stepping towards his father.

Alexei squared up to him. 'Look at you. We should never have let you come here so young for this culture to warp you. For you to mix with disgraceful people. Now you speak to your own father like this. Would you hit me too?' They stared at each other for a short eternity, disdain etched across their faces. Alexei shook his head and walked away, turning back halfway out of the room. 'It's not just our lives you're ruining. Wind that news back a few minutes.' He carried on out of the room, Andriy and Iryna giving him a wide berth as he tore past them.

Dmitriy stood rubbing his forehead, the air almost hissing out of his nostrils with each outbreath, as Iryna and Andriy edged in towards him. Iryna shaped to hug her son.

'One minute,' said Dmitriy, walking away from her and fetching the remote control. He wound the news back a few minutes and pressed play upon seeing the start of the sports segment.

Fifteen minutes later after watching the segment and gathering some necessities, the couple were in Andriy's Aston on the way to his place. Dmitriy dialled a call through the in-car system. The rings gave way to a gruff Russian voice. 'Hello.'

'Kazimir,' said Dmitriy.

'Who's this?'

'What did you call me? Your "prime export". The player to "lead you into a golden era" I think you said.'

'Ah . . . Dmitriy,' said Kazimir sheepishly. 'How are you?'

'Fresh,' he said with punch to his voice. 'Not playing as much football as I'd like, you know? Might have to look at getting my phone fixed because it seems like I'm not getting calls and messages from people I should definitely be hearing from. How about you? You enjoy those draws in the first round of qualifiers?'

'Dmitriy . . . please. Calm yourself,' Kazimir replied in a quiet, soft tone. 'I understand your frustrations. My decisions are purely tactical. We just wanted to try some other systems.'

'Other systems as in the same formation with an inferior player in my position?' asked the playmaker.

Kazimir stayed quiet for a moment. 'Look. I am the manager. I don't have to justify my selection to my players.'

'No, you don't,' replied Dmitriy. 'But you will have to justify your failure to qualify for the World Cup next year to the fans and the Federation.'

'Some justifications are easier to make than others here,' said Kazimir flatly.

Dmitriy swapped a look with Andriy. 'Yes. Yes, they are. You remember when you took us for that caviar dinner?'

'I do.'

'Do I recall you telling me how much you'd love to manage in one of the big footballing countries at some point?' asked Dmitriy.

'I do,' clipped back Kazimir, his tone changing.

'I'll be honest with you. At home, I can see how your current squad selection decisions play out for you but in most of the big football countries, I can tell you they look very different. They're not going to look favourably on managers leaving out big players for certain non-football reasons. I think there'd be big questions raised over his judgement, both footballing and moral. But a man in your position – imagine what the big leagues would think of him if he were to take a stand, even if just on a football basis, knowing there may be consequences. What would they think of a manager like that?'

A long pause passed. 'What do you want?' asked Kazimir.

'All I want is for you to watch me. This current squad is set, I get that, but for the next one, I just want to know that you watched me. If you haven't seen what I've done so far this season, watch what

I do today, then in the next game, then in the next. I want to know you've watched.'

'I've watched plenty,' said Kazimir. The call cut.

Dmitriy looked across at Andriy then smashed his hand against the dashboard. 'FUCKING COWARD!' He stared ahead out of the window, his rage morphing a little more into despair with each breath. Andriy laid a comforting hand on his lap. 'What the fuck am I supposed to do?!'

'There's only one thing you can do,' said Andriy as he turned the car right. 'Make it blindingly obvious to the world what a coward he is.'

The streets around The Cooperative were awash with anticipation. Rainbow shirts bobbed around in a vast sea of sky blue and white jerseys. The general hubbub of the crowd came into sharp focus outside of The Old Mill turnstiles where a cluster of fans stood, around two hundred strong, a few of them taking turns to blow whistles over the slow boom of a bass drum. All these fans had their faces half-covered with scarves or wore cardboard masks of McGlynn or Dmitriy. Many wore grey jackets, some in a camouflage pattern. One at the front brought a megaphone to his mouth scarf-covered mouth and waved his Weavers-badge flag. The whistles stopped.

'Whose badge is this?' bellowed Rory whilst revering his flag.
'Our badge!' chanted the protestors.
'Whose home?'
'Our home!'
'Whose club?'
'Our club!'
'And who can go'n fucking whistle?'
'MCGLYNNN!' screamed the protestors, before breaking into a zealous round of 'Bring our badge back.'

A few packs of police officers stood by, watching on like hawks. After a few minutes, the protestors quickly dispersed into the general crowd, and headed in every possible direction. The police watched as many of them crouched and re-emerged maskless and with scarves down.

Inside the stadium, both teams were out on the pitch warming up. Cas waited just inside the dark mouth of the tunnel, soaking up the swelling atmosphere as he looked out at the bright white floodlights through his swirling, frozen breath. He laid a hand on the white breeze block wall, its vibrations tickling his bones for a moment, before he cupped his hands together, blowing into them and walking back towards the dressing room. Walking from the other direction was Magnus.

'Is a crisp one this evening,' said Cas, rubbing his hands together. 'I think maybe the big coat comes out.'

'This is practically summer back home,' said Magnus. 'Big coats all year round.' The two men reached each other just outside of the Surgeons' dressing room for the day and shook hands. 'Here's to a good game.'

'To a good game,' replied Cas.

Magnus stepped backwards, pushing the door open with his body. 'And one of those English post-game managerial tipples afterwards?'

'Yes,' replied Cas. 'Sounds good.'

Magnus leaned back against the door, fully opening it whilst closing his eyes and smiling as a warm stream of air from a heater above the door hit him. 'Thanks for being a hospitable host and giving us a toasty dressing room. I may be used to the cold, but my old bones will take the warm any day.'

Cas's eyes were drawn past Magnus to something in the dressing room. Amber was treating a player. In her fitted teamwear, her stomach protruded. An early bump.

'I'll see you out there,' said Magnus, giving Cas a thumbs up and walking into his dressing room, the door closing behind him.

Cas's blood ran cold.

Out on the pitch, the Weavers finished their limbering drills and sauntered over to a coned rectangle near the sideline. Dmitriy noticed the electronic advertising boards at pitchside were showing the slogan 'Claim Our Game' on a rainbow background. The text suddenly changed to 'NothingButPrideMag.com'. Steve tossed half the outfielders some bibs and began a possession game. The intensity rapidly ramped up, as the team with the ball pinged it around, mostly in one or two touches, and their opposition pressed and harried them, trying to steal it. Dmitriy tore around at game-level ferocity, sprinting at nearby opponents when they took the ball. After a few possession turnovers, his fervour had not dropped. As the ball arrived at the bibbed Finney's feet, Dmitriy was all over him like a rash. Although still not up to full speed, the club captain used his rangy frame to shield the ball from his snappy opponent and sent it successfully to a teammate, taking a minor bump as he followed through.

'Welcome back,' said Dmitriy with a grin, which was met by one from Finney as they moved away from each other.

'Look at you, spring in your step. Heavy hung the armband,' jibed Finney.

The ball circulated twelve more passes before returning Finney's way. Dmitriy was straight on him, but the ball was gone with a deft touch. The playmaker could not stop himself bundling into his captain, who playfully shoved him away.

'Oy, Taz,' Steve shouted Dmitriy's way. 'Leave some tornado for the game.'

Dmitriy nodded his way and slowed to a walk as the ball moved to the other side of the zone. Pass pass pass. The ball turned over to the other team who lost it immediately to a strong toe from Charlie. The ball skidded in the direction of the gap between Finney and

Dmitriy. Both darted for it. Dmitriy launched into a slide tackle, taking the ball and cleaning Finney out with his follow-through.

'Woah!' shouted Steve from the sideline as the rest of the players instinctively moved towards their floored teammates. Dmitriy climbed to his feet as Finney grabbed his knee and took a deep breath. 'Sorry, Fin. You OK?' asked Dmitriy as he crouched and offered Finney a hand up. *Whack*. Something bounced off Dmitriy's head. Before he could fully register what it was, Victor shoved him into a stumble forward past Finney.

'The *fuck* you doin', dickhead?!' roared Victor, whose hand had slapped the back of Dmitriy's head a moment earlier.

Dmitriy spun round and launched himself back at Victor, the two shoving each other simultaneously before their teammates stepped between them and pulled them apart as they tried to pull free and go again.

'HEY!' yelled Steve as he arrived at the scuffle with a few of the other coaches, shoving players aside to tend to Finney on the floor as Neil ran towards them. 'You alright, Ian?' he asked softly as Finney gingerly sat himself up. 'All of you,' the assistant manager said, speaking back towards the rest of the players, 'warm-up's done for now. Get inside.'

The dressing room was devoid of chatter as some of the players continued warming up and stretching while others made final touches to their kits, boots, and taping.

In a toilet stall, Finney gazed down at his scarred knee, examining it with his hand. Did it feel worse than it had been the last few weeks? It was hard to tell. He popped a yellow pill in his mouth, gulped it down, and flushed the toilet before leaving the stall, and swigged some water as he washed his hands. As he walked back into the main area, all eyes were on him.

'You alright, Clooney,' asked Charlie.

'*I'm* alright, Chaz. It's those two,' he said, gesturing towards Dmitriy and Victor, 'we've gotta be worrying about. Oy!' he called over to them. 'Do you remember who the actual opponent is today?'

They lifted their sunken eyes his way and nodded.

'This is massive. Be men and act like it,' he said as he sat and shook his head.

As Steve briefed Cas on what had happened on the way from his office to the dressing room, Cas registered the news but still reeled from what he saw in the away dressing room. They reached the hushed dressing room and Cas took his place in its centre, peering down at his shoes and twiddling his wedding ring with his thumb.

'All . . . we have . . . is each other.' He scanned around the sober faces of his players. 'Look around at your teammates.'

The players looked between themselves, some more comfortably than others.

'We are a family. We spend the most of our time together. We sweat together. We bleed together. We laugh together. We are there for each other when the times they get hard. When we sign the contracts and put on this shirt, we make the commitment to each other and the fans . . . that we do these things absolutely one hundred percent together.'

Neither Dmitriy nor Victor could look at their manager.

'I know sometimes, even with the people they are the closest, people we say and do things, bad things, that hurt each other. Maybe the closest ones, we hurt them the most, we push them the most. But we can't let it break us. If we break, you suffer, he suffers, we all suffer, and the people with our scarves and shirts out there, the thousands, maybe millions that depend on us, they all suffer. Not just now, but forever. We have to stay *together*.' A pair of tears rolled down Cas's face. 'Please. We are all we have.' His lip quivered. 'You know the plan. We have to do it *together.*' The tears streamed now. '*Hala, Weavers!*' he pushed out as his voice broke.

The chant echoed back resoundingly as the players rose. They headed over to their boss, mobbing him with hugs and handshakes. His tears would not stop no matter how much he willed them to.

Victor reached him, visibly upset. 'Boss man. Yo. I'm sorry,' he said, embracing him.

'Victor, please,' he said as they parted. 'This man,' he gestured with his head, triggering Victor to turn and see the approaching Dmitriy, 'he is your brother. You have to make this right or it will make you trouble for the rest of your life.'

Victor broke eye contact with Dmitriy, lowered his head, and nodded.

'If you don't make this right, you won't realise how good you two can be together until is too late. You have to be good with each other, *simpatico,*' he implored, wiping the tears from his face.

'You got me framed nicely?' McGlynn asked the TaloVision crew, setting up a few stairs above him in the director's box.

'Just a minute,' said Michael as he altered some of the camera's settings.

'Andy, while we have a second, do you mind if we speak about that invoice?' asked Adam, shrinking as he did. 'It's just, it's pretty tight, is all.'

McGlynn frowned. 'Adam, my boy. A tip from the top of the business tree to a fledgling entrepreneur. It's something called timing, yes?'

Adam nodded and bowed his head.

'We ready?' asked Michael.

'Like PJ and Duncan. Actually, one second.' McGlynn moved across the step to the other side of the camera frame. 'Good side. There we go. Ready when you are.'

'Action.'

'So, here we are, January second, bringing in the new year with a top of the table clash with the Surgeons here at The Coop, packed to the rafters with our amazing fans. Just listen to that support.' McGlynn welcomed the camera to pan to the crowd.

An ear-piercing whistle sounded from below the director's box. 'Shove those new stadium blueprints right up your dickhole, McGlynn,' somebody bellowed at the tops of their lungs.

McGlynn put a hand up to obscure the camera and signalled for it to cut, air-slicing his throat vigorously. 'Stop there. We'll go again. Did you get which little . . . who said that?'

On the pitch, the Surgeons passed the Weavers, each of them shaking hands with Finney before making their way down the line-up. As Goldwasser, the visiting team's most prolific striker, shook hands with the Weavers' captain, Finney's eyes malfunctioned, twitching and blinking erratically, and he pulled their hands to one side. Goldwasser let go, disconcerted.

'Have a good game, mate,' said Finney with an awkward smile, rubbing his eyes and closing his fist a few times to re-establish control over it.

Dmitriy panned around the crowd between handshakes. No boos or whistles had come his way yet. Finney was probably partly to thank for this, having wrapped an arm around him and playfully ruffled his hair on their way onto the pitch to show no ill feeling over the warm-up tackle. The playmaker glanced past Charlie beside him towards Victor. The striker's cold gaze awaited him. After a couple of seconds, they broke off in time with each other.

On the sidelines, Cas and Magnus came together to shake hands ahead of kick-off. 'See you on the other side,' said Magnus with a warm smile. As Magnus turned away, Cas looked beyond him to Amber on the bench, wrapped up in a padded club winter jacket. She self-consciously smiled and nodded his way. He grinned back through a grimace.

COLIN

After that scuffle in the warm-up, it's all smiles here at The Cooperative ahead of kick-off between these two teams tied neck and neck at the top of the table. An intriguing contest awaits us with the free-flowing football of the supremely talented Weavers against the ultra-organised, relentless-running soccer of the Surgeons.

CHAPTER 20

Five minutes in, after a give-and-go and beating the Surgeons' right winger, Dmitriy won a corner off their right back. As he jogged to retrieve the ball from beside the boards in front of The Old Mill end, a horrific shriek sounded from over his right shoulder in the crowd. Déjà vu overcame him as he turned to look. He could not find the sound's source but suddenly it amplified, coming from multiple places at once. He squinted as he searched the faces in the crowd. Nobody was screaming, yet many of the fans were also squinting at the shrill, ear-splitting screech. He was not imagining it. He looked back at the players assembling in the penalty area, who were squinting too. The noise disappeared in an instant, leading many fans to search around themselves confusedly. He let his thoughts of it go and dribbled the ball over to the corner flag, setting it right on the edge of the arc before studying the positions of his teammates assembling in the penalty area. He raised a hand, signalling to Finney and his other tall teammates that he was aiming for the back post. As he ran up to swing the ball in and planted his kicking foot, the multidirectional shriek burst back to life for a second, putting him off, and causing him to hit the ball into the side netting for a goal kick. He ran over to the referee, telling him of the shenanigans in the crowd.

'I heard it. If it happens again, I'll take a look,' assured the referee.

Dmitriy peered back over his shoulder as he jogged back towards his own half and apologised to his teammates.

PETE

The pace of this game is astounding. After struggling to build more than a five-pass move for the first fifteen or so, the Weavers have found a rhythm now and are moving the ball as quickly as I've seen them playing in any game. They're managing to beat that first press and get the ball into the middle third, but that swarm of Surgeons' bodies aren't letting them move the ball into any real dangerous spaces yet.

COLIN

If anybody can find half a yard of space against this unabating unit, you'd fancy it's Velasquez's men. The ball comes into Finney. Juliansen is breathing down his neck, not giving him an inch to turn. Li presses him from the other side and Goldwasser cuts off his angle to play back to his other centre back. Finney dummies to turn left and then clips a ball out wide to Allen. He's having to work hard every time he gets it to keep that ball flowing from front to back under immense pressure. Welcome back to the Alpha League, Ian Finney!

PETE

I think he just had a sneaky look up at the clock to see how much longer before he can take a breather. Can't say I blame him.

COLIN

And that's why you're sat here with me. Allen runs into the red wall and passes back inside to Finney, who plays a one-two with Lebedev. Make that one-two-three! Lebedev finds a rare yard. Ezemonye's pulled off his marker. He's calling for it into feet. Lebedev holds it a fraction too long but still finds the pass, although the space is gone now. Can Ezemonye turn him? He tries, but he's crowded out. He plays the only pass he can see, out of the mix back to Finney.

PETE
Lebedev found a yard then lost it there. He's not going to get many of those this evening so if they're going to threaten, him and the rest of the Weavers' attackers are going to have to move around each other with the timing and precision of cogs in a Swiss watch.

For the next twenty-three minutes, play proceeded at a brutal pace. The home side forced the issue, with Dmitriy occasionally breaking the red midfield line and charging on goal or finding balls to his wide forwards in decent positions. While Victor battled against the red backline, using his strength and pace to get a yard here and there, Dmitriy did not find him in any good positions, often holding the ball a fraction of a second too long.

The Surgeons defended resolutely and were dangerous on the break, moving the ball at speed into space whenever given the chance. Many of their forays forward were snuffed out by the excellent Finney, who received more taunts than usual from the opposition crowd. While he was not back to his pre-injury nimbleness, his positional play was second to none, at least until around the thirty-fifth minute when he began to slow markedly due to fatigue. His legs would no longer carry him to the spaces he knew he needed to occupy on time every time and the Surgeons created two half-chances in the last eight minutes.

'His legs have packed in, guv,' said Steve to Cas on the edge of the technical area. 'We swapping him out at the break?'

'We see how he feels,' said Cas, keeping his eyes on the game as Finney sent the ball out left. 'Maybe the break gives him the second wind.'

As Cas's eyes followed the ball out to Nixon, Steve's stayed on Finney as he rested his hands on his thighs and gasped for breath. 'Maybe,' he mumbled.

Nixon progressed the ball ten yards and as he met the defender, he did a double stepover that bought him no space, so he played the ball inside to Victor, who bounced the ball back to Dmitriy. First time, he spun a ball over the head of the Surgeons' right back for Nixon to charge onto and cross. Victor spun and bolted towards the middle of the box. One of the centre backs followed him only to lose him after a drop of the shoulder and check out towards the near post. Nixon wrapped his left foot around the ball, swinging the ball in towards the onrushing talisman. His attempt at a left-foot volley was thwarted by the centre back, who managed to recover and block the ball out for a corner. The Old Mill fans behind the goal rose and roared as Victor collected the ball from the boards, passed it towards the corner flag, and carried on his run towards it. Dmitriy arrived there first and gathered the ball.

Just as Victor called, 'Short one, Dimmy,' he flinched at something colourful landing by him. He looked at it as some jeers and whistles began. It was a banana. His mind instantly flashed back to Chuka's face in his final game a few years back when a banana landed beside him. A red mist descended. Victor's head spun in the direction the banana came from to see who had thrown it. A few rows back, many of the fans' gaped at a middle-aged black guy in a

Weavers' hat and a grey camouflage jacket, who was waving his hands desperately to signal some sort of gross misunderstanding.

'What the FUCK, fam?!' boomed Victor at him, stepping towards the boards.

The man kept waving his hands as he shouted some sort of objection, but Victor could not hear him over the din. The fan eventually pointed towards the corner flag. Victor turned. He was pointing at Dmitriy.

Victor watched as his teammate realised that he was the target. The striker felt sick to his stomach as he caught his playmaker's gaze. The second-long look between them felt like an eternity to him. He darted back over to the banana, picked it up, and cocked his arm to throw it back where it came from. Dmitriy grabbed him just in time to stop him, snatched the banana out of his hand, and skimmed it along the grass to the boards behind him.

The referee arrived on the scene and encouraged the duo to step away as he spoke to a steward by the boards. As a few stewards assembled at the front of the stand, it quietened apart from a few pockets of fans, who began chanting 'Bring our badge back' on loop. The stewards made their way to the row of the banana thrower and after a short dispute, led him away from his seat towards an exit, to the applause of half of that stand and most of the rest of the stadium. The majority of the Weavers' players and the referee checked in with Dmitriy as the crowd settled. Victor stood by shellshocked, studying Dmitriy's all-too-familiar glum expression.

The referee pointed to the corner spot, triggering the players to take up their positions. Victor jockeyed backwards into the penalty area, keeping his eyes on the dejected set-piece taker until he arrived at the penalty spot.

Dmitriy measured up the corner, raised his hand, and at the last split second before he made contact with the ball, the shrieks blasted again. This time, as the sounds disappeared, his cross curled towards the back post as desired. As a Surgeon headed the ball out to the right wing, Dmitriy tried to find the offenders in the crowd. A few shit-eating grins were scattered throughout the general area where the sound seemed to emanate from. He grabbed his badge and yelled, 'We're your team. Support us!' towards them before running into the box, followed by a smattering of boos.

'We think they have some sort of alarms in their pockets. The people, they are analysing the video and telling the stewards to go move these people out,' said Cas as they stood in the corner of the dressing room. 'Do you want to continue?'

Dmitriy nodded.

'Are you sure? You don't have to put up with this,' said Cas.

'Fuck them. Idiots,' replied Dmitriy.

Cas laid a hand on his shoulder. 'If you change your mind, just let us know.'

As Cas walked away, Victor snook a look past Charlie at Dmitriy then made the sign of the cross as he lowered his eyes to the floor, his brow furrowed.

At the sinks in the toilet area, Finney stealthily downed another pill, gulped some cold water from the tap and splashed some over his face, gasping at its freshness as he tried to get his breathing under control.

'How are you, Ian?'

Finney ceased splashing and saw Cas and Neil in the mirror waiting behind him.

'I'm alright, gaffer. Blowing but alright. You counted to make sure there are only eleven of those cunts out there?'

'I'm pretty sure,' smiled Cas. 'Do you have some more in you?'

'As much as you need. As long as you only need another fifteen or twenty,' replied Ian with a wry smile.

'Ha. We take that,' said Cas, patting him on the back before leaving.

Neil hung back. 'You sure you're OK?' he asked, keeping his volume low. 'You're looking a bit peaky.'

'That's cos I'm having a blinder.'

Neil did not crack a smile.

'Seriously,' said Finney. 'I'm alright. Just haven't been ran like this in forever.' Neil eyed him suspiciously, then nodded and moved off only for Victor to come over sporting a concerned look.

'Big man, I heard what they're singin'—'

Finney cut him off. 'Not now, Easy. We've got bigger fish to fry.'

A few minutes later, Cas addressed the team. 'Is good, guys. Is good. Hopefully, the stewards they stop the circus. Do your best to keep the focus. Keep the pace. These guys, they don't drop off, they cover the gaps quick, but we can find the way through together. If we play with one brain, one picture, they cannot cover those gaps quick enough. Together, guys. *Hala,* Weavers!'

The team bellowed it back his way. As they geed each other up and began moving out, Victor looked across again and saw Dmitriy's empty eyes.

COLIN

After those ugly scenes just before half-time, it took a while for the crowd to calm down but listen to that noise now! None other than Gunnar Magnusson reared his head from one of the executive boxes a moment ago and took his seat for the second half.

PETE

That, Colin, is the sound of pure vitriol. I'm surprised he's been let in the place outside of a game, to be honest.

COLIN
I don't think we needed the temperature cranking back up in here, but the players make their way out to an inferno of noise wondering what's going on.

As the Weavers emerged from the tunnel, they looked around at each other confused as their adrenaline levels climbed.

Finney chatted tactics with Dmitriy and Charlie, as Victor followed in another group. Over the hubbub, a shriek sounded nearby. Dmitriy ignored it.

'Hey, faggot!' came a call in Russian.

Dmitriy's head whipped round. A few rows back in the crowd was the caller, dressed in a grey camouflage jacket and a cardboard mask holding a cardboard banner overhead. The mask was of Emily's face. The sign was written in Russian.

RAPE HER LIFE, RAPE OUR GAME

Before Dmitriy knew it, he charged towards the stand like a rabid dog. His teammates' confusion turned to horror in a heartbeat. Victor's déjà vu rooted him to the spot.

Dmitriy leapt clean over the rainbow-coloured advertising board just by a steward, who had not realised quickly enough what was going on to stop it. His studs clattered up the concrete steps. The man in the mask threw his banner towards the steps Dmitriy was charging up and tried to run along the row away from him. He scrambled over the man seated next to him as the wild-eyed player reached his row. The fan at the end of the row leapt out onto the steps, allowing Dmitriy in. The next few jumped bolt upright, unable to get out of his way fast enough as the man tried to force an escape route.

As Dmitriy got three seats along the row, a long arm reached up from the row in front and grabbed the front of his waist. He tried to rip it off him to no avail. Then a second hand locked around like a rugby tackle. He kept pulling forward, but the human anchor made hard work of it. Two other arms wrapped around his torso, halting his progress completely as yellow-jacketed stewards dashed up the steps at both ends of the aisle.

'DIMMY!' cried Charlie in his ear. 'Dimmy, stop!'

He snapped out of his craze and peered down to see Finney's face squashed against his midriff. The captain's arms were clamped around him and Finney's body was sprawled across a fan on the row in front. Charlie was hanging on to the playmaker's upper body like a koala on clinging onto a tree during a storm.

Along the row, the man had leapt down to the row in front and gotten tangled up with some fans, who had taken exception, grabbed him, and wrestled him to the ground. The stewards were making their way towards him and a handful of police officers were running over.

Finney let go, got off the fan, and apologised to him. 'Dimmy. Come on. They've got it,' he said as he squeezed his midfield partner's shoulder.

'Come on, fella,' said Charlie, relaxing his grip but encouraging him backwards with his hands.

Tens of thousands of pairs of eyes gawped his way. His body deadened as his adrenaline dumped. Trembling, he turned and let Charlie lead him out of the row. They met Finney on the steps and walked down past the discarded cardboard banner. At the foot of the stairs, the referee waited. He lofted a red card overhead.

The crowd erupted in a chorus of boos apart from the travelling fans and a few pockets of fans in The Old Mill, who clapped and jeered.

In a daze, Dmitriy took a pat on the back and some words in his ear from Finney and trudged towards the tunnel, which Cas and Steve were jogging out of, having heard the explosion of noise whilst making their way out after chatting in the dressing room. They saw Dmitriy's state.

'What's happened?!' asked Cas.

'I'm sorry, boss. I'm sorry.' He walked straight past them.

Cas looked concernedly at his assistant and back after his playmaker. 'You start with them,' he said, pointing out to the pitch. 'I see what's happened.' He jogged after Dmitriy.

Steve watched them for a moment then marched towards the pitch. As he exited the mouth of the tunnel and saw his players all in concerned conversation by the Weavers' bench, two police officers hurtled past him.

CHAPTER 21

Cas listened on as Dmitriy recounted the incident – what the sign said, who the mask was of – to the officer.

'If you'd have gotten much closer, they may have had grounds for attempted assault,' said the officer.

'And what about me? They can say these things and it makes no problem?' asked Dmitriy, still fuming.

'Well, I'm guessing it'll make a problem here at the club for them but criminally, with his message not referring to your sexual orientation, those terms aren't covered by our hate speech legislation so it's not a police matter. I'm sorry, Mr Lebedev. As vile as it is, there's nothing we can do about it.'

The officer wrapped up the chat and left. Cas gathered his thoughts as Dmitriy took off his shirt and bundled it in his hand, the rainbow badge staring him in the face.

'Is horrible, Dmitriy,' said Cas. 'You shouldn't have to put up with it. I'm sorry.'

'It not your fault. But you see there are too many of these things,' said Dmitriy, flinging the balled-up shirt at the base of the laundry bin with no intention of getting it in.

Cas's mind was momentarily overcome by the image of a black and gold shirt zipping by his feet. 'I do. The club will take care of him.'

'And the banana?'

'Of course,' said Cas.

'And the alarms? And the whistles? And the songs? And, and, and?' He eyed Cas. 'Too many things. Maybe it's not possible to control. But maybe the club loses control because it goes too weak.' He pulled his boots off. 'You speak to McGlynn yet?'

'Not yet. Tomorrow,' replied Cas.

'Please, boss. Make him see.' Dmitriy rolled down his socks and took off his shinpads. 'Go. It's finished. They need you out there.'

Cas watched his dejected playmaker heave himself to his feet and peel off his underlayer. 'Is not finished. We pick it up after.'

COLIN
And Velasquez re-emerges on the touchline to find his team pinned back by the visitors. His ten men have held them at bay for the first ten minutes of this second half, but the Surgeons are really dragging them around, probing for the spaces to slice through.

PETE
Cas is conferring with his assistant Steve Frank as the subs continue their warm-ups. His wide forwards have dropped back into the midfield to somewhat compensate for Lebedev, but he has an issue here. Finney's looking leggy – he was struggling towards the end of the first half, after very little football since his return, and this frantic start to the second hasn't helped him. If Cas replaces him with fresher legs, that leaves them very inexperienced in the middle.

COLIN

Yes. And with Xavier out, they lack a player of his type too. The Surgeons' move breaks down on the edge of the area and the ball goes wide to Allen. That high press is straight on him, covering the angles down the line and back to Cope. He plays inside to Finney, and again there's that pressure, from the front and the back. The best he can do is a hopeful ball forward towards Ezemonye. And the Reds win the header and come again.

PETE
It's just wave after wave after wave.

A few minutes later, during a pause in the game when one of the Surgeons received treatment, Cas trotted over to Finney, who was slurping a drink on the touchline, his chest heaving up and down as his lungs tried to pull oxygen in. 'Ian, I take you in a few minutes, yes?' Cas said, patting the captain's shoulder.

'Nah, gaffer, I'm good,' said Finney before drawing in a few deep nose breaths and covering his eyes with his free palm.

Cas watched him with suspicion. 'How does the knee feel?'

'The knee's grand. It's my lungs burning a hole through my chest, but it's good for me. Can't get match fitness without matches, eh?' he said as he opened his eyes. 'Besides, who else is gonna hold this together?' he asked, obscuring his mouth from the cameras.

Conflicted, Cas eventually nodded. 'You wave us if is too much.'

Finney took one last slurp and threw the bottle to a teammate. 'Gaffer . . . I'm Luther Vandross here,' he said, smirking then clapping to the few teammates nearby as he jogged back on to the pitch.

COLIN

Juliansen plays it up to Goldwasser on the edge of the area. The striker plays it first-touch out right and Organon plays it immediately to the overlapping Bragg. The box floods with red shirts. Bragg cuts them all out, chopping it back towards Juliansen, who's stayed free on the edge of the area. Another last-ditch block from Finney! The Weavers clear it for a red throw as Vaucanson helps his captain off the floor.

PETE
Look at Organon sprinting to take the throw. They smell blood here.

COLIN
Bragg gives it back to Organon, who switches it to the other wing, dragging the weary Weavers across again. Panizzon plays it forward to Li, who bounces it back out to Juliansen. Panizzon's bombing after that. He gets the cross in. And once more, Finney cuts it out and clears his lines, giving his team a moment to reorganise.

PETE
Again, look at that hunger and energy to retrieve the ball just for a throw-in. That's unwavering loyalty to the manager's vision.

COLIN
Oh wait. There seems to be a problem in the Weavers' penalty area.

He fell like a Redwood, dully thudding the earth without any warning of 'Timber'. As his teammates and opponents ran towards him and waved frantically towards their benches, Finney's limbs flailed violently. His entire torso convulsed, arching and flexing forcibly and erratically, as his eyes rolled around in his skull. As the arm-flailing died down for a moment, Charlie rolled Finney onto his side and tilted his head back, opening his mouth.

The medical staff of both teams ran on, trailing Cas, who sprinted on in a blind panic. As he reached the crowd assembled round Finney, he stopped and eased people aside for the medics to get through. As the convulsions began to calm and Chris, Neil, and the Surgeons' team doctor tended to the unconscious midfielder, Cas caught eyes with Amber before pulling his attention back to his captain.

After a few minutes of care, the medical staff stretchered the now conscious but bewildered and exhausted Finney off the pitch to a small chorus of taunts from the Surgeons' fans. The Weavers' players were almost as pale as their home shirts as they watched him go past the warming-up substitutes along the sideline before disappearing down the tunnel. Cas called the potential replacements over, conferred with Steve, and asked one to ready himself.

'Is he gonna be alright, Cas?' asked Charlie, who was at the head of the group of players now gathered near the bench.

'I hope so. He's awake. They say is good. He's in good hands.' He paused and looked around his downcast players. 'I know at the time like this, is difficult to bring our minds here, but we have to. The game will not stop. The fans, they are still here. Ian, you saw how he fights today. He wants the win. We need a big last section, guys. A big performance.' After imparting some new tactics and much-needed energy to his players, a question came from the back of the pack.

'Who's skipper now, boss?'

Cas scanned around the faces in front of him. 'Dom, do we have another armband?'

The kitman dug around in a bag, emerged with a rainbow armband, and passed it to Cas, who walked into the pack. 'You ran them very hard,' he said as he fastened the band onto Victor's arm, much to the striker's surprise. 'Keep it going. Lead the guys with the example. Show the captains who aren't here what He made you of,' he said, pointing skywards. He patted the striker's arm, faced back out to the pack, and clapped loudly. 'C'mon, guys. We give it everything for the ones who are gone!'

A short, sharp applause and yell came back his way. The players slapped hands and first bumped as they jogged out, most still somewhat pale-faced and haunted. Victor pulled his armband up, peering at the dazzling colours against his off-black sleeve as his mind churned.

WEAVERS 0-4 SURGEONS
FT
(HT 0-0)

Lebedev (45' ■)

Organon (79')
Li (83')
Goldwasser (87')
Nixon (OG 90')

'Unlucky, Cas,' said Magnus as he shook his opposite number's hand after the full-time whistle. 'You can't account for happenings like that. Is your captain OK?'

'I don't know,' said Cas. 'I have to go see.'

'Fingers crossed. We'll take a rain check on the drinks. Go.'

Cas trotted away, giving Amber a cursory nod before disappearing into the tunnel. Magnus adjusted his glasses as he looked up to the executive boxes. He spotted his son, who was standing to leave, and waved his way. Gunnar saw but just carried on along his row.

The players and Cas jogged back into the dressing room. Finney sat on a physio table over near one of the benches chatting with Chris, Dmitriy – now in his casual clothes – and a few staff, including a nervous Neil, nearby. He looked depleted but his eyes were alert.

'You alright, Fin?' asked Charlie as everybody moved the captain's way.

'Are *you*?' asked Finney, baffling Charlie. 'How many fingers am I holding up?' said Finney, raising his two fuck-off fingers on each hand. *Jesus*, lads.'

'Cloons. Come on, fam,' said Victor. 'Ten men. Then you doing the electric boogaloo. And dem man . . . fuck, fam . . . they were relentless like dat liquid metal don from Terminator.'

'Terminator two,' corrected Finney.

'That was a cognitive test, fam.'

The guys chuckled.

'So, what's the news?' asked Victor. 'You epilatic or somethin'?'

'Epileptic, you mean?' laughed Finney, raising an eyebrow.

'Cognitive test two, fam. You passed with flying colours.'

Finney turned to the medics. 'I think he needs to come in with me.' He turned back to Victor. 'You ever thought of a name change from *Easy* to *Simple*?'

'Ha ha *ha*,' fake-laughed Victor as the others laughed at Finney's comment. 'C'mon, big man. My mum epilates her tash.'

'Just for me,' replied Finney.

'My man goin' to hospital or what?' Victor asked Chris, drawing a nod. 'Best get him there. Man thinks he's funny. Full psych eval necessary.' He hugged Finney tightly. 'I'll pray for you, fam.'

'Ha. Cheers,' said Finney. 'It's just something daft. I'll be grand.'

The players let out a collective sigh of relief as more wished him well.

Cas made his way through to Finney. 'You have us worried there, Ian. You sure you OK now?'

'I think so,' said Finney. 'Obviously gonna get the once-over but looked worse than it was.'

Cas hugged his captain's head to his chest momentarily. 'I come to the hospital after if they let me.'

'No need, gaffer. I'll be sound,' replied Finney.

'Rest well,' said Steve, shaking Finney's hand before making his way out with Cas.

Finney shook Dmitriy's hand. 'No more hulking out while I'm gone, yeh?'

Dmitriy nodded as he smiled wryly.

Finney eased himself off the table and grabbed his bag that Neil had packed. As he turned, his heart stopped. Walking in was Mr Davis with his clipboard and cool bag.

'Good evening, gents,' the tester said to a lukewarm reception. 'Can I borrow you for a few minutes?'

'Me?' blurted out Finney as every muscle clenched.

'Not today, Mr Finney,' he said, pointing past him. 'Mr Nixon. Come with me please.'

A wave of relaxation overcame Finney as Nixon trundled past him towards Mr Davis. Finney faffed for a moment to allow Mr Davis time to get out of sight before he said goodbye to the team and headed out with Chris, Neil, and the medics.

The players went to their places and began undressing. Dmitriy sat at his, peering at the floor.

'*You* alright?' Charlie asked as he untied his boots.

Dmitriy nodded, still looking at the floor.

'Did that fella have a mask on of that lass you . . .?' Charlie trailed off.

The other side of Charlie, Victor's ears pricked up as he began to lift his shirt.

'Uhuh,' muttered Dmitriy.

'What did his sign say?' asked Charlie.

Barely raising his head, Dmitriy answered, 'It say "You rape her life, you rape our game".'

'Fuck me,' replied Charlie, stopping what he was doing. 'That's bang out. No wonder you were gonna tear his head off his shoulders.' He resumed taking his boots off. 'Some people are mental. You can't let the crazy shit they say get under your skin. Easier said than done, like.'

Dmitriy nodded, his mouth scrunching to one side.

The other side of Charlie, Victor stood with his shirt half over his head, as he had been for the last ten seconds. A text notification sounded in his bag, snapping him back into motion. As his shirt came off, the armband dropped to the floor. He stared down at it for a long while before picking it up.

Half an hour later, the dressing room was almost empty and completely silent.

'We will solve it,' said Cas.

Dmitriy blew out a big, hopeless breath. 'I know. You speak with McGlynn tomorrow.'

As Cas sheepishly nodded, Steve looked his way, puzzled.

Andriy stormed in through the dressing room door. 'I'm so sorry. They wouldn't let me through with all the trouble,' he panted. He carried on over to Dmitriy and wrapped his arms around him. 'Come on. Enough of this place for today.' The agent stoically nodded to Cas and Steve – a downgrade on his usual pleasantries – as Dmitriy grabbed his bag.

'Tomorrow?' said Dmitriy to Cas, in a tone more demanding than asking.

'Tomorrow,' replied Cas. 'Rest well.'

Dmitriy and Andriy left without a goodbye, leaving the manager and his assistant gravely looking at one another. As they turned out into the corridor, McGlynn and the film crew came their way.

'Boys, boys. Glad I caught you,' said McGlynn, picking up his pace and triggering the crew to up theirs too.

'Not now, Andy,' said Dmitriy.

McGlynn put his brakes on. 'Guys. I'll take care of this for you. I just need—'

'Not now,' snapped Dmitriy as he and Andriy strode past the owner and his crew.

'Dmitriy!' called McGlynn after them, to no response.

Andriy parked the Aston outside Dmitriy's house and unclipped his seatbelt.

'Stay here. I'll only be ten minutes max. I'll say hello to Mama, pack a bag, and be straight back out.' said Dmitriy.

'No,' said Andriy, opening his door. 'I'm coming to say hello to Iryna. Neanderthals aren't going to drive us out of every fucking space!' He climbed out of the car before Dmitriy could object and slammed his door.

Dmitriy unfastened his seatbelt and rushed out. 'Relax. I just want to get in and out. We can unwind at yours.'

'I am unwound,' said Andriy as he yanked his scarf loose with his leather-gloved hands and unbuttoned his overcoat.

'Mama,' called Dmitriy as they entered and moved through the hallway. 'Mama.'

'Dima,' came a sob from down the hallway.

The couple looked at each other and sped up. They reached the kitchen to find Iryna sat at the dining table, make-up cried down her face, a couple of empty wine bottles in front of her, and one of Alexei's architectural models on a seat beside her.

'He's gone,' she howled, picking her near-empty wine glass up off the roof of the model.

Dmitriy swept the glass out of her hand, laid his other arm around her, and pulled her close. 'Gone where?'

She sniffled against his scarlet jacket. 'Back to Russia.'

CHAPTER 22

Black hood up, Victor got out of his Focus, closed the door gently, and crept round to open its boot. After checking over his shoulders to see the poorly lit street behind him, he heaved two of the six holdalls out onto the tarmac, softly shut the boot, and locked the car. He slung one bag over his shoulder, picked the other up by its short straps, and scurried towards the front door. Dumping the handheld bag, he fished a key out of his pocket, opened the door, pushed the bag on the floor inside with his foot, and edged in, delicately closing up behind himself. He flicked just one light switch, bathing the hall in a low glow of yellow light, and carried on in, leaving the two bags under a pew. Two more tiptoeing round trips later, carefully and stealthily locking every door he opened behind him, he shoved the last of the bags under the pew and went to open the church's back door. As he came back in, he turned off the lights, lit some candles near the lectern, and sat over the bags. He bowed his head, interlinked his fingers, and mumbled, 'Please.'

Fifteen minutes passed before he heard footsteps at the back door, sitting him up straight. He lifted himself off the pew, tiptoed into the aisle, and sat himself two rows back as the footsteps loudened. Out of the dark corridor that led to the back door emerged Jack in his ten-gallon hat, his arms outstretched at his sides.

'Though I walk through the valley of the shadow of death,' he rejoiced as he sauntered to the lectern. 'Come on. Finish it for me, fellow child of God.'

Victor eyeballed him. 'I will fear no evil.'

Jack clapped his hands slowly and grinned. 'I'd have bet my house *again* on you going with the Coolio version. It's definitely more fitting for you . . . boy.'

'Yo, fuck you, man. Just take your dollar and go,' said Victor.

'That's not very Christian of you, *Easy*. Remember, your pastor told me I'm welcome here any time. I think I'll stay a while,' he said, running his hands down the sides of the wooden stand ahead of him before opening the cover of the large Bible sat on it.

'C'mon, man. The bags are here. They been here for months. I'll carry 'em to your car myself. Just let's get you paid, get out, and draw a line under it,' pleaded Victor.

Jack flipped to the first page proper. 'In the beginning, God created the heaven and the earth. You know, I never actually read this shit. It's meant to be pretty good. Five stars on Godreads,' he smirked. 'And the earth was without form, and void; and darkness was on the face of the deep. Darkness. Deep. And the Spirit of God, yada yada . . .' he flipped a page, '. . . here we are . . . so God created man in his own image, in the image of God created he him . . . bit repetitious . . . God said unto them, be fruitful, and multiply . . . fellas!'

Two hefty men, both dressed in camouflage jackets and balaclavas, stepped out of the shadows of the back corridor.

'. . . and replenish the earth, and *subdue it*.'

Victor leapt to his feet. 'Yo. What the fuck is this, man? Your money is right there!'

'Victor. You had the chance for this to be just about the money. That time's long gone. I don't just want your money,' said Jack as he strutted out from behind the lectern and joined the masked men, who strolled in Victor's direction.

Victor eyes darted past them towards the back corridor. 'Yo, Chuks!'

As Jack and his men turned to look at the empty doorway, Victor sprinted towards the church's front door. As he got there, footsteps thundered towards him. He fumbled for his key. Got it. Towards the lock.

'Fuuuuuck,' he yelled as they grabbed him. The key flew out of his hand as they wrestled him to the ground.

'Best say your fucking prayers, boy,' said Jack as he pinned Victor's head against the floor with a hand on his forehead and duct taped his mouth shut.

'HEY!'

Everyone's head turned towards the back corridor where Chuka stood, eyes bulging as he spotted his brother on the floor under the knees of the two balaclava'd men. 'Get off him!' he roared as he marched in before tipping the Bible off the lectern and yanking the wooden reading stand and post off its base.

Jack stood up and laughed. 'Now now, Pastor. We just have a bit of business with your little *bro*. Let's not make his sins yours.'

Chuka kept coming, the post held over a shoulder as his free hand pulled his purple necktie off and shoved it into his pocket. 'A friend loves at all times, and a brother is born for a time of adversity.'

Jack tapped his men on their shoulders, pinning Victor's throat with his knee as they stepped forward, and pointing Chuka's attention towards his holstered hunting knife. 'Really? You're going God squad in a moment like this? You got no better last words than those?'

Chuka upped his pace. 'Ezemonye for life, bitches.'

The two men pounced his way. One took a jab from the lectern post square to his face, sending his stumbling backward. The other man became more measured in his movements as Chuka spun the post to attack next with the reading stand end. He swung it like an axe a few times, pushing his opponent back but missing, and then began jabbing with it again. His opponent lunged forward and tried to grab the post, but the pastor slipped his grip. Stepping backward, he spun with the post like a hammer thrower and cracked his assailant round the head with the stand, stunning him.

The first man, blood trickling from his mouth hole, came again. Chuka shoved him off with the post, only for the man to come again and grab it in a tug-of-war. After struggling for a few seconds, Chuka let go, causing this opponent to fly back and stumble over the pews. Wrapping his removed necktie around both hands, he scrambled after the fallen man, mounted his back, and began choking him. As the man spluttered and struggled to escape, Chuka smashed his head repeatedly off the nearest pew.

The other assailant grabbed Chuka's foot out from underneath him, trying to pull him to the floor, but as the pastor kept hold of his necktie chokehold, the pull lifted his body almost horizontal. Chuka spun along the axis of his captured foot and the tie and, with his free foot, smashed the assailant in the head, crashing him to the ground.

As Chuka's ankle got free, his horizontal, rotating body fell, pulling his necktied opponent crashing down with him, bouncing his balaclava'd head off the solid floor. Chuka released the chokehold but kept the tie, rolled to his feet, and punted his floored opponent in the back three times. He turned to face the other balaclava'd assailant, who had just climbed to his feet and raised his fists like a boxer.

Chuka raised his in kind and looked through the ceiling to the sky. 'Forgive me for what I'm about to do to this filthy *mumu*,' he said, flipping into the thick Nigerian accent his brother enjoyed mocking with.

Still pinned under Jack's knee with a blade near his face, Victor could not help but wheeze out a chuckle.

The assailant poked out a few range-finding jabs, then darted forward and swung a big overhand. Chuka dodged in and *crunch* – front kicked his opponent's kneecap a few degrees backwards, toppling him with a squeal. Chuka turned to his brother and Jack, who waved the hunting knife his way.

'A-fucking-men,' said Jack. 'It appears we're at a bit of a stalemate here, doesn't it?' he continued, toting his knife back towards Victor. 'You want little brother safe and well. I want my money, a nice hot chocolate, and bed.'

'What money?' asked Chuka.

'There are a few bags under the benches near the front,' said Jack. 'Let me and the fellas get those, and we'll be on our way.'

Chuka looked at the two groaning men picking themselves up off the floor and then back at his brother and the knife. 'Get out and never come back.'

'Not a problem,' replied Jack as he stood and let Victor up, pointing the knife towards Chuka now. 'Better things to do with my Sundays, anyway.' As he smirked at his own comment, Victor volleyed his legs out from underneath him. Walloping the floor, the knife bounced out of his hand towards Chuka, who rapidly reached down for it.

'You FUCKIN' DICKHEAD!' roared Victor as he smashed Jack in the face, violently aborting his effort to get up. 'You couldn't just fuckin' leave it!' he bawled as he stuck the boot in again as Jack tried to slide away. Victor stamped on the side of his ribcage before his older brother pulled him away.

'Watch them,' Chuka ordered his younger brother, pointing to the men in the balaclavas and passing him the knife, before thumping two more kicks into Jack's back, leaving him writhing in agony with his hat off and a wig on the floor. Victor glanced over; his eyebrows raised high at seeing Jack's bald head.

Chuka pulled the tie out of his pocket, wrapped it round both hands, quickly span it twice around Jack's neck like a makeshift noose, and began dragging his writhing body along the smooth floor. As he kicked and struggled for breath, Jack's face trickled a trail of blood that smeared as he slid. Victor caught up with him, wielding the knife to drive the other men back.

'You think you can come into my church, God's house, and hurt MY BROTHER?!' bellowed Chuka as he hauled Jack's flailing body along like a sack of potatoes. Jack spluttered an unintelligible answer as his men backed up. 'I see you again, I see anyone who walks like you, or even breathes the same as you, any of you, and I swear I will come find you and end you. Do you understand?!' Chuka boomed, enunciating each word with aplomb.

The balaclava'd men nodded. Chuka stopped and bent down to eyeball Jack, still with the tie tight around his throat. 'Do *you* understand?'

His eyes protruding, Jack coughed as he nodded desperately. Chuka released the tie and threw him to the pew where the holdalls were.

'That their money?!' Chuka asked his brother, shocked at the number of stuffed bags. Victor sheepishly nodded. Chuka disapprovingly shook his head and sighed. 'Take it, go, and never, ever cross our paths again.'

Jack clambered to his feet and grabbed two of the bags. 'Come on then!' he yelled at the other two, kickstarting them to grab two each. Battered and bloodied, they lumbered out with the heavy bags in hand, one of them almost hopping. Chuka and Victor, still with the knife, following them right out of the back door. As they headed to their blacked-out Vectra, Chuka mentally registered the license plate number.

'Ezemonye, motherfuckers! Ya dun know!' hollered Victor at them as they got in the car, drawing a sharp nudge from Chuka.

The brothers kept their eyes on the car until it was out of sight and only went back inside when it was out of earshot.

Victor plonked himself down on the front pew, dropped the knife by his lap, planted his face into his hands, and exhaled all the way down. 'Jeeeesus, fam,' he said, lifting his gaze. 'Still got it.'

Chuka shot daggers at him. Victor quickly made the sign of the cross and mouthed 'sorry' to the ceiling.

'Thanks, bro. That wasn't good.'

'Wasn't good? Wasn't *good?*' said Chuka with absolute incredulity, rendering his brother speechless. The elder brother shook his head and stared at his junior. 'Go get the dustpan and brush and the mop out of the storeroom. You can help me clean this mess up.'

Victor's knee jerk reaction was to suck his teeth, but he quietly quelled the action, barely making a sound, before getting up and strolling to the storeroom. As he was gone, Chuka wandered over to the pew and picked up the hefty hunting knife. He held its blade up to reflect the candlelight behind him, moving it to admire the glimmer dance across its high sheen surface. As he altered its angle, he pointed it towards the back of the church and, beyond its tip, noticed the ten-gallon hat and wig near the front door. A thought dawned on him. He caressed his finger along the knife's blade, then ran it along again harder. The blade was completely dull.

Victor returned, put the cleaning equipment on and against the pew, and tapped his brother's shoulder. As Chuka turned his way, he threw his arms around him. 'Ezemonye for life, bro,' he said, holding his senior tightly.

After a long embrace, Chuka tapped the knife's blade on his brother's back. 'This thing's a fake, you know. Might be able to chop an apple with it if you're lucky.'

'Don't mess, fam.'

'I'm not,' replied Chuka. 'Straight up fugazi. You just got jacked by some plastic thugs.'

Victor let go and Chuka passed him the knife to inspect.

'How much cash was in those bags?'

Victor pressed his finger against the dull blade. He looked up at his brother, mortified, before his eyes flickered towards the fund thermometer.

'How much?!'

The rain rolled down Cas's windscreen. Set on slow, the wiper eventually swept the sheet of rainwater aside, exposing the grey skies ahead. He turned the radio on. The host wrapped up her chatter. The first three piano notes of John Legend's 'Ordinary People' sank his heart. His finger hovered over the off button for a moment before he left it to play.

She answered the door in an oversized chunkily knitted cardigan and an open scarf that covered half her torso. 'Come in,' she said, giving him a wide berth to enter past her.

'Can I get you a coffee? I can do you a *Bombón*?' she asked as they sat across from each other in the living room.

'No thank you.'

'Tea? Water?'

'Is fine. I'm fine,' he assured her.

She settled her fidgeting and took a deep breath.

'Is OK. Relax,' he said to her. 'Is us.'

'It's us,' she echoed back, nodding.

'You look beautiful,' he said, causing her to break her eye contact momentarily.

'Thank you,' she meekly replied. 'You look nice too. The all black actually works better with that hair for some reason.'

'I'm glad you like. So, you want to speak?'

'Well, yes,' she said. 'I think it's overdue, a proper talk. Not by text. In our best states to talk.'

Cas winced. 'I'm sorry about your office. I shouldn't come to you like that. Maybe I shouldn't come at all. But Magnus, he invite me. It was very nice of him.'

'He is nice.' She paused. 'You don't have to apologise. What's done is done.'

'What's done is done,' he said, trailing off as his eyes glazed over momentarily.

'By the way, is Ian OK?' she asked.

'I think so,' said Cas. 'I go to see him last night. He seems fine himself. They say they do some checks, maybe he's out today or tomorrow if all comes back clear.'

'It's horrid to see somebody just drop like that out of nowhere,' she replied. 'So scary. Life can be so fragile and short.'

'I know,' replied Cas.

'And Dmitriy?'

He tilted his head and his mouth contorted. 'I'm just glad Ian grabs him. You know what that sign says?'

She nodded heavily. 'They translated it on the news.'

'These people are animals. Maybe he deserves Dmitriy to get him . . . the bully gets his medicine.'

'Maybe,' replied Amber. 'I just don't know where that ends.'

'Me too,' agonised Cas before looking out of the window for a long while. 'Is good to see you.'

'It's good to see you too. I miss you.' Regret swept across her face the moment the sentence left her mouth.

'I miss you too. I just want to be here with you.'

She averted her eyes. 'I don't trust you.'

'I know you don't. There's nothing I can say to make you do it,' he said animatedly. 'Please let me show you that you can trust in me again.'

'It's not that simple,' she said.

'Is simple if you want it to be.'

'It's not. There are other things.'

'I know,' he said.

'No,' she replied. 'There are things you don't know.'

'Amber – I don't care about the guy or the baby. I want to be here with you.'

Her jaw dropped. Her face jittered as she processed her new understanding. She rested her hands on her hidden bump. 'How . . . how do you know?'

'I see you at the restaurant with him months ago,' he said. 'Then I see your bump yesterday when I walk past your dressing room.'

She raised her hands to her face and dragged her fingers down her forehead, the bridge of her nose and her eyes splitting them apart as she sighed.

'I love you,' he said. 'Is it serious with this guy?'

In shock, her head began shaking a few seconds before she got her answer out. 'I . . . I don't know.'

'So be with me. He doesn't matter.'

Her eyes searched for her words. 'He matters. I'm having his baby.'

'He can see his baby,' Cas said, rapid-fire. 'But me and you, we are together. We raise it.'

'Cas—'

'I know how much you want the baby.'

'It was an accident, I swear,' she said.

'Is OK. I want to be with you. I will look after the baby like is mine.'

'But it's not your—'

He cut her off again. 'Doesn't matter. I make the commitment to you. For better or worse. I love you and everything that is yours.'

Pained, she tried to interject again. 'Cas—'

'I will show you. I promise.'

'I want a divorce,' she blurted out.

Her words knocked the wind out of him. He had to look away. He did not want those words attached to her image. He eventually looked back. She looked deflated too. 'But I . . . I want to be with you. I want to raise your child.'

She peered down at her lap. 'And so does its father.'

They sat in silence. Cas gazed off into the distance, through the walls, his mind's eye finding the playhouse in the garden. Its bright tiles shone in the sun, but a quick glance at the window reminded him it was actually pouring with rain. He rose to his feet. 'And so does your husband. Till death. *Infinitamente,* remember?' He headed for the door.

'Cas.'

He ignored her call.

'Cas,' she repeated, no louder but brimming with emotion.

He stopped and turned.

'I'm sorry.'

He carried on out.

CHAPTER 23

His chubby little fist, adorned with gold sovereign rings, knocked on the double door. 'Come in'.

Arnold ran a hand through his strands of hair, adjusted his suit jacket lapels, and entered. Sat at the head of the boardroom table was the Warrior's manager.

'Gunnar! How's it hangin'?' Arnold schmoozed. 'Happy New Year!'

'Happy New Year,' Gunnar replied in kind, a smile plastered across his face. 'Please . . . take a seat.'

'Umm, I'd love to chit-chat but I'm not actually sure I'm in the right room. I think I was meant to see Malc and maybe Salih.'

'They pass on their apologies. They're unable to attend but please, take a seat,' he said in a customer-service voice. 'They're perfectly happy for me to act on their behalf. How can I be of service?'

'Hmm, I appreciate you taking the time to be so welcoming, especially with your busy schedule and all, but unfortunately, I really think I need Malc and Salih. I'll reschedule with them.'

'No, you won't,' said Gunnar, his friendly tone persisting as he stood.

'Excuse me?' said Arnold.

Gunnar strolled in his direction, eyes and smile on him all the way, and pulled out a wheelie boardroom seat just ahead of him. 'You came all this way,' Gunnar grinned. 'Let's speak of this important business you bring. Sit,' he said, offering the seat to Arnold.

'Honestly, I really think I *need* those other two. Sorry for the inconvenience, Gunnar.'

'It's no inconvenience,' said Gunnar, with the disposition of a Stepford Wife. Hands gripping the top of the seat's back, he rolled it behind his creeped-out guest. 'Because you're going to,' he laid his hands on top of Arnold's shoulders and shoved down, buckling the agent into the seat, '*sit.*'

The perturbed Arnold watched his host saunter around in front of him and sit himself on the table, where he towered over him.

'What can I do for you, Arnold?' asked Gunnar, his eerily friendly grin still strong.

'You know what, Gunnar. This is about what I can do for you,' said Arnold, pointing his two stubby index fingers at the looming Icelander.

'Ooo. You can do something for me? It's not every day somebody offers to do something for me. What can you do for me, Arnold?' asked Gunnar, his glinting eyes wide.

'Well, you have some valuable inventory that is maybe surplus to your requirements. I can get you top dollar for it – a tidy profit – if we act fast. There's nothing like shelf-space and a fat stack of Benjamins to fill it as you please.'

'Everybody loves a fat stack of Benjamins,' said Gunnar, rubbing his hands together gleefully.

'Damn fucking straight,' replied Arnold, nodding like the sales manuals told him too.

'This valuable inventory,' said the Icelander. 'Are we by any chance talking about Bryan Lawler?'

'We are. Judging by the minutes you've been giving him this season, it seems like your plans for the team lie in a different direction. You're a winner. You know what you want, you know what works for you. If Bryan no longer fits your picture, I'm sure I could get him off your hands. Player of the year for the league champs. Overseas club so he doesn't strengthen a domestic rival. Like I said, you get a big payday and the opportunity to bring in somebody fitting your desired profile. My client gets some minutes, a decent payday, and maybe even a bit of sunshine if he's lucky. Win-win!'

'Win-win!' Gunnar parroted back, even his expression matching Arnold's.

'So, what do you reckon?' asked Arnold.

'What do I reckon?' Gunnar lowered his head as he considered the situation. 'How tall are you?'

Arnold recoiled in confusion. 'Five four. Why?'

'Five four. Wow. What a world we live in,' marvelled Gunnar.

'How's that?' asked Arnold.

'You almost couldn't write it. These chairs in here. Divine, aren't they?'

Arnold frowned in befuddlement. 'Very comfortable,' he said with a shrug.

'We had this guy come in. Custom chairmaker. Ergonomics expert. Italian leather and all that. He told us this story about going to do a chair fitting for some sheikh or some oligarch . . . I forget . . . but this guy wasn't in. Just his wife. Absolute little bombshell. She shows him to the office, giving him the eye while he's doing his fitting. His tape measure is *up*, you know?'

Arnold nodded along, wrapped up in the story.

'So, he has this model chair that he brings in to check against the height of the desk, which he told me is exactly the same height as this desk here, and she sits in this model chair and licks her lips his way and tells him to come sit on the table in front of her.'

'No.'

'Yep. She sucks him off on her husband's desk. Takes it all.'

'Jesus.'

'And this man, this expert in ergonomics, you know what he buzzed off most?'

Captivated, Arnold shook his head.

'That in that height seat,' he pointed at the seats around the boardroom table, 'with him sat on a desk of this height,' he tapped the desk, 'with the perfectly angled lean forward, her upper body was the perfect proportions to give him the perfect blowie.' He locked eyes with Arnold. 'She was *five four*.'

Arnold slowly recoiled again. 'What the fuck is wrong with you?'

'Just laying out my terms,' he said, tilting his head gleefully. 'If we act fast, of course.'

Arnold pushed his feet into the ground to roll his seat back, but Gunnar leaned forward, grabbed its arms, and held it in place. 'You feel that, you greasy little globule? That's where Bryan's going,' he said as Arnold tried in vain to budge. 'Fucking nowhere until I say so.' He pulled him a few inches closer, looked the little agent up and down, and sneered. 'Now fuck off.' He shoved Arnold back in his chair, crashing it into the wall behind him. Arnold sprang out of it and scurried out of the boardroom.

As Cas stormed out towards the training pitches, Steve struggled to keep pace with him. 'When's the news about Dimmy's ban landing?'

It took Cas a moment to register that Steve had spoken. 'Sorry. What?'

'Dimmy. His ban. When will they announce?'

'Umm, tomorrow I think.'

Steve nodded and continued speaking.

The words reached Cas's ear drums but fell short of his brain. The final word of Steve's question had triggered a sickening feel and a mindless twiddling of his wedding ring. 'Ian?' was the next word he tuned back into as they arrived at the staff huddle on the sideline next to the players limbering up. 'Ian, yes. Maybe just the man,' he said, gesturing to Chris. 'I videocall him earlier. Did they make any more news since after breakfast time?'

'No, not yet,' replied Chris.

'Actually, there is. They gave me his bloodwork results to pass along,' interjected Neil. 'They said it was an isolated episode and that he should be out later today or tomorrow at the latest.'

'Gracias a Dios,' Cas said, looking to the heavens before raspberrying out a sigh.

'Do they know what caused it?' asked the team doctor.

Neil rubbed his stubble. 'Yes, they do. I'll fill you both in on the details after the session, yes?'

'OK, OK.' Cas turned to look at his players skipping along. 'Actually, can we do here now? Put the minds at ease?'

Neil's face reluctantly tightened. 'It's probably best after. Besides the boys are into their session now.'

'Is OK,' replied Cas. 'We don't have to interrupt. They are focused now. You can tell us though.'

Neil gurned and removed his glasses. 'It's nothing, really. Just a reaction to some medication he's been taking.'

'Medication?' asked Chris.

'Yes,' replied Neil. 'For the knee.'

'Is that in my records?' asked Chris.

Before Neil had a chance to respond, Cas chimed in. 'The knee medications make the things like this happen?'

Neil wiped his glasses on his jacket and dropped them. 'It's not common but I can go into the detail of it with you later.'

'What detail?' asked Cas as Neil picked his glasses up. 'Was it a painkiller or . . .? Do we have to worry about any of the others?'

Neil sighed as he slid his glasses back on.

'What were you giving him?' probed Chris.

'Yes, what is it?' asked Cas.

'It was for his knee, but it wasn't something we usually give for an injury.'

The team doctor raised an eyebrow as the huddle listened intently.

'What do you give it for?' asked Cas.

Neil paused. 'It's generally used for things like Parkinson's and Alzheimer's, but it helps the tendons heal faster.'

'So why you don't want to tell me?' asked Cas, seeing Chris shaking his head out of the corner of his eye. 'What's the problem?'

Neil gritted his teeth. 'Well, it's pretty heavy-duty stuff, as you saw, and . . . it produces something that *could*, if not monitored properly, have had him fail a drugs test.'

Cas shouted a whisper. 'Is illegal?!'

'No, no. But it increases growth hormone and if you have too much of that, they can ban you.'

Cas stepped closer to Neil. His volume raised. 'Why you give him something risky like this? You risk his career, his life.'

'He begged me to. His career was on the line anyway. He has no contract beyond the end of the season. Then Xavier got hurt. He just wanted to be back in; to help.'

'So the player tells the physio his job now? And you give him drugs?' Cas rasped.

'Cas, please,' said Neil, his palms up.

Cas turned to the doctor. 'Did you know about this, Chris?'

The doctor shook his head. 'First I've heard.'

'Look,' said Neil, 'I know what happened was awful, but I made an oath to help my patients and, unfortunately, helping them isn't always black and white.'

Cas encroached Neil's space. 'An oath? AN OATH?!'

The players slowed, all their heads turning towards the shouting.

'You don't know what an oath is! He fell down to the grass like he would die, and you tell me you make the oath to look after him?!'

'Cas, he asked for treatment,' replied Neil, speaking in his most calming tone. 'I monitored him closely. I honestly don't know how this happened, but sometimes, with the variability in people's reactions, these things just happen. Nobody meant for this.'

'These things just happen?!' Steve laid a comforting hand on his manager's shoulder, but he batted it away. 'You play with his life and these things just happen?! Get out,' Cas ordered. 'You're done here.'

Neil looked over to Chris and received a regretful shake of the head. The physio lowered his gaze and much like a player who had just received his marching orders, raised an apologetic hand to the team and trudged towards the training complex.

His former colleagues and patients watched on sorrowfully, having never seen their manager shout somebody down with such ferocity before.

The Spaniard turned to his players and pounded a pointing finger into his palm repeatedly. 'We sign the contract here. We wear the badge together. We should mean something to each other. We should mean something to each other and act like it, always.'

Steve laid his palm on Cas's shoulder again, this time calming him. 'Go on, lads. Back to it,' he said to the players, setting them in motion again.

Dmitriy dropped a shoulder left and darted right, taking the ball away from the mannequin, then hammering it over the plastic wall a few yards inside the penalty area. At full stretch, Cope fingertipped the ball onto the bar.

'Quality,' called Dmitriy, clapping his colleague before turning and strolling back towards the balls a few yards along the empty training pitch. He gathered one and looked up to see Cope back up and ready in the goalmouth.

'It's time,' came the call, stopping Dmitriy just as he was about to set off. Andriy and Cas were walking towards the pitch. 'Make this last one a good effort though, yes?' Andriy added with a smirk.

Dmitriy grinned back, thumbs-upped the 'keeper, and took off. A different dummy at the mannequin, another piledriver of a shot over the wall. At full stretch, Cope could not get to this one, but it ended with the same sound – a clang off the bar – anyway.

'Had it covered,' said Cope as he rolled to his feet and Dmitriy jogged his way, drawing a little chuckle.

He bro-shook his goalkeeper's hand and jogged towards the duo waiting on the sideline.

'I thought you'd at least finish with a shot on target,' said Andriy with a wry smile.

They briefly greeted the seated TaloVision crew as they passed and entered the boardroom, where McGlynn waited at the head of the table.

'Gentlemen. How are we all?' he said as he got up to greet them, receiving nods and small-talk answers. 'How are you today?' he asked Dmitriy with a more sombre tone.

'I'm OK,' said Dmitriy flatly as they shook hands.

'Please,' said McGlynn, gesturing towards the seats.

As everybody sat, Andriy looked over at McGlynn. 'Are those guys just waiting outside or . . .?'

'Yep. Part of the job. On hand in case of good news,' said McGlynn with a winning smile.

Andriy nodded back and grinned reservedly.

'OK. First thing's first. Yesterday was obviously an embarrassment to the club,' said McGlynn, sliding his notebook towards himself. 'The idiot with the mask and the sign; he's been given a lifetime ban. He wasn't a season ticket holder. He'd bought a ticket for cash and we don't even know if he was a Weavers' fan.'

'Was he Russian?' asked Andriy.

'I don't think so, no,' answered McGlynn. 'Probably thought he was a smartarse and knocked it up with Google Translate. Anyway, it's obviously raised our attention to the possibility of people sneaking in abusive signs in different languages so we're banning all non-English signs apart from those for visiting fans in European ties.'

The Russian couple looked at each other tentatively.

'What about the foreign fan clubs who are always here? The ones they have the flags every week?' asked Dmitriy.

'Unfortunately, they're going to have to get new ones. One cretin spoils it for everyone,' said McGlynn.

Troubled, Dmitriy sat with it for a moment. 'But maybe I'm not here soon so what's the point?'

'We'll get to that,' said McGlynn. 'Let me just get through a few other points first. Obviously, we'll be releasing a statement condemning the perpetrator and saying something to the effect of "we don't support violence in any way, shape, or form, but we support our player as a person unconditionally during these difficult times during his victimisation by the hateful and intolerant minority that football must eradicate". Maybe not the word *eradicate* but something along those lines, anyway. That sound alright?'

Dmitriy shot Andriy a consultatory glance, cueing him to respond. 'I'm sure something along those lines will be fine.'

'Good, good. Obviously, there's a ban coming for you. We'll appeal it if it looks like we have grounds to. I'm hoping it's not too strong given the context.' McGlynn opened his notebook. 'Between us, I'd love to see cunts like him get a slap.' As he flipped to the relevant page, the three across from him all gave each other a little look.

'Here we go,' said McGlynn. 'Onto those God-awful personal alarms.'

'Personal alarms?' asked Dmitriy.

'Yes. You know, those devices ladies carry in their bags in case they end up . . . in trouble,' said McGlynn.

'He's making a hash of trying to say *rape alarms*,' said Andriy in Russian, clearing up Dmitriy's confusion.

'Yes,' said Dmitriy.

'They were the things making that terrible racket that you heard. As they're only small and they all look different, we can't guarantee that one will never get in the ground again, but we will be employing more search staff for outside The Old Mill, and they will be looking for devices like them during their searches.'

'Thank you,' said Dmitriy as his brow furrowed. 'What about the ladies who have them for the real purposes?'

McGlynn shrugged. 'Hopefully our environment's safe enough that there aren't many who feel the need to bring them in.'

'I think is more for after the matches,' Cas chimed in.

McGlynn shot him an irritated look. 'Yes. Well, I imagine there's a mobile app or something.'

Dmitriy turned to Andriy. 'If an app can do the same, you can't stop it anyway,' he said to him in Russian before turning back to McGlynn. 'Mr McGlynn.'

'Andy,' McGlynn corrected him.

'Andy. Thank you for trying to make all these things better for me, but really I think it's best for me to go,' said Dmitriy. 'Many fans here, they don't like me now, they think I change the club, and it makes me tired. I don't want to fight them, I don't want to change the rules for them; I just want to fight on the pitch for the wins. I gave you everything I can these last years. Please, let me go.'

McGlynn closed his notebook. 'Dmitriy. I'm going to do everything in my power to make this all better for you. While it might be a game of catch-up while these idiots find new ways to show their stupidity, as we show more and more we're not going to take it, they're going to see there's nowhere to go with it. We can tough this out together.'

Dmitriy drummed his fingers on the table. 'It's past this, Andy. I don't feel good here anymore. I don't know how to say. It's like your wife, she has an affair in your bed. You never want to sleep in it again.'

Cas's eyes glazed over as his fingers clawed into his thighs.

'Ha. *Nobody's* banging my missus in my bed, but I take your point,' said McGlynn. 'Look, Dimmy. We're on the edge of something special here. Look at where we came from. Remember some of those shitholes we had to play in a few years ago? Look at the stadiums we play in now. Look at what we could call our home in a few seasons time. We were a Beta League team through and through. Look at us now, challenging for the biggest league title in world football for the second season in succession! You helped us get here. We need you to help cement us here. Cas and I spoke all about it last week and I've had a big think.'

Dmitriy curiously eyed his manager, who had said the conversation with McGlynn was yet to happen.

'I want to show you how much you mean to us all, the fans included.' He turned his notebook over, opened its back cover, pulled out a handwritten slip of paper, stood up, and slid it across the table to somewhere between Dmitriy and Andriy. 'Let us show you.' He sat down as Andriy turned over the slip and read it.

4 more years. Double your money.

Andriy peered long and hard at the slip before looking at McGlynn.

'Biggest contract in club history by a country mile,' said McGlynn, beaming proudly.

Andriy nudged the slip over to Dmitriy, who picked it up and read it.

'Can you read my handwriting there?' asked McGlynn as he examined Dmitriy's impassive face.

Dmitriy nodded. 'Yes. It's big number. But you're not listening.' He tore the slip in four, dropped the scraps on the table, and stood. 'This is not about the money. It's about my life.'

Andriy stood with him and buttoned his suit jacket back up. 'Thank you for the very kind offer, Andy, but it's just not what we're looking for. Have a good day, gents.'

Astounded, McGlynn watched them to the door.

Dmitriy turned back his way. 'If the big offer comes for me. Please take it. For all of us.'

The duo exited, leaving Cas, his hands linked behind his head, opposite the owner.

'Win him round. I want that signature. You understand?' said McGlynn.

Cas raised his eyebrows. 'You see him. I try my best but maybe here there's no winning.'

McGlynn glared his way. 'What the fuck would you think if one of your players said that to you?'

Cas tapped his fingers against the table and began a miniscule nod. 'You're right.'

'I know. He's your player. Our player. Practically irreplaceable. Find a way,' demanded McGlynn.

Cas nodded as the owner closed his notebook. As McGlynn looked at the fragments of paper across the table, he chuckled to himself.

'What is it?' asked Cas as he rose from his chair.

'Just something he said earlier,' replied McGlynn. 'Banging *my* missus in *my* bed. Hilarious.'

CHAPTER 24

'There he is, the baddest man of the cloth. Layin' the wrath down,' hollered Victor as he closed the church door behind him.

Chuka looked up from the new lectern he was screwing together, shaking his head but with half a grin on his face. 'It's nothing to be proud of, little brother. And even if it was, pride is a fool's game.'

'I know, man,' said Victor as he swaggered in and removed his shades, 'but gotta take some pride in helpin' out your flesh and blood.'

'Well, I've prayed for His forgiveness,' Chuka said as he twisted in the last screw, 'but I take no shame in it.'

'*My* man,' said Victor.

Chuka put the screwdriver on the lectern, rolled down his shirt sleeves, and picked up his suit jacket off the back of a nearby chair. 'Where are you taking me then? San Carlo's? Ella Canta? The Araki?'

'Nah, man. We stayin' in. I got a real treat for us.'

A quiet five-part knock sounded on the church front.

'It's open,' called Victor.

In walked a young girl, no older than eleven, carrying two stuffed, unbranded plastic bags. 'Here you go, mister,' she said, bringing them towards Victor, who walked her way.

He took the bags out of her hands, snook a quick look inside them, and nodded. 'Yes, fam. Pleasure doin' business with ya.' He palmed her a fifty-pound note. 'Go get yourself somethin' nice, yeh.'

She pulled the fifty taut and held it up to the light.

'C'mon. You really gonna play me like that?' asked Victor.

She shrugged. 'Business be business.' She pocketed the note, turned, and as she headed out of the door, flashed a peace sign over her shoulder.

'Victor. What have I just witnessed?' said Chuka.

'Don't worry yo' head, *my brudda*. That was just her tip. Price for contraband. Worth every penny.' He put the bags down on a pew and lifted one of its contents overhead like a trophy – a bucket of Shabzy's Fried Chicken.

Chuka's jaw fell open. Then he chuckled. 'I thought you were taking me somewhere fancy?'

'Peri fries. Curly, fam. What's fancier?'

Five minutes later, they were side by side on a pew, elbow deep into their fried chicken feasts.

'No askin' for a selfie, an autograph, or nothin'. Safety in demographics, innit?' said Victor.

Chuka shook his head as he rotated a drumstick and slurped the breaded skin off it. 'You're not alright, brother.'

Victor reached out and pinched Chuka's bucket. As he went to slide it towards himself, his brother stopped him. 'Alright enough to know you weren't sayin' no to this. When's the last time you reckon we had some a dis?'

Chuka ripped some chicken off the bone and chewed away as he thought. 'Wow. It's been time, you know.'

'That's what I'm sayin'. I know our bodies are temples but in moderation, man can't tell me fried chicken isn't God's love.'

'Stop chatting that madness. Especially in here,' said Chuka, shaking his head and smiling gently.

'Sorry, man,' replied Victor, making the sign of the cross with a drumstick in his hand before realising what he had just done. He threw it back into his bucket, shaking his head before lowering it. 'Does He really forgive us? No matter what we done?'

Chuka looked over at his brother, whose tone and demeanour had transformed. 'If we truly ask him to, yes.'

'I been aksin', man. For time now,' said Victor. 'I ain't feelin' forgiven. Shit hasn't just washed out.'

Chuka threw his stripped bone into his bucket. 'I'm sure having that . . . *situation* hanging over you this last half year hasn't helped. Do you feel any better now it's done?'

Victor sighed. 'Relieved, yeh. Better . . . pff. It's mad, ya know. I bet a man *his house*. His house, fam. Was I gonna turf man out on the street if I won?'

'You think you would have?' asked Chuka.

Victor played with the drawstring on the neck of his hoodie. 'Honestly . . . yeh, I probably would. I'd have been like *fuck this ejat*. Man fronted up. Now he's gotta pay up. Wid a house like that, he can afford it.'

'What's it like?' asked Chuka.

'What's what like?'

'That *mumu's* house.'

'Must be an absolute crib for that dough,' replied Victor.

'You haven't seen it?' asked Chuka, an eyebrow raised.

'Nah, man.' Victor saw his brother's sceptical face. 'But he had a bag fulla cheddar and a crispy whip so—'

'And a fake knife,' Chuka interjected.

'Nah, man. You don't think . . .?'

Chuka shrugged.

'FUCK, man.' Victor sat gobsmacked for a long moment. 'Fuck. Guess I'll never know fo' sho. That cash, man. I'm in debt now. I'm gonna be paying for time. That's cash not helping the fam. That's cash not helping your ting,' he said, pointing to the fund thermometer.

'Back there's *our* ting, little brother,' interjected Chuka.

'Whatever, man. Point is, that'd've been boxed off many times over. Case closed.'

Chuka restrained his nod.

'And the team. I sold them out, fam. You know how hard they all worked? You know many people were depending on us? And I sold them all out cos I'm a stupid pussy'ole. He,' Victor pointed through the ceiling, 'mighta saved me but *I* . . . I was a pussy'ole. I chose not to bag, fam. I chose. I can't take dat back. Not ever. We coulda won that league, fam. That's on me.'

'Brother,' said Chuka. 'You could have played at one hundred for the entire game and it could have gone a different way. Maybe you'd have scored more, maybe less. What's done is done. You can't change that.'

'So, what do I do with it now, man?' asked Victor.

'You ask Him for forgiveness and do everything you can to win the next one,' replied Chuka. 'This Shabzy's aside, are you on that? Doing all you can?'

'C'mon, fam. You know me,' said Victor, his voice half an octave higher than usual. 'Puttin' the yards in. Gettin' myself in positions. Tryna live right.'

Chuka reached into his bucket and emerged with his peri curly fries, which Victor stole one of and sucked the salt off it. 'You didn't answer me. Are you doing *all* you can?'

A light feeling trembled in Victor's chest and arms as he considered his answer. 'You see what happened at the game yesterday?'

Chuka bit the end off a fry and nodded.

'Man, when that landed by my feet, well . . . you know,' he said with a heavy heart, looking away from his brother. 'And then I realised it was for him. I dunno, man. I dunno. And then when he went for that guy wid the mask. I was right there next to him. That don is lucky Cloons and Charlie stopped Dimmy cos man was vexed. I seen that look before.' He paused, his eyes flickering towards his brother. 'They stopped him. I just stood there.'

'Do you feel like you should have stopped him?' asked Chuka.

Victor cupped his face then ran his hands down it. 'Maybe.'

'Then why didn't you?'

A cocktail of contradictory thoughts shook around in Victor's mind. 'I dunno, man.'

'I think you do,' said Chuka.

Victor drumrolled his fingers on the pew. 'It ain't fair, man.'

'What's not?'

'Where was all this when that banana came at you?' asked Victor.

Chuka's nostrils flared and his lips narrowed. 'What's done is done, Vic.'

'What's done is done?!' said Victor. 'We should have been together, man. Ezemonye back to front. How many fucks were given then?'

'They cared, Vic. They tried to convince me. I just wanted out.'

'They could've made you stay,' replied Victor.

'Made me,' laughed Chuka. 'My mind was made up. Tell me, how's a grown man going to have his made-up mind changed?'

'They should have showed you they gave a shit more, showed everyone,' said Victor as he grew more exasperated.

'There's nothing they could have showed or said,' explained Chuka.

'There'll have been somethin'.'

'Do you know why I turned back? Why there's nothing they could have said?' asked Chuka, drawing a shake of the head from his brother. 'Because when I confronted that guy, I saw pure hate in his eyes. To him, I was absolutely subhuman. I was the shit on the bottom of the shit he'd trod in. I could have shouted at him all day, reasoned with him, whatever, and it wouldn't have changed a thing. He hated me. And I saw that, and I hated him. I saw myself killing him. I saw myself cracking him and stamping on his head until I couldn't see that hate in his eyes anymore. That's when I turned around. And that's why they were never going to get me to turn back.'

Victor witnessed his brother's seriousness. 'But it was one man, fam. You let one idiot change it all. You let him win.'

'He might think he won but I won too,' declared Chuka. 'Idiots like that, they don't want to change. They don't want the world moving in a positive direction. MLK said "the arc of the moral universe is long, but it bends towards justice". He was right. I wanted to help that bending, to be better than when I was young but for me, that wasn't the place. I want to be around people who want to change, who are open to it. Here, I am. That's my win.

Honestly little brother, I don't know how to help change the hearts and minds of those who don't want to change, who want to hate on others for things that they can't change and don't matter anyway.'

Victor dipped his head and gulped. 'You reckon those people, the racists and that, the ones who've done shit but maybe now they're questioning what they did and what they thought, you reckon they can change?'

'I do,' said Chuka. 'If they want to, they can.' Chuka ate another fry.

'You miss it, fam?' asked Victor as he pulled a box of crispy strips out of his bucket.

'The game? I ain't left it, little brother. Still boss you in fives, *innit*?' Chuka said.

'Pray on,' replied Victor.

'I'd be lying if I said I didn't miss some of it, but I'm good here and I think one of us is in the league is all it can take.' Chuka nudged his brother's shin with his shoe. 'Find peace, brother. Do *all* you can.'

Gunnar rolled the pushchair out of the patio door into the brisk evening air, gently closed it behind him, then slowly pushed Joki over to the garden table and sat. Apart from some bushes rustling and an owl hooting somewhere in the distance, silence surrounded them. Gunnar looked down at his son, whose eyes struggled to stay open. Feeling that watching would somehow jinx his sleeping, he turned his eyes away for a few moments, keeping an ear on the faint sound of the baby's breathing. When he looked back, Joki's eyes were shut. Relief washed over him. He arched back over the chair then relaxed before looking out into the dark woodland surrounding the back of their garden. Like a magnet attracted them, his eyes were drawn back to his son. Uncomfortable at the lack of control he felt in their movement, he moved them back towards the trees. The owl hooted again. As his concentration returned, he realised his eyes were back on his son. He let them stay this time. Sensations fluttered inside him; his heart beat a little quicker than usual, his neck and cheeks felt warm even though he could see his breath, and his stomach and throat felt strange.

Joki's face was the picture of peace. Something fell onto the tip of his nose. It was a snowflake. Gunnar looked up. Floating white flakes danced across the navy night sky. The icy crystal still sat atop his son's tiny nose as others drifted down onto him, mostly resting on his clothes and hat. Gunnar took out his phone, opened his camera, and snapped a photo. Night mode would not capture the scene in its serene glory. He turned on the flash, decided against it, and put his phone back in his pocket.

'So, you still do have a fucking phone then,' came the whisper out of the darkness.

Gunnar rose instantly, his eyes scanning the garden for movement.

'Relax,' said the voice again, a little louder this time, as Gunnar spotted a man limping across by the bushes towards him. 'It's just me.'

'What the fuck are you doing here?' whispered Gunnar, having recognised the voice.

'Nice to see you too. What choice do I have when you've gone AWOL?' asked Ted, his bald head catching the light first as he emerged out of the shadows.

'Keep it down,' said Gunnar, nodding to the pushchair. As he sat back down, he paused halfway. 'What the fuck happened to you?'

he asked as Ted's face appeared, both eyes black, gauze and tape over the bridge of his nose, and his right cheek profusely swollen.

'Team fucking Ezemonye,' whispered Ted loudly as he walked onto the patio. 'Look at this little bundle,' he remarked, sneaking a peak at Joki before helping himself to a seat.

'You let Victor Ezemonye do that to you?' asked Gunnar with a chuckle.

'I said *team*. His brother, mostly.'

'The one who used to play?' asked Gunnar, smirking.

'Yeh. He wasn't fucking playing about last night.'

'No,' said Gunnar, impressed and amused in equal doses. 'He wasn't. Maybe I should get the chequebook out.'

'Do what you want. I'm just here to say I'm done. I collected and he's off the hook. I didn't sign up for this,' he said as he gestured to his pummelled face.

'Oh, you're done, are you?' taunted Gunnar. 'At the first sign of trouble, you pussy out? It's your own fucking fault, anyway.'

'Fuck you. How's this my fault?' asked Ted.

'You got lazy. You found what you thought was a plump, easy target – pardon the pun – and you milked her and milked her till her bull showed up and saw red. You think I've got sympathy for that?'

'Honestly, it doesn't surprise me that you don't,' said Ted. 'A man who'll bring his own baby out to catch its death in the freezing cold isn't a man of much warmth now, is he?'

'Where I'm from, we put children to sleep in the cold. It's good for them,' said Gunnar. 'So they don't grow up to be little bitches.'

'Charming,' replied Ted. 'Anyway, I'm not sure it's the Weavers you want to be worried about this season.'

'Are you honestly going to try to tell me how to do my job?' asked Gunnar, amusedly incredulous.

'No,' replied Ted. 'I'm just saying what we started last season has snowballed. They've got bigger problems than their striker being off the boil.'

'Ted, you'll get what I owe you. You can stop selling me. And boring me,' said Gunnar.

Ted sat back and took a deep breath. 'What are you going to do about your dad?'

'Don't worry your battered little head about it,' said Gunnar. 'Out is out.'

Ted frowned. 'After all this, you're not going to tell me?'

'No. All I'll say is that our little tricks wouldn't work with him. He'd know it was me. And I'm guessing he'd know your face,' said Gunnar.

'Possibly. They have just ordered a few more bars from me.'

Gunnar nodded and pensively looked out into the shadows. 'So, you're well and truly out. End of an era. What's on the cards . . . aside from getting that horrific face sorted out?'

'I'm going to sell up and get out of dodge. With my little starter fund, there are sunnier, larger lands in which I can grow my empire.'

'So, this is *really* it?' asked Gunnar.

'Let's hope so,' said Ted.

'Let's,' said Gunnar with a tinge of bittersweetness.

Ted grimaced as he pushed himself to his feet. Gunnar got up with him and extended a hand across the table. Pained, Ted lifted his and shook it. Gunnar looked his accomplice in eyes, a hint of a smile and a nod emanating from him.

After the struggling man stepped away from his seat, he looked in on Joki again. A warm, wide smile fought its way on to his immobile face. 'No little bitches, ey?'

Gunnar grinned back his way. 'No little bitches.'

Ted limped away across the lawn.

'Hey,' Gunnar whisper-shouted after him, causing him to stop and turn. 'You'll be alright in a week or two. Kruggo's on that cane for the rest of his days,' he said, grinning ear to ear.

Ted slyly smiled back his way then continued hobbling out.

CHAPTER 25

His studs clawed up the concrete steps. He glared down the row. All those between him and his target stood bolt upright, making a clear path for him. All those the other side of his target blocked any escape from the row. The man stood dead still facing him, Emily's mask on and his cardboard sign held aloft.

Dmitriy tore along the row and decked the masked man with a huge right hook. As he jumped on top of him, the din of the crowd and the shrieks loudened but all his attention funnelled itself into the dull thuds of his fist repeatedly pummelling that mask, blood seeping out from underneath it as it crumpled under the weight of his blows. *Thud thud thud.* His fists were numb as he rained down shot after shot, dyeing the concrete beneath the man red. The crowd cheered on his brutal attack as the smell and taste of iron saturated the air. Finally, as his victim stopped moving, Dmitriy ceased and sucked in a few deep breaths. As he went to pull the once-beautiful, decimated cardboard mask off, the man somehow wriggled over onto his front and tried to crawl away. Dmitriy, still on him, grabbed the nearby fallen sign, its red-lettered message glaring him in the face. As the man tried to clamber forward along the blood-soaked floor, Dmitriy wrapped the sign around his neck and pulled it tighter and tighter until the struggle was done. The crowd were as loud as he had ever heard them, baying for blood. He let the sign go and rolled the man over to face him. The mask of Emily was a bloody pulp. He took it off, kissed it tenderly, pressed its forehead against its own, then dropped it into the seeping pool of blood below. Staring up at him was the crushed face of his father.

Dmitriy shot up out of bed, gasping for breath. Andriy was gone from next to him and the room was fairly light. He looked at the clock. 10:11. He jumped out of bed, threw a T-shirt and jogging bottoms on, and rushed downstairs. 'Why didn't you wake—'

'Because you slept wretchedly and it would have changed absolutely nothing,' said Andriy as he passed Dmitriy a freshly brewed espresso.

'Did they call yet?' asked Dmitriy as Andriy began to lead him over to the table where Iryna sat, her empty breakfast plate ahead of her.

'They did,' replied Andriy as Iryna pulled her son's face towards her for a kiss on each cheek, wishing him a good morning in their language.

'And?' asked Dmitriy.

Andriy pulled him out a seat and gestured in such a way that Dmitriy knew he would get no answer until he obeyed. He took a deep breath, sat, and pulled himself into the table as Andriy wandered round it and seated himself. 'Four matches. The club said they'll consult legal, but I think with it being a fairly conservative number of games, they won't appeal it.'

'Fuck,' he muttered as he stared at the dark, rich-smelling liquid in his cup, and downed it in one.

'It'll be OK, darling,' said Iryna. 'Four games will fly by. You could do with a rest with all this madness going on.'

'I don't want a rest, Mama. I want to show my worth so I can get out of all this as quickly as possible,' said Dmitriy, setting the cup down and springing to his feet, ready to head off.

'But rest you must, superstar,' said Andriy. 'Today is an off-day . . .'

'I'm going in to train anyway,' said Dmitriy.

'And Cas has given you an extra day off tomorrow,' continued Andriy. 'He said to relax and come back raring to go in a couple of days.'

Dmitriy shook his head and slumped back into his chair.

'He doesn't want to see your beautiful face until then,' Andriy carried on. 'They might not have been his exact words. He might have said arse.'

The words startled Iryna. Her wide eyes shot to Andriy. Andriy looked apologetically across at Dmitriy. Then Iryna burst out laughing. The guys blurted out relieved laughs of their own.

She wiped a tear from her cheek. 'Oh,' she said, catching her breath. 'We can have a laugh without that miserable oaf here.'

The guys smiled back at her, Dmitriy bittersweetly.

'Dima,' said Iryna, hesitating before carrying on. 'Your boss. He's not . . .?'

Dmitriy's brow furrowed. 'Not what?'

'Not . . . like you two boys?' asked Iryna.

'Noooo, Mama,' said Dmitriy. 'What made you ask that?'

'I don't know. He just looks like he might be, but then I didn't know my own son was. It's a whole new world to me,' she responded.

'He's married, Mama.'

She raised her nose and eyebrows with true scepticism.

'I think your,' Dmitriy flipped into English for a single word, '*gaydar* needs some calibration.'

'What's this? A *gaydar*?' asked Iryna.

Andriy chuckled. 'I'll tell you all about them later. Speaking of whole new worlds, not only do we you have some time off so we can all do something fun together, you and I have been invited to a party tonight, Mr Lebedev.'

'What party?' asked Dmitriy.

Andriy grinned. 'One where it wouldn't matter if your *gaydar* was calibrated or not.'

'Taxi for Finney!' came the call of a gruff Cockney voice.

Finney looked towards the door of his hospital room and laughed. 'That was pretty good for you,' he said to Victor. 'Does this make me Miss Daisy?'

'From the porno?' asked Victor.

'You what?' asked Finney, utterly baffled.

'Drive In Miss Daisy. Zum zum in de pum pum,' replied Victor.

'Wow. You do know that was a film about a little sweet old lady?' asked Finney.

'Not the one I saw, big man,' replied Victor. 'Times is changin'.'

A few minutes of shit-talking into their drive to Finney's house, Victor stopped at a red light as he grooved away to the radio. The billboard ahead of them scrolled to a new advert for Finney's wife's new album. Scantily clad, Nova looked over her shoulder, right into their car with her smoky eyes and pouting lips, with each of her hands resting across a bare male chest. Even though both men's faces were partially cut off by the photo, the dreadlocks laying on the shoulder of one of the men, combined with his skin tone, made Finney fairly certain this was Jiro, Nova's choreographer he met last season before his injury.

Victor looked over at his friend. Finney averted his eyes and peered out of his other side window as if he had seen nothing.

'Yo. Is she fo' real, man?' asked Victor.

'What?' replied Finney, maintaining his gaze away.

'Fuckin' 'Trois Trois Trois', big man. She's all over the news chattin' about poly . . . I dunno man, polystyrene or somethin'. Please tell me this is just some crazy clickbait viral marketin' shit?'

'Has it changed yet?' Finney asked, pointing out the front window but still refusing to look.

'Nah, fam,' said Victor, checking out the poster. 'She's larger than life.'

'I meant the light, you dickhead?'

'Ah shit!' said Victor as he glanced across to see the green light, right as a car behind them honked. He put his foot down and moved off, taking the billboard out of sight. 'Two of them?'

Finney kept his eyes out of his side's window, eventually sighing and nodding.

Victor shook his head and sucked his teeth. 'What the fuck, man?'

Finney combed part-way into his grey streak then slid his hand down over his face, covering his mouth.

'At the same time?' asked Victor.

'How the fuck should I know?' snapped Finney.

'Sorry, big man.' Victor paused for a long moment. 'This is just some fucked up shit, fam. She took your daughter with her to be around this?'

Finney shook his head. 'Lulu stayed with me. My Mum helps. A nanny too.'

'You fuckin' kiddin' me, fam? They were talkin' 'bout her like she's Mother Theresa,' said Victor. 'Brave. Unconventional lifestyle ting. Bitch abandoned her little girl. They ain't sayin' shit about dat.'

Finney shrugged. 'She wanted to take her, but I wasn't having it.'

Victor clenched the wheel. 'She left her own daughter, fam. Of her own accord!'

Finney nodded.

'How you so fuckin' chill, big man? She's making a fool of you.'

'She's making a fool of herself,' replied Finney. 'Nothing I can do at this point but leave her to it.'

'She's your wife, man. She made promises. She can't just do you like this,' insisted Victor.

'She is though, isn't she?'

Victor shook his head, flabbergasted. 'Literally puttin' it on show to the world, fam. Wid one man, the press'd be slaughtering her. But this bitch is gettin' brownie points cos it's with these two Village People. Shit's backwards, fam. And they're taunting *you* wid that shit!'

he said, trembling with incredulity. '"Nova, she takes it up the trois" on loop, fam, even when you were being stretchered off. How come they lettin' people disrespect you like dat yet they shuttin' down songs about Dimmy's shit?'

Finney finally turned to Victor. 'You think it makes a difference? Polyamorous, monoamorous? Whether those fuckboys fuck each other or they just take turns on her? She could be fucking three goats and a unicorn, all of different genders, one straight, one gay, one bi-curious, and one fucking Peter Pan sexual, for all I care. She's gone. That's it. Gone. Me moaning about all this pointless extra shit, what's it gonna achieve?'

Victor had no answer.

'You hear me? *Pointless extra shit*. What's it gonna achieve?'

'I heard you, Cloons,' said Victor, clamming up.

'Did you though?' asked Finney. 'Did you really?'

Victor glanced his way, hearing his annoyance.

'You think I haven't seen you these last few months? How you've been with Dimmy?'

Victor fixed his eyes on the road ahead.

'We knew if anybody was gonna give him chew it was you after how you were with Andriy. Lemme ask you this: what fucking difference does it make to you? You think he's checking out that sweet package of yours in the changies? You could go to any gym changing room in the land and have to get changed next to a gay man from time to time. And do you know what? You probably always did, you just didn't know it.'

'Would you have that with a woman, fam?' said Victor.

'What do you mean?' asked Finney.

'A woman in our changies?'

'See what I mean? *Extra shit*. We don't have a woman. We have Dimmy. What . . . are you scared he's gonna bum you?'

'Fuck off, fam,' Victor bit back.

'Are you scared he's gonna take a mental snapshot and keep it in the bank for a sesh later with One Eyed Willy?' asked Finney.

'What's wrong wid you, man?' asked Victor as he turned left.

'Wrong way there, rudeboy. And there's nothing wrong with me,' said Finney. 'How many people you reckon you've stashed away in your wankbank over your lifetime?' He examined Victor's reticent face. 'Can't count that high, can you, smart arse? You reckon all of them would approve?'

'You wanna get an Uber, fam?' asked Victor.

'You wanna stop being a bell-end?' asked Finney, prompting Victor to slow the car. 'Woah. Come on, Vic. You know I love you. I'm just saying this is extra, unnecessary shit. It's always been around. It's always been extra. Check out your good book. There's that story about those village folks who want to bum those angels to death. What's the village called?'

'I don't know what the fuck you've been smoking,' replied Victor.

'Come on. You must know the one?' said Finney.

Victor shook his head. 'Ain't in my book, man.'

'Nope, it's definitely in there. I went to a C of E school. It's *definitely* in there, cos there's another story just like it later on with a woman, and they actually do it to her.' He looked across at Victor's stony face. 'You haven't even read it, have you?'

'Course I have, fam,' shot back Victor.

'Course,' said Finney, nodding dubiously. 'This has been extra shit since Bible times and well before. If you believe in a man in the sky running this show, do you really think he gives two fucks about this?'

Victor shrugged.

'And even if he does, isn't it only him that's meant to judge?' asked Finney. 'Aren't you just meant to be treating others like you want to be treated? Like you'd have wanted your brother to be treated?'

Victor side-eyed Finney then turned his attention back ahead. 'You talk more than Chuks. You done, man?' He turned the radio volume up.

'And now,' announced the radio host, 'back at number one, with the release of her album by the same name, is Nova with the scorching 'Trois Trois Trois".

Victor turned the volume down immediately.

Finney reached across and turned it back up. 'Yep, I'm done. Are you?'

He held the butt of the rifle tight against his jaw and shoulder, gazing through its scope at the yellow target far off in the distance. Adjusting his camouflage-clothed body against the mat he laid on, he steadied himself and slowed his breathing. He laid his finger on the trigger as softly as an insect landing on a blade of grass. In. Out. In. He squeezed on the out. Even with the ear protectors, the bang blared and rattled through him. *Pop.*

'Yes, Cas!' said the instructor from behind him, admiring the dented target on the hillside around one hundred yards away. 'Excellent form, brilliant shot. Are you sure you've never done this before?'

Cas looked up over his shoulder with a grin and nudged his ear protectors off. 'Sorry?'

'Excellent, I said,' repeated the instructor. 'Are you sure you've never done this before?'

'I think I remember if I did.'

A few of the others along the row of shooters exchanged sour-faced glances as the instructor walked along to the next one. 'Whenever you're ready.'

A while later, as everybody headed towards the table of Thermoses and mobile phones, Cas rubbed his hands vigorously, trying to warm up. As a few of the shooters fished their phones out of the waterproof bag, Cas found his Thermos.

'So, none of you guys like football?' Cas asked the group around him.

'More of a rugby man myself,' said a hefty guy with a neck wider than his head. 'The gentleman's game,' he said with a smile as he opened his phone.

'I'm more motorsports,' said a lanky guy the other side of Cas. Like a bit of a tinker under the hood. When the missus lets me.'

The group chortled.

'How about you?' Cas asked an even taller man opposite him. 'They must have tried you in the goal when you were young, no?'

'Not really,' he replied. 'I was more of a tennis player until I filled out and then I was in the boat at five thirty every morning.'

'You know, I don't remember the last time I was with the people who don't follow the football. Is like a whole new world,' said Cas, thrilled.

'I think one or two of the younger lads are fans but as you can see,' said the rower, nodding over towards a few stragglers on their phones, 'they're not the most sociable. And their bad habits are contagious,' he continued, nodding towards the broad-necked rugby fan on his phone.

'You say your team's the Weavers, sharpshooter?' asked the hefty fella, his brow furrowed.

Cas nodded, then looked up to notice the concerned expression on his fellow shooter's face.

'Like this,' said Andriy as he pulled his scone apart with a slight twist, neatly detaching its top from its bottom.

Iryna copied him and smiled jubilantly as hers cleanly pulled apart.

'And now we go with the jam,' he said as he splodged a clump of raspberry jam onto one half of his scone.

Dmitriy stared at the dark red mass as Andriy spread it with his knife.

'And then the clotted cream.'

Iryna delightedly followed suit. Her son still had not touched his and was looking round the room, seeing if anybody was watching him.

'Relax,' Andriy assured him. 'We're just a bunch of tourists in here, treating our mother to the finest afternoon tea in the land. These aren't really our demographic,' he said, referring to most of the other diners being women around Iryna's age and older.

Iryna lifted her teacup. 'Cheers to that,' she said before taking a sip. 'If you would have told me this thirty years ago, that I would be in Britain drinking afternoon tea with the crème de la crème in a place like this, I'd have laughed you out of the room. You know what my first job was in the place I worked?' she asked Andriy, who shook his head. 'They wouldn't let me on the machines right away. I was the tea girl for, oh, about my first six months there. I didn't have one of those beautiful service trolleys and nothing like this,' she said, caressing the ornate teapot in front of her, 'but the water was piping hot and that was all that mattered. That factory was so draughty.'

'Here comes the nostalgia,' said Dmitriy. 'Look at those dreaming eyes.'

'Hey, don't tease. I loved that place. So did you. You were warmed through by many a cuppa in there while you waited for me after practise, gabbing away with some of the younger girls. I never should have left, you know. Those girls were like a second family to me.' She savoured her first bite of scone and made herself wait to speak until she had swallowed. 'Delicious! I imagine your work's a bit like that too?'

'What – like a sewing factory floor in the Ukraine? I think that English tea's gone to your head,' said Dmitriy.

She tsk-tsked his way. 'I mean with the guys. You've grown up with some of them. They must feel a bit like a second family?'

Dmitriy pulled his scone apart and jammed its insides.

A waitress pushing a silver service trolley holding patisserie cakes galore pulled up beside the table. 'Can I get you anything else at the moment?'

Andriy flipped into English. 'No. We're fine, thank you very much.'

'Fantastic,' said the waitress, wheeling away a yard before stopping again. 'I hope you don't mind me saying you guys are amazing.'

Andriy and Dmitriy smiled at each other and then at the waitress. 'That's very nice thing of you to say,' replied Dmitriy.

'Do you think you'll come?' she asked, her voice quick with excitement.

'Pardon?' Dmitriy asked.

'To No Man's Land?' she replied.

Dmitriy's brows drew together. 'Sorry?'

The waitress laughed at herself. 'Silly me, putting you on the spot like that. The tea lady trying to get the next scoop. My apologies.'

'No. It's OK,' said Dmitriy.

She gratefully nodded. 'Let me know if I can get you anything at all.'

As she moved away, Dmitriy turned straight to Andriy.

'I'm on it,' he said, already opening his phone. His mouth moved as if he was going to speak at any moment, but it took a full twenty seconds of clicking and scrolling before the words came. 'It's all over the news but I have nothing from the club.'

'What is?' asked Dmitriy.

'It's just talk, Cas. We've had no offer,' said McGlynn down the phone.

'Is not just talk when OmniSport and all the other big ones are saying it, is it?' asked Cas, keeping his volume low having found some space away from the group of shooters, a few of whom could not help but notice his intensity.

'Granted, they're usually solid. But there's nothing. It's probably those arseholes over there planting the story, just trying to add fuel to the fi . . .' McGlynn trailed off.

Cas heard an unusual sound down the line as McGlynn's silence persisted. 'Andy?' The next thing he heard was McGlynn shouting for somebody to come quick. 'Andy. What's happening?' All he could hear was rustling. Then a door closed.

'You rolling?' asked McGlynn, mouth away from his phone as something like a printer came to life in the background.

'Rolling?' asked Cas. No response came. Still sounding distant, he heard McGlynn call 'let's go.'

'Cas. You still there?' asked McGlynn.

'Of course I am,' replied Cas. 'What's happening?'

'I've just received a fax of a written offer for Dmitriy from the Warriors. Eighty-five million, just like the news said.'

Cas stopped breathing. 'Andy . . . please. I know is a lot of money but remember Bryan. We can't give them another.'

McGlynn paused. 'Yes. I couldn't agree more. There's no amount of money they could offer. Dmitriy is an invaluable member of our team. Thank you, Warriors . . .' said McGlynn before tearing something up, '. . . but no thank you.'

Cas shut his eyes and breathed a deep sigh of relief.

'I'll let the press know their money's *no bueno* here. Transfer denied. *Adios, amigo.*'

Cas covered his eyes as the call ended and wiped his brow before heading back over to his Thermos crew.

'Everything OK there?' asked the rower.

'Yes. Phew. How they say? Disaster aborted,' Cas said to the group before sharing in a collective chuckle.

A few minutes later, they were called to convene back with the instructor, who explained their next task. As the group picked up their mats off the grass and headed down the hill to their next location, Cas hung back to chat with a straggler at the back of the pack. 'How you like it until now?'

The straggler shyly bowed his head. 'It's alright.'

'Your first time?' asked Cas.

'Nah.'

'You just done the long shooting or the other things?' said Cas, trying to draw more conversation out of the awkward individual.

'All of it. The handguns. Clay pigeons. Crossbows.'

'Ah nice,' said Cas. 'Which is your favourite?'

'This.'

They walked on, wordless for a moment.

'I'm Cas. What's your name?' he asked, smiling the straggler's way.

'Winston. I'm Winston,' replied the straggler, adjusting his glasses over his slightly crooked eyes.

Suze laid her glistening cheek and arm across Lawler's chest as she snuggled up to him under the covers. She went to say something but instead just laid a kiss on his skin and gathered his nearest arm around her. Half sat up with a few pillows propped behind him, he gazed down at her peaceful, satisfied face and kissed her crown. She tilted her head back to look his way. Again, she went to say something but changed her mind, kissed him, and pulled his arm in closer.

A pang of guilt rose within him. 'Shall I shot some tunes on?'

'Yeh, go 'ed,' she said. 'The remote over your side?'

He spotted it on his bedside table and as he rolled for it, Suze grabbed him, trying to stop him reaching. 'C'mon, girl,' he laughed.

'I'm keepin' you nice and close,' she said, cutting him enough slack to allow him to get it.

As he turned the TV on and hit the menu button to search for the music app, Dmitriy's face was on OmniSports. The volume was low, so he scrolled along the app menu at a snail's pace to try to get a sense of the story.

Suze turned to the TV. 'Poor bastard,' she said. 'He should've twatted that div the other day. Maybe then they'd think twice.'

The story cut to footage of Gunnar. Lawler jammed the volume up and shoved himself more upright.

'. . .and if the bid is successful, Dmitriy Lebedev will be the most expensive signing in Alpha League history. Would his signing see him partnered with his old midfield partner, Bryan Lawler, who has found minutes harder to come by this season?'

Suze turned back his way. 'Would 'im comin' be good for you, hun?'

Lawler hit select, loading the music app. 'Since soft lad Arnie shit his whack yesterday, I'll take any change I can get.'

CHAPTER 26

Andriy dusted off Dmitriy's navy blazer shoulder and primped his baby-blue dress shirt collar. 'Look at you. Properly dressed for your night at the ball.'

'Piss off,' chortled Dmitriy, relaxing back into the car's back seat.

'I just wish you'd have picked a more colourful one,' Andriy said, pressing the collar's fold down even crisper.

'I've had enough colour for a lifetime,' said Dmitriy. 'And besides, are you really going to lecture me on colour?' he said, grabbing Andriy's black lapel. As always, his full outfit was black, but for once his shirt was without a tie and down two buttons, and blazer and trousers, still immaculately cut, had a velvet finish.

'I'm giving you a preview of a certain other team's colours,' Andriy said, running his hand along his sleeve before flashing his gold watch, 'just in case'. They turned the corner and began slowing. 'The moment of truth. Are you ready?'

Dmitriy shrugged. 'How about you?'

'I have a confession to make,' said Andriy. 'I've been to one before.'

'When?!' asked Dmitriy.

'When you did your summer trip back home the day before me the other year, before the team got promoted.'

Dmitriy raised his eyebrows. 'Why didn't you say anything?'

'Because I knew I shouldn't have gone and opened us up to any risk whatsoever. I'm sorry, my love,' Andriy said, taking his hand.

'Ah well. Doesn't matter now,' said Dmitriy. 'But you have insider knowledge. How was it?'

Andriy leaned forwards, raised an eyebrow, and laid a hand on his chest. 'An experience.'

The car pulled up.

'I'd say don't do anything I wouldn't do, but fuck me, that'd be a shit night for you,' said Barry from the driver's seat. 'Lap it up, fellas . . . just keep it out the papers.'

The guys grinned, thanked him, and got out. The queue along the front wall was long. As Andriy began towards the head of it, Dmitriy paused. Andriy looked back, saw his trepidation, and extended a hand to hold. The two walked hand-in-hand for the first time outdoors since their summer holiday and the first time ever on British soil towards the brightly lit sign of the club, Sod'em.

The blare of carnival music grew louder as they walked through the dark corridor. Opening the doors at the end, the darkness gave way to dazzling light and colour. Even though it was only 22:30, the place was heaving and the dancefloor was packed. Dmitriy had not frequented many clubs in his life, but he had never seen one with so many people dancing so early. And dancing so joyfully.

Having spied a cordoned-off area towards the back corner, Andriy began into the crowd, keeping hold of his partner's hand. As they eased their way between the gyrating and frolicking bodies, smiles beamed their way. Dmitriy was used to being smiled at by masses of people but they were always smiles of recognition. Here, he could tell half of these people did not know who he was. The ones who did appeared extra excited.

'Maybe we overdressed,' said Andriy with a grin as they passed a couple, one in just leather suspenders, hot pants, and knee-high Doc Martens, and the other in a leather chained biker's cap, tiny denim shorts, and work boots. His torso was painted with a glittery lightning bolt and he blew the whistle in his mouth with gusto.

Dmitriy smiled back with a mixture of bewilderment and amusement as they kept going as the occasional hand reached out to paw at him.

They eventually emerged from the lively crowd at the velvet roped-off section. The gigantic bouncer, who looked like a Hispanic version of Barry but wearing purple glittery eyeshadow, smiled broadly, unhooked the rope, and invited them in. Everybody here knew them and were delighted to see them as they continued in.

'Oh my God, oh my God, oh my Gooooooood!' came the familiar shout as the angular-haired receptionist popped out of a booth as they passed. 'I can't believe you guys made it!'

'It's good to see you again,' said Dmitriy with a big smile, offering his hand to shake.

The receptionist ignored the hand and dived in for a hug before kissing the slightly taken aback Dmitriy on each cheek.

'Shakes are for fakes,' he chirped as he let go and swooped on Andriy. Dmitriy spotted Paul making his way over.

'Guys! Guys! Welcome!' Paul shook both their hands. 'Thank you so much for making it. We saw that atrocity the other day. Are you alright?' he asked Dmitriy.

'I'm OK, thanks,' replied the player.

'Good. Tonight's a night to forget all that shite. Come on over,' he beckoned, gesturing over to a booth. 'Champagne awaits!'

'Do you have some orange juice or maybe some water?' asked Dmitriy as they followed.

'For you, I'm sure we can find some somewhere,' said Paul, turning back with a huge smile.

A flute of orange juice and champagne later, the chat was flowing. 'So, you never snook into one of these places in a hoodie and shades?' asked Paul.

'Not once,' replied Dmitriy. 'The risk was too big.'

'Well, this isn't the most glamorous place you'll ever go but you should have a fabulous first night *out* out here and we're privileged it's with the NBP gang. If ever we were to use the term 'guests of honour', it's for you guys.' Paul raised his glass. 'Everyone,' he shouted as he climbed to his feet on the booth's leather bench, trying to attract the attention of everybody in their section. 'To the brave ones that changed the game . . . and the world. Cheers to Dmitriy and Andriy.'

Everybody raised a glass or a fist to the toast and echoed his cheers. Dmitriy and Andriy clinked their empty flutes together and smiled gratefully around the section.

Paul gave a thumbs up in the direction of the DJ booth. As he sat down, an announcement came.

'This next one,' said the DJ, 'is for a very, very special couple.' He mixed the current song into Ricky Martin's 'Cup of Life.'

Dmitriy and Andriy smiled gratefully to Paul and around the group, who boogeyed away.

'Do you know this?' asked Dmitriy in his partner's ear, trying to mask his confusion.

'No,' replied Andriy in his ear, keeping his smile wide, 'but it sounds like that chap Ricky Martin.'

Lots of chatter and a couple of champagnes later, a tune came on that caught Andriy's attention. Sat in the end of the booth, he slid out to stand and offered Dmitriy his hand. 'May I?'

'What?' asked Dmitriy, his expression falling.

'Have this dance?' said Andriy.

Dmitriy shot him a look.

'Darling. You've done scarier things. Please. I love this song.'

Dmitriy grimaced and looked at the faces around him, all willing him on. Andriy smiled like a kid in a sweet shop at him. He gulped, found a smile, and slid out of the booth, much to the delight of everyone else around.

The two strolled beyond the velvet rope onto the main dancefloor, which was even busier now. Swimming through a sea of smiles and nods and winks, they eventually found a pocket of space. Andriy immediately moved to the beat. Dmitriy tentatively followed his lead. His body loosened a little as he went, but his attention leapt from point to point around the dancefloor. Plenty of fellow dancers met his eye contact in a friendly manner. A sizeable minority appeared more than friendly. Even the ones who were not looking directly his way were restraining themselves from doing so, at least in his mind.

'Hey,' said Andriy, pulling him close. 'It's just you and I.'

Dmitriy half-smiled and held Andriy a touch closer, using the movement of his partner to tune his more resonantly with the rest of the song. Closing his eyes, he could enjoy the music, Andriy's touch, and the energy of the room more without feeling so self-conscious. Under the darkness of his eyelids, he even kissed his partner for the first time in public. As the song eventually changed, Dmitriy fell out of rhythm and parted from Andriy to look at his face. 'Maybe more later?'

'Of course,' said Andriy, winding down and nodding towards the velvet rope. 'Let's go.'

'You don't have to come,' said Dmitriy. 'Stay. Dance. Enjoy it.'

'You sure?' asked Andriy.

Dmitriy nodded, slipped Andriy's blazer off, and kissed his cheek, before patting the shoulder of a guy in a dance circle next to them. 'Can you look after my friend? It's only his second time.'

Andriy laughed as the circle welcomed his and winked at Dmitriy as he walked away, heading back towards the magazine's private section. On his way, something out of the corner of his eye caught his attention. His heart skipped a beat. A polka dot dress and a checked lumberjack shirt beside each other. The dress was worn by a voluptuous drag queen, the shirt by a bear of a man. He carried on towards the roped section, trying to breathe out the sick feeling that had arisen.

'How are you finding it?' asked Paul as table service brought Dmitriy a new orange juice to the otherwise empty booth.

'Everybody's very friendly. It's nice.'

'He looks like he's enjoying himself?' said Paul, nodding out towards the dancefloor.

'Yes, he loves to dance.'

'And you?' asked Paul.

'Not so much as him.'

'I bet it's in there somewhere. You just haven't really been granted the opportunity to find it.'

'Maybe,' said Dmitriy, to be polite.

'And how is everything else?' asked Paul.

Dmitriy shrugged. 'Could be better but could be worse.'

Paul looked at him long and hard. 'It's OK not to be OK, you know. Very few people have ever been in the position you're in right now.'

'I'm OK,' said Dmitriy.

'We're here for you, all of us at NBP, you know. We've all had our little slices of hell. Maybe we can help you digest some of this. Maybe we can help you fight back.'

'I not need to fight,' said Dmitriy. 'It only gets me in trouble. You see, yes?'

'I saw. But you don't have to fight with your fists,' replied Paul. 'There are too many of those hateful creatures to go about it that way. They want you to snap like that. "Look at little Nancy boy trying to act tough". In their eyes, it'd just give them even more permission to be even more violent towards you.'

'So how you fight them then?'

'With your words,' said Paul, locking eyes with Dmitriy. 'They can scream and shout and send you horrible messages galore, but you have a louder voice than all of them put together. Your voice can take their voices away.'

Dmitriy swilled his juice around its glass. 'The club, it already makes the bans for the fans it catches. Really, I don't know what more they can do for it. Maybe it's the best for me to go somewhere else, try again with the people who know what they get with me.'

Paul sighed and gave Dmitriy a heartfelt look. 'I can't imagine how hard it is for you. All those judging eyes. All those voices. I know your country haven't recruited you yet this year. But I can't imagine it'd feel great letting all those hateful vermin know they won either.' Paul paused and mixed his cocktail with his straw.

'Your voice and your image can drown it all out. Do you have any idea how many people are craving your words?'

Dmitriy shook his head.

'We've had to have work done to bolster out website, it crashed so many times with the traffic to people watching your interview. If you keep speaking out about it all, your club, the league, the governing bodies, the government, they're going to have to act. With your profile, if you can stick it out, you can do more for hate against gay people here than has been done in decades.'

'What do you mean?' asked Dmitriy.

'I mean that more of these people and their hate can be stamped out. Take, for example, that abominable sign that thug had the other day. Under the current laws, that sign isn't classed as criminal. We all know it was based on your sexuality, we all know that "fuck your rainbow" is homophobic, and the clubs can choose to fine and ban people for those things, but it's not enough. You've had to hide who you were most of your life so far because immorality isn't illegality. These people are trying to force you out of a sport you've given so much to. Force you out of your livelihood.

I'm saying you can fight these thugs with your words and your image. The more you speak and put yourself out there, the more seriously all the authorities will have to take this. The more serious the punishments are for acting in such vile ways, the less willing they're going to be to act. They want you out of your livelihood, but would they dare act on it if they knew it would cost them theirs? If they risked jailtime for trying to be even slyly homophobic?'

Dmitriy took a sip of his drink as he mulled over Paul's words.

'We have relationships with civil rights lawyers and campaign groups. We can give you as much airtime and column space as you want. Our front cover is still waiting for you if you want it. They need to know their savagery can't be tolerated anymore. If you're willing to push through, we can put a stranglehold on all this. All the other Dmitriy's in the game can know that this is our game too.' Seeing that Dmitriy was growing uneasy, Paul took a sip of his drink. 'Ooof, sorry I got so heavy there. It just really gets me sometimes, what you're going through. But tonight isn't about that. Tonight is about you being able to be you around a bunch of people who you can be completely yourself around. Tonight is about love. Go find your treasure of a man out there. Be with him.'

Dmitriy nodded, downed his drink, bid Paul farewell, and shuffled through the swaying bodies until he found Andriy, his black shirt drenched in sweat as he boogeyed away with his new friends. As he kissed him on the cheek, Andriy took his hands and tried to lead him into dance.

'I'll be back in a minute. I need the toilet first. You want a drink from the bar when I come back?'

'Ooo, please. Something long and wet,' said the tipsy Andriy.

Dmitriy grinned and shook his head, kissed his cheek again, and headed through the crowd to the toilets. As he unzipped himself and began using the urinal, an unmistakeable sound came from one of the stalls behind him: flesh slapping against flesh. He kept his eyes on his stream of urine as the sounds grew faster and groans began. As he zipped himself up and turned, the stall door was wide open, showing the two men inside going at it. The man closest to the door, trousers down around his ankles, looked over his shoulder at Dmitriy and grinned his way, before the player averted his gaze. He washed his hands, dried them on his trousers, and raced back out to the bar.

Whilst waiting to be served, Dmitriy noticed a miserable thirty-something year-old woman leaning against the bar, her mascara smudged a little. She swirled the ice cubes at the bottom of her glass as the rest of her body swayed before she looked up and locked her stare on Dmitriy. After a few seconds of awkwardness, he smiled her way. 'Are you OK?'

Her glower persisted.

'Can I order you a water or something?' he asked her.

She pointed her empty glass at him then plonked it on the bar behind her. 'You.'

'Yes,' he said. 'I'm Dmitriy. What's your name?'

'Emelia,' she said. 'Emelia Shields. I know your name.'

'Can I get you a water or a Coke or something?' he said.

'My husband follows your team. Season ticket. He loves you. If he was here right now, he'd be proper fanboying you,' she said with a slight slur. 'He'd want a selfie with you or your autograph.'

'Please tell him thank you. I appreciate all the support,' he said as the barman came over. 'Just three bottles of water please.'

'On his cock,' she said.

'Excuse me?' said Dmitriy.

'He'd want your autograph on his cock,' she said.

Her let her strange, drunken comment go.

'You know, I fucking love these places,' she continued. 'Came with the girls plenty. I even brought him a few times down the years, I like them so much.'

Dmitriy recoiled slightly.

'No! Listen to me. Listen to me,' she said as her eyes teared up. 'I love you people. But it's not fucking fair . . .' she said, trailing off.

'What?'

'What you do to us. What you did to that poor, gorgeous girl. What he did to me. He saw . . .' her lip quivered, '. . . when you came out, and he cried. I sat with him on our sofa while tears rolled down his face, saying it was amazing what you did, saying he couldn't believe how brave someone could be. Then a week later, I come home and he's got his bags packed. He can't do it anymore, he says. He can't lie to himself anymore. And he leaves me.'

Dmitriy was flabbergasted. 'I'm so sorry. I . . . I—'

'Nine years I was with him. Nine. Do you know what that does, having somebody pull the rug out from underneath you like that?'

Dmitriy shook his head as a cringe to hold of him.

'All those "I love you"s. All that life we shared together. All those promises,' she said, twisting her wedding ring. 'All those doubts I had about how attractive I was cos he barely wanted to touch me as the years went on. It was never the right time for kids, but it was fine to buy a house in *my name* that's pulling *me* under now,' she despaired. 'And now *my* job's at risk cos I called him a gay bastard to a colleague one lunchtime and they reported me. I just said the words next to each other. He's gay and he's a bastard, and they reported me! I work for a bloody cancer charity. Where's the bloody compassion for *me* when I need it?'

The bartender put three waters on the bar and held out the card machine, jolting Dmitriy out of his horrified trance. He scrambled around his pocket to fish his bank card. 'I'm so sorry. It's awful what's happened to you,' he said to her, barely getting his words out.

'Happened to me?' she barked. 'It didn't *happen* to me. He did it to me! He chose ruining my life over him coming out. It's not like we live in Saudi or somewhere! And now he's livin' la vida loca, out half the nights of the week enjoying himself, and I'm a fucking husk. He won't even speak to me. I have to come to places like this to try to catch him to make him speak to me. Nine years,' she said, angry tears streaming down her face.

Like a zookeeper passing meat into the big cat enclosure, he offered her a bottle.

She slapped his hand back. 'You think that's gonna wash it all away?'

'No. I—'

'You make me sick,' she said. 'Ruining people's lives, then acting like you've done something heroic. Piss off and take your baseless pride to someone who can't see straight through it.'

He grabbed two bottles off the bar and hurried off into the crowd, his heart racing. He yanked the top of a bottle, chugging half of it down in an attempt to cool himself. His irritation grew as he tried to make his way through the bopping bodies. As he made it to the space where Andriy had been, he saw a man in full glitter face paint drop a small white pill into a flute of champagne and gave it a swirl. The man passed it over his shoulder to another behind him. Dmitriy watched as it got passed again in the direction of Andriy, who was lost in the music. Dmitriy shoved his way through the crowd, drawing hacked-off looks from his victims, reaching Andriy just as he lifted the spiked flute for a toast with the friendly dance circle.

'Cheers, my dears!' Andriy called out. Dmitriy whipped the glass out of his hand. Andriy peered at him, shocked and confused.

After a moment to think, Dmitriy went to down the drink, missing his mouth and drenching the front of his shirt. 'Can we go, please?' Dmitriy asked in Russian, wiping the booze off.

'What was that all about?!' asked Andriy.

'Please,' said Dmitriy, offering his hand with a serious expression. 'I'll tell you outside.'

Andriy accepted the hand. 'Sorry, guys. Got to go. Thanks for taking care of me.'

As they fawned over Andriy and begged him to stay for a while longer, Dmitriy glared at them before pulling his partner away. They proceeded to say some hasty goodbyes to Paul and the magazine staff, then Dmitriy dragged Andriy by his hand through the crowd.

'What's the rush, mister?' asked Andriy as they burst out of the exit. 'It's freezing out here. Is Barry here already?'

'Come on,' said Dmitriy as he stormed along the pavement ahead and texted Barry. 'We're better waiting out here.'

'Are you just messaging him now? He's going to be ages!' said Andriy with a tipsy lilt.

'Just come on,' Dmitriy said, reaching back a protective hand, encouraging his partner forwards. They stopped just around the corner from the club.

'What's going on?' asked Andriy.

Dmitriy sighed deeply and wrapped his arms around his partner. 'That's just no place for us.'

Andriy heard the concern in his voice and hugged him tighter.

'Oy oy!'

The two separated to see who had shouted from across the street. It had been one from a group of five drunken men, a couple of them with beer bottles in hand.

'Do you have to bring that shit out here for people to have to see?' sneered one of them as the others chatted amongst themselves.

Dmitriy eyeballed him for a moment before Andriy cupped his face and brought it to face his. 'Ignore them. They're pissed idiots,' whispered Andriy.

One of the group squinted across the road at them. 'Fuck off. Have you seen who that is?' he asked his pals.

Dmitriy turned his face further away.

'It's only fucking Dmitriy Lebedev and his bender agent!' The attention of the entire group turned towards the couple.

'Fuck me!' said another.

'Don't fucking encourage them,' laughed another. 'That one takes twenty percent and a hundred percent of your anal virginity.' The group cackled like hyenas as they began to strut across the road.

Andriy tugged at Dmitriy's hand. 'Let's go,' he whispered.

Dmitriy yielded to another gentle pull and began walking.

'Yeh, that's right,' shouted one of the men. 'You fucking run. No one here to pull you back so you look hard in front of everyone. Only thing hard about you is your cock for that fucking mincer's stinkpipe.'

Dmitriy halted, dropped Andriy's hand, and turned back towards the men.

Follow the story to its thrilling conclusion in

TARGET MAN
The Second Half

If you enjoyed this book, please post a review on the book's page at
www.amazon.co.uk

www.artonjames.com

Printed in Great Britain
by Amazon